Learner Services

Please return on or before the last date stamped below

CITY COLLEGE
NORWICH

2 3 OCT 2009

2 4 FEB 2010

2 5 MAY 2010

− 6 OCT 2010

2 5 JAN 2011

1 4 NOV 2011

2 8 JAN 2013

A FINE WILL BE CHARGED FOR OVERDUE ITEMS

Critical
Issues
in
Child
Sexual
Abuse

Historical, Legal, and Psychological Perspectives

Editor

Jon R. Conte

Sage Publications
International Educational and Professional Publisher
Thousand Oaks ■ London ■ New Delhi

For information:

 Sage Publications, Inc.
2455 Teller Road
Thousand Oaks, California 91320
E-mail: order@sagepub.com

Sage Publications Ltd.
6 Bonhill Street
London EC2A 4PU
United Kingdom

Sage Publications India Pvt. Ltd.
M-32 Market
Greater Kailash
New Delhi 110 048 India

Printed in the United States of America

Library of Congress Cataloging-in-Publication Data

Critical issues in child sexual abuse : historical, legal, and
psychological perspectives / edited by Jon R. Conte.
     p. cm.
Includes bibliographical references and index.
  ISBN 0-7619-0911-7 (cloth) — ISBN 0-7619-0912-5 (pbk.)
  1. Summit, Roland. 2. Child sexual abuse. 3. Sexually abused
children. I. Conte, Jon R.
  HV6570 .C75 2002
  362.76—dc21

                                          2001004077

01 02 03 04 05 06 10 9 8 7 6 5 4 3 2 1

Acquiring Editor:	Nancy Hale
Editorial Assistant:	Vonessa Vondera
Copy Editor:	Amy Kazilsky
Production Editor:	Claudia A. Hoffman
Typesetter/Designer:	Denyse Dunn
Indexer:	Molly Hall
Cover Designer:	Jane Quaney

Contents

Roland C. Summit

Editor's Introduction

For professionals new to child abuse and especially child sexual abuse, it may seem hard to imagine a time when the problem was not viewed as important, deserving of professional attention, and often the subject of clinical discussions, research reports, or public media accounts. And yet, it was not more than two or three decades ago that child sexual abuse was, in fact, not seen as a significant problem.

From the very beginning of the modern rediscovery of child sexual abuse, physician Roland C. Summit had an integral role in shaping how professionals and the public came to understand the problem. Rol, as he is known by friends and those who look up to him, had a profound impact on the field. As a teacher, consultant, author, and confidant, Rol could be counted on to speak powerfully and clearly to the concern presented him. Among many positive attributes were his ability to use language to communicate with passion and insight, his strong support for the idea that responding to child sexual abuse required the efforts of many professions, and his willingness to give his time, energy, and wisdom to other professionals, parents of abused children, adult survivors, and those in the public who sought him out. Perhaps the greatest attribute Rol exemplified for us all was the ability and willingness to speak for those who could not themselves speak, the young and most traumatized of victims of child sexual abuse.

The authors in this volume continue the tradition of Roland Summit and provide stimulating, current, and far-reaching thoughts about child sexual abuse today. Rol is actively enjoying retirement but I know that he is grateful to the authors and he wishes that all of us concerned with child sexual abuse will be stimulated and helped by the ideas that follow.

— Jon R. Conte, PhD

1

An Interview with Roland Summit

David L. Corwin

Dr. Corwin: Rol, why don't you just start at the beginning in terms of talking about your training, your interests, and how it is that you were drawn into this field of interest and concern?

Dr. Summit: That's a question that I've asked myself. And I've had to realize, looking back, that part of it is just who I am and what went into growing up. But then a lot was the circumstance of where I came into the field and at what time, and so I look at a series of kind of coincidental things that have added up.

One thing that I've seen as important is that my father was a guidance counselor. He spent his career working with young people at the high school level, and then, later, in Palm Springs when I was in high school, he was Director of Guidance and Child Welfare for the school district, and he essentially did social work for troubled and disadvantaged families. He would share some of his stories, one of which was a very complicated incest family that he dealt with. And so, the theme of incest was not absolutely strange to me.

EDITOR'S NOTE: This chapter is an edited version of an interview with Roland C. Summit, M.D., conducted by David Corwin, M.D., on June 21, 1996 and August 13, 1996. In the interest of space, the interview has been edited to consist largely of Dr. Summit's comments.

Another thing, there was a book I read in high school that made a tremendous impression on me for what I would now call community mental health. It was called *Kings Row*. It was a remarkable profile of character pathology in a small town. And I read it when I was 15 years old, and prone to personal romantic idealization of some of the people in that book. The central character was a young man who grew up to become a psychiatrist. A series of his girlfriends evoke a personally significant kind of sympathy.

One was his inseparable childhood playmate, who was beaten and banished from his life when her brutal father observed an otherwise quite charming and innocent first sexual encounter. I experienced a pathetic idealization of that relationship turned suddenly awful by the parental abuse. Then a beautiful young woman fell in love with him. She was intensely sexualized, and desperately dependent on him for reasons that weren't exactly clear until she became the victim of her father's murder-suicide. I was appalled to discover that the girl had been the prisoner of incest. Her father had been the mentor to the young man, a physician who prepared him for medical school. I wrote an impassioned book review for sophomore English class, protesting that no one community could contain, let alone conceal, so much psychopathology, especially incest.

Some of those issues have paralleled my own life. I realize that in some way my life choices were drawn out of that book. It was very subtle. I didn't realize until reading the book afterward how I might have idealized the thinking and the positions that this young man took. At the time I read it, I had no thought of ever becoming a psychiatrist. So there were numbers of things that kind of burned incest issues and lost love and tragic losses of potential related to sexual abuse, before I ever got into mental health.

A couple of my patients in the training years were incest victims. One in particular [in 1962], a young teen who came in following a suicide attempt and confided, probably for the first time, that she was locked in an incest bondage with her father. I naturally turned to my mentors, my supervisors, with this dilemma, and I was told, "Don't pay any attention to it. No matter what's going on, there's nothing you can do about it, and if you did try and do something, she'd probably go home with her father anyway." And sure enough, that's what happened. That was before the battered child syndrome, before our reporting laws. And it represented a pretty typical psychiatric standoff. I was clearly told to stay out of this.

I did an elective in my last year of psychiatry in community psychiatry, and pursued a little research project on the impact of parenting and the role of fathers. Parenting was clearly a more important issue to me than to most, for whatever reason. I certainly had a lot to learn from my own experience with my mother and father and the influences each of them had on me, and I just—I was struck at that time with a sense of paradox. I rejected a lot of the psychoanalytic tenets of Oedipus theory. It didn't jibe with my sense of how kids grew up. But I was also struck with the coincidence of some kids who make it and some kids who don't. And what are the influences that allow kids to grow up, especially in the growth of their capacity for intimacy.

It was essentially a coincidence that when I got out of psychiatric residency I was at risk of being drafted, having deferred service through the late-Korean and mid-Vietnam eras. So I didn't feel I could open a practice as I had expected because it was likely to get aborted. My residency child psychiatry supervisor, Rita Rogers, was based here, at Harbor, and she put in a word with the chief, Peter Castelnuevo-Tedesco. Peter offered me a job and said, "We've got this new idea we're developing here, the Community Consultation Service, to try and relate to agencies in the community on a premental illness consultation basis, and you can come to work for us. It may help defer you further from the draft or, if you do get drafted, at least you're not losing the overhead of a practice."

I really had no idea of what I was getting into, but I came to love that kind of work. I was introduced to community agencies. I began to learn from these consultations the many styles of coping that people had beyond the standard psychological defenses and breakdowns and mental health treatment.

Most of the people in the community who were mentally ill weren't getting treatment. They were coping in family peer groups, alcoholism, whatever else. But I had to discover there were all kinds of alternatives to psychiatric care, and self-help was one of them. I got quite interested in self-help, especially as I became involved in what was then a new problem, the use of mixed drugs by teenagers. And that was my main focus for three or four years [1966 to 1970].

So there was no focus on child abuse originally, but among my early experiences was a regular consultation with Child Protective Services in Long Beach. They were dealing with abused children and we didn't know what to do with them. I evaluated a couple of accused abusive families without much confidence that I knew what I was doing. I had a lot more confidence in drawing on community resources for drug abuse. Really, I had a pretty intense and gratifying experience in that field.

I probably would have stayed with the focus on drug abuse except for an event in October 1970, four years, or a little more, after coming to Harbor. A newspaper writer was doing a story on the carousel animals in our collection. She told me she had just interviewed somebody who was trying to put together a self-help organization for child abuse and was looking for professional endorsement or support, and I might be interested in talking with her. I said sure, and that led to a meeting in my office with the woman who called herself Jolly K. She was founding what she then called Mother's Anonymous, finally Parents Anonymous.

She told me her story that day: A sexually abused, foundling child, living through a series of foster homes and becoming self-abusive and sexually disordered until she married and found that she was trying to kill off the slut that she saw in her young daughter. The slut that she saw was her self-image, and she knew it, yet her daughter was the innocent scapegoat.

She gave me a very clear dynamic of intergenerational revictimization, and a whole other view of what child abuse can be in a projective, psychodynamic sense. There wasn't much professional awareness of that out there at the time. Her story also recalled for me these little bits and pieces of incest concern that had been incidental thoughts over the years.

Well, I became the first of the board members of Parents Anonymous and lived through the growing pains of that organization, and, probably most important, became acquainted on a quasi-social basis with abusive parents who would share with me their fears and their backgrounds that they'd never tell a protective service worker or an examining mental health specialist. Their guard was down and I was a trusted ally. An incredible majority of them had been sexually abused as children.

Then Jolly commissioned me to write a piece for their training manual on sexual abuse. I felt I had no place to go with that. Earlier, we had really had a verbal knock-down-drag-out fight about the issue of sexual abuse. She, out of her own childhood, knew that sexual abuse was integral in child abuse. But that wasn't part of common knowledge or a professional acknowledgment back in the 70s, so I was the bright young psychiatrist who told Jolly that sexual abuse wasn't a part of this issue and certainly wasn't a legitimate part of treatment within a self-help program. I said these are character-disordered people, pedophiles, who have a deep-seated problem and are certainly not amenable to self-help therapy. With the wisdom of personal experience, Jolly said, simply, "You're full of shit." She knew better than I what the issues ought to be in that group, and ultimately I conceded to try to write an incest piece for the manual.

It turned out nobody else was writing about sexual abuse in 1973. That little piece came to the attention of people in Washington who were funding Parents Anonymous. It also put me in touch with Kee MacFarlane who was the Federal Officer with a special interest in sex abuse prevention. She asked to republish it in a compendium that she was putting together. All of a sudden I was an expert in child sexual abuse for the mere fact that there were no other psychiatrists with a visible interest.

One day I agreed to talk about sexual abuse at a conference on child abuse at Children's Hospital in Los Angeles. And then, again, I was the last hope for anyone who would talk about this. I put together my sense of a spectrum of degrees of severity of sexual assault, from incidental kinds of contacts within an almost normal home environment to child rape and exploitation. I had had some consulting contact with that whole range.

I gave a talk, really, after scribbling out those topics on a piece of scrap paper in the hospital parking structure. Dave Freidman, who was a pediatrician out at Children's, encouraged me to write that up. Actually, it was already recorded and transcribed and printed in the proceedings of that meeting. The only reason I took the plunge to publish was because the nub of the paper was already there. It helped, also, that Dave was on the editorial board of the *Journal of Orthopsychiatry* and offered to put in a word for me. So that's how the first paper came about, the *Clinical Spectrum*, in 1978.

The publications extended beyond my L.A. County beat into contact with the scattered national community of people who were dealing with child sexual abuse in one capacity or another.

All of a sudden, in August of '78, a dozen or so people found themselves together in Washington, DC to talk about how to deal with sexual abuse. Was it a significant problem? And if so, what should be done about it? Kee MacFarlane had badgered the Feds into sponsoring a consultation conference. She also compiled the list of could-be experts. The list included people I knew—Hank Giaretto and Lloyd Martin—and mostly people I had never met: Ann Burgess, Nick Groth, Judienne Densen-Gerbor, Sue Sgroi, and Lucy Berliner, among others. All of these people were suddenly together brainstorming. It was an intoxicating moment in the midst of the prevailing isolation of the time.

I'm reminded of Lloyd Martin in this story because there was a time when child sexual abuse was pretty much defined as father/daughter incest within the model of intrafamily abuse. I was more or less totally preoccupied with that aspect, especially through Parents Anonymous, through ICAN, our Los Angeles County network of child abuse agencies, and especially through a close affiliation with the Giarettos and the San Jose model of Parents United child sexual abuse treatment.

Lloyd Martin, on the other hand, was entirely concerned with street prostitution and pedophilia on a male-to-male basis, and he was concerned that I was really misrepresenting the field in talking about father/daughter incest as the core. You really have to give him credit for the initiative of reaching out and drawing me to the streets and into the world of other kinds of sexual abuse, especially boy-seeking pedophiles and career criminals. He literally took me to the streets, talking with prostitutes on the street as well as meeting with a couple of his own informants.

A few years later, we all found ourselves in Boston at the invitation of Ann Burgess for a conference that she had put together involving law enforcement, customs, pornography intervention, and mental health. We all gave presentations. And that meeting was picketed by NAMBLA, the North American Boy Love Association, who brought young men out to extol to people on the street how much they loved the experience of sex with older men. NAMBLA tried to take Ann Burgess's job—attacking her for consorting with law enforcement and entrapment of law-abiding pedophiles.

They really hit Lloyd Martin with broadsides as a rogue vice cop who was trying to make a career for himself, busting loving innocent people. I sure got a piece of the "gentle" side of pedophilia at that time, the would-be loving man-boy relationships. And I guess actually the first taste of backlash in terms of how this work can be abrasive even when you think you're doing something that is constructive and positive in the world.

I guess something else out of that was the necessary recognition that sexual paraphelias in general, and sexual abuse of children in particular, were not the exclusive domain of mental health. They were the stepchild of mental health. The people who were making gains in this field were people outside of psychiatry and often outside of the mental health professions altogether. The cops and the vice officers knew more about this field than we did, and we needed to learn from one another.

So, most of the people who had any visible interest and association with the topic of sexual abuse were suddenly in touch with one another after August, 1978. If it hadn't been for that intensity of discovery and interpersonal support, nobody would have emerged with any expressed ideas because there was no audience for those ideas at the time. We were each other's audience, really, and we'd speak long into the night at meetings, and I was certainly involved in a lot more correspondence then because that was the only place to share.

I should mention that one of the early consults specific to sexual abuse was with a place called Cedar House in Long Beach. Two visionary social workers had put together a residential day care center for abusive families. A wonderful model, I won't get into it now, but it was very influential to me for its neighborhood focus and counterpathological approach to abusive families. It provided a secure place to be cared for and accepted in the midst of a therapeutic process.

The presence of Cedar House in Long Beach allowed for a kind of a volunteer network of concern for child abuse in that city. A number of women's organizations picked up on child abuse as a focus for education and funding. It was out of that context that one of the first conferences on child sexual abuse was sponsored by the Long Beach Child Trauma Council, which I attended regularly. It was actually nationwide in scope in terms of the invited speakers: Ann Burgess, Kee MacFarlane, and others.

It's interesting that I hadn't written the accommodation syndrome yet, but the elements of the accommodation syndrome were everywhere. We were all dealing with the same phenomenon.

So much was going on in those years. It was an explosion, an idea whose time had come which had been neglected for so long that everything was spilling out together. Talking about a period of years between 1975 and 1980. That was the real explosion. A lot of people don't understand that there was much going on then. They date sexual abuse awareness to the 80s, and often mid-80s, and it gets contaminated with the whole *McMartin* phenomenon, and what was a frenzied media attention then.

My first testimony in court was in December of '78 in a child protection matter. I've been characterized sometimes, usually not in a flattering context, as a dupe to the prosecution as someone who enjoyed testifying to put people in jail. That has really never been my intent and my sole interest, but I have testified in some of the high-visibility cases, and more lately the accommodation syndrome is core to one particular rebuttal argument for children.

Dr. Corwin: What argument is that?

Dr. Summit: The legitimate argument for the accommodation syndrome, as I've come to understand the conservative place of expert testimony in a field that isn't loaded with data, is simply to introduce as a rebuttal the argument that if children have not immediately complained about sexual abuse, or if they give an inconsistent development of reporting, and even if they retract on prior statements, that's not inconsistent with the reality of sexual abuse.

That concept was driven home for me in June of 1980, when a parent called me from a little town in the eastern Sierras called Big Pine. She told me about a case involving their children, where all the boys in town had been molested by a school teacher/administrator in that little district.

Big Pine taught me more than I ever wanted to know about community denial and the ability of one sex offender to use a trusted position to evade suspicion. I mean, he was active for about six years within that school district with well over a hundred boys who never disclosed. And once the whistle was blown on this, through a series of almost impossible coincidences, virtually none of those families sought the mental health treatment that was offered for the kids. It just fell underground, every step of the way. The Big Pine case began to prepare me for multi-victim and ultimately multiperpetrator allegations.

We had to learn that incest offenders could pose an out-of-family threat as well. But the intrafamily dynamic and the family treatment model was current at the time. It was very offensive to feminists. That was one of the times when factions began to split. Feminists saw no quarter for encouraging a child to live with a rapist. Family treatment, family reunification programs were an anathema to feminists who saw all offenders in the same light and tended to want a strict "put 'em in prison and throw away the key" model.

That doesn't work either. At least it's not acceptable in court channels and the presumption of innocence and all those things. It ignored the problem that anyone who was going to be put in jail on a stiff sentence was going to be put there on the testimony of a child with no other corroborating evidence. We began to split on the relative emphasis of prosecution at about that time.

One major development locally, which paralleled experience in other places, was the need to develop a straight-through kind of vertical prosecution for offenders. We found in our Los Angeles County-based treatment program that individuals who denied molesting children (most of our experience in that program was incest families), individuals who denied and who got a good attorney, could escape prosecution and punishment. Individuals who entered our treatment program, acknowledged they really did it, and were cooperating in treatment tended to be put away with harsh sentences.

Prosecutors coming in fresh to this saw the opportunity to salt these guys away. And there was a double standard. If you admitted you did it, you're going to go to prison. And our whole treatment premise was to present prosecution and incarceration as the stick against which the carrot of acknowledgment and treatment looked more appealing.

So, in the summer of 1981, I chaired a succession of high-level, interagency meetings leading to a lot of recommendations. The one which was adopted was the formation of the vertical prosecution unit in the DA's office, so that the same people could take a case from discovery through the process and make judgments as to proper charging and disposition without new people coming in with their own aberrant ideas.

I guess that would be the next era of the whole issue of how to define the field of sexual abuse of children. There had been an evolution of thought beginning with incest, father/daughter incest specifically, to mixed kinds of victimization involving boys within families and out-of-family sexual exploitation, child pornography, and pedophilia. The concept then moved rather suddenly to trying to deal with the question of sadistic abuse. There the apparent motivation had less to do with sexual gratification and less to do with trying to develop a quasi-positive relationship with a child victim, than an apparent pleasure in hurting children and exploiting a grotesque kind of sexual gratification through cruelty and suffering.

I need to go back to 1980 for another epochal that came from a different base event for me, and also the fact of that experience. Although a lot of what I talked about and a lot of what I drew from as a consultant was third person kinds of experiences from therapists or investigators who were themselves dealing with children, I was also treating a couple of people as outpatients here at the hospital.

When I first came to Harbor in 1966, I was assigned to take over the ongoing therapy of a patient who had been abandoned by a resident leaving the program. This young woman, whom I've pseudo-named Stephanie and, later, Stevie, had experienced a psychotic, suicidal break while she was a student at age 17. Now, at the age of 20, she was back in treatment with a delusional system involving voices from the devil and visual hallucinations of things turning into monsters. It was a very graphic, apparently schizophrenic, process.

She was so paranoid and fearful that we spent years establishing even basic communication and trust. I prescribed ever-higher doses of medications, trying to get hold of this psychotic process. By 1980, after 14 years of supportive therapy, we had established a rich, complex relationship. But we still hadn't gotten a handle on this continually suicidal, self-mutilating, and delusional picture. In discussing Stevie's dynamics with Mike Durfee, we discovered she had dissociative issues in common with someone that he worked with in a quasi-therapeutic relationship. She had taught Mike about her own dissociation and her history as a child of ritual abuse. Stevie's history was not suggestive of cult ritual, but rather of extreme cruelty, mind control, and sexual abuse at the hands of her father. And Kee MacFarlane, who was in town by now, was also working closely with a young adult woman who described all kinds of sadistic torture at the hands of a neo-Nazi, fanatical father.

We had these experiences in common of people really deeply and seriously damaged by sadistic child sexual abuse exhibiting dissociative phenomena. We didn't understand dissociation, as opposed to psychosis, until somebody really gave a name and a background to it.

I had worked with Stevie for 14 years—'66 to '80—dealing with all kinds of dynamics that I called schizophrenic. But then I attended a lecture by Pamela Reager detailing dissociation as the outcome of life-threatening abuse. And the next time I saw Stevie she exhibited a frank out-of-body dissociative experience where she saw her arm suspended in space, moving apart from her own volition. She was scared to death. At first, I thought she was having another psychotic break, but then I remembered Pam's lecture. We talked the episode through as a dissociative phenomenon. We could both be reassured that this was "normal."

From that moment on, we began working with a dissociative treatment model where I could view her whole behavior as the norm for a child loaded with fantasy and unrationalized fears, and for the adult who reverted to childlike behavior and a childlike view of the world, where things changed into monsters and people became menacing on a switch of mental outlook. And out of that came my sense of what I call the *hidden child phenomenon* as a dissociative quasi-alternate identity.

Our whole treatment was founded on that. And, ultimately, Stevie, after many fits and starts, totally recovered. On her own she gave up all the medicine I had been giving her, which she once viewed as a poison. At one point she was convinced that she made up her own stories of symptoms so I would poison her with more drugs; again, this dissociative in-and-out reality.

None of that could be conceived or worked with before we had the knowledge and collegial permission to view dissociation as a recognizable post-traumatic phenomenon. But what is sad about that is that no matter that Stevie recovered through that process; no matter that it was the threshold of memories of frank sexual abuse, which were so important in her resolution; no matter that people developed successful treatment regimens to deal with adults who had first-time memories of sexual assault in the process of therapy; the concept of dissociation has been trashed by clinicians and lawyers who view it as a sure sign of misguided intervention.

But what was crucial then was the change in my own outlook: I began viewing Stevie not as schizophrenic with a chronic and intractable organic mental disorder, but as someone with a post-traumatic affliction that was subject to recovery. Once I didn't see her as permanently and chronically mentally ill, we began developing another kind of optimism. That's an optimism I think that's being denied therapists now, who aren't free to work at that level or who are self-conscious for the fear of suggesting new pathology into their troubled clients and patients.

The backlash view, expressed so articulately by the people out of the False Memory Syndrome Foundation and its advisory board, has returned to this skeptical view that multiple personality disorder, dissociative identity disorder, all of this is artifactual: a tidy little arrangement concocted between hysterical clients and overzealous, inquisitive therapists. While this may be a hazard, it's not what we need to learn from a genuinely post-traumatic process.

Back to the context of those three people that we were working with, Kee MacFarlane, Mike Durfey, and I. Kee's client went on to recovery. My patient went on to recovery, and Mike's—you know, Mike was never her therapist, he was a resource to her, and she was quite dependent on contact with him, and he drew a lot from the conversations and understanding her phenomena. This young woman's course is of historic interest for whatever it may mean in the long run. Working with a variety of top-notch therapists in the dissociative disorder field, she went on to develop an increasingly complex system centered on satanic ritual abuse.

She had begun describing her experiences with a sadistic minister father who would take her out on forays murdering babies. That crystallized into descriptions of satanic circles and mind control. And she became one of the demagogues, if you will, in the survivor community of survivors of satanic ritual abuse. In a sense, she may have defined some of the criteria and phenomena. I don't want to say that too strongly because I've seen so many different nuclei from which this information has developed. I don't think she was solely responsible for the scenarios. But she certainly reinforced a lot of the imagery of organized neighborhood-based satanic cults.

I had occasional contact with her through meetings and lectures as the whole area of ritual abuse developed. And to get way ahead of that story, but to stay in the context of the evanescent reversibility of memories of abuse and the complexities of dissociation, the last time I saw her, almost two years ago, she was lecturing in a different manner with a much more solid quality and none of the artifacts of abuse or mysticism. Very solid, down to earth, she was helping people recognize the difference between abuse effects themselves and artifactual affects of defenses against abuse.

She met me for lunch and wanted to explain to me that she felt she was quite recovered, that she had begun taking an antidepressant and had come to the realization that she was addicted to the dissociative process as her first response to stress. She began withdrawing from dissociation, not allowing herself to fall into this realm.

And through that process she came to believe—and I don't know which is the truth of her experience, but this is certainly opposite to what she said for so many years—that she had never been a part of any organized cult abuse. Her father was not a high priest of Satan. He was a cruel and sadistically abusive man, and that her defense against that intolerable incest was to distract herself with imaginings of what could be even worse in her experience, so that her experience with her father wouldn't seem so bad. And out of that came a habit of creating her own world of atrocity experience.

I've had a similar experience with another survivor who stays in touch with me on the phone, who was also one of the potential leaders of the satanic ritual survivors groups, who now believes she was never satanically abused, and that was her. She asserts that the satanic was just her own dissociative way of redefining her incestuous experience.

For both of these individuals, it's the process of dissociation that has to be mastered, not the content of the memories.

In a sense, we assign a life warrant of pathology to survivors when we interpret their behavior as character-based or mental-illness-based when it is, in fact, reactive to trauma and re-enacting of trauma and a playing out of the addiction to trauma. There was so much to learn. I just hope we don't lose that enlightenment.

The other thing, before we leave this subject, is the fickle nature of abuse memories. We have learned that the typical, and by all rights, *healthy* response of children to severe abuse, when you're betrayed by an environment and by caretakers who can't take care of you, the best way a child can deal with that is to set it aside and keep it out of consciousness and to learn one way or another to get distance from that experience, even as it's happening. Later memories of that experience may be literally accurate or grotesquely symbolic. There's no gold standard for accuracy.

Dr. Corwin: In the chronology of your work, I can remember in 1980, perhaps, it might have been 1981, you first presented the child sexual abuse accommodation syndrome at UCLA, and I was there at the Grand Rounds where you presented it. That may not have been your first presentation of those concepts, but if you could—

Dr. Summit: The phenomenology of what crystallized in the accommodation syndrome was just bread and butter stuff that we were all dealing with. The thing was, we were all dealing with it but the world didn't know that. And especially the court world didn't know that. Children were being impeached and attacked by attorneys for not telling right away.

As I began to realize that, by going to court and seeing that happening, I began to realize that there needed to be some way to express this, these paradoxes in language that would stop punishing kids for their normal behavior.

In 1979, in response to a case in disciplinary review, a sheriff's officer accused of molesting his daughter and discharged for that reason, and then appealing that discharge, I was testifying, and a number of issues were cogent there, where the young woman was impeached for not making an immediate complaint.

And, in support of my testimony, I put together an essay on what I called "Typical Characteristics of Father/Daughter Incest." It drew on what I knew and on some of David Finklehor's work in terms of disclosure and nondisclosure. And I think there were seven categories that were selected as being paradoxical, commonsense notions that weren't true.

And the first five categories in that list, literally, right then, in July of 1979, were secrecy, helplessness accommodation, delayed disclosure, and retraction. Those five categories just sort of clustered together in front of your eyes as something to be talked about. And I began lecturing off of that scheme even before it was called the accommodation syndrome, ever since 1978. By '79 I was calling it the child sexual abuse accommodation syndrome.

I remember one conversation, again with Kee, where I was trying to write this thing for publication in 1979, and I liked the alliteration of "incest accommodation syndrome," and discussed with Kee what this ought to be called. It was a choice between incest and child sexual abuse, and Kee said, "Oh, don't stay with incest, this is much too broad for incest." And by that time I had accumulated a much broader experience. But I was almost—there's my problem sometimes being more attracted to the style of language than to the broader meaning.

By 1980, I know on record that I was calling it the accommodation syndrome. A meeting in Vancouver was transcribed and published as proceedings. These proceedings represent the first published version of the accommodation syndrome by name. That presentation also included an extended discussion on dissociation as one of the paradoxical defenses.

I had a strong sense, reinforced all over the place, that the accommodation syndrome was critical for understanding. When I would lecture on it, people would have a kind of an "aha" experience. Survivors would come forward and say that they felt for the first time they had permission in their lives for their failure as children in not coming forth, not making it stop. Perhaps unfortunately that community clinical understanding was picked up quickly was an explanation of inconsistent behavior in criminal court cases.

Dr. Corwin: And your main intent, the purpose of that article, was what?

Dr. Summit: The purpose of the article was to allow children their own normalcy in dealing with sexual assault. Ideologically to not require them to behave like perfectly self-protective adults, to kick somebody in the balls and run out screaming that they had been molested. Because that's what was expected of them. When they didn't fit that standard, they were dismissed as liars or inconsistent.

The whole public prejudice left child victims revictimized by their own normal response. There was virtually no willingness to concede that a normal child would submit to sexual assault without complaint. And at the same time nothing is coincidental and nothing is unique, to my thinking. It's not entirely coincidental that at the same time the women's movement had been fighting to rescue adult rape victims from a parallel prejudice.

In the published version of the accommodation syndrome, I acknowledge Ann Burgess's work in the rape trauma syndrome. Both papers gave a kind of a benediction to victims who kept their victimization as a private issue and then were discredited for that privacy. Both concepts, the accommodation syndrome and rape trauma syndrome, are dealt with identically in legal precedent, to be thrown out as offers of proof, but to be allowed as rebuttal issues for education of the jury to the dilemma of victims as a class.

Dr. Corwin: What are your current thoughts and reflections on the choice of the word *syndrome?*

Dr. Summit: I'm not about to be too apologetic for that. The problem is in the interpretation of the word in its particular context. For me, *syndrome* was a list of items that are observed together without a known etiology, without even a recognizable connection until the list is made. In time it may be possible to discover what makes these things happen.

I don't believe I ever meant syndrome to mean a diagnostic entity that proved the abuse, although it was certainly a pedantic implement to help people not disbelieve the child in the process of disclosure. The accommodation syndrome always has to be considered in terms of double negatives. It's not that it proves the abuse happened, but accommodating behavior doesn't disprove that the abuse could have happened.

It gives a potential advocacy for a respectful attention to the child's statements.

By now, the word advocacy is as troubled in my choice of words as syndrome. And I don't think it would have been a problem except for the way the legal profession looks at the word syndrome. In common use, not only in medical use, syndrome is a much more vague and open concept than *disorder* or *disease*. In popular literature, syndrome is used for all kinds of phenomena that aren't psychopathological.

My whole wish, in fact, was to make this not a disease entity but a normal set of behaviors. So, as I saw it, and as I will still maintain, syndrome was not meant to be a specific diagnostic trigger.

However, lawyers who write about trials and evidence have their own take on what a syndrome is. And they call "syndrome evidence" derisively the same thing as "character evidence," an improper attempt to characterize fuzzy logic as something specific and identifiable, used improperly for the purpose of biasing the trial process. And so, if psychiatrists are to introduce a syndrome as explanatory for something, it is fair game for being attacked, for not being scientific and not being diagnostic.

Dr. Corwin: What is your sense of the current dilemma?

Dr. Summit: I really hate to sound pessimistic in the face of what should be seen as a huge amount of progress in the field. But rather, I get phone calls from parents who want a therapist who can deal with problems of abuse in a custody dispute, and I have to advise them not to pursue these complaints because there's no way the judge is going to listen to them.

I have running conversations on the phone with women who have been knocked around in the family law court for a couple of years as their influential husbands have prejudiced the court into blaming the mother for inventing the complaints of sexual abuse. And then I'll hear a moment of great optimism where this woman will phone in and say, "We got the case changed to another courtroom and this is a really nice judge, and he wants to review all these papers and he really wants to hear about the case." Wonderful.

The evening of the next day a message is recorded on my voice mail saying, "I just wanted you to know that the judge threw out everything and awarded full custody to my husband and restricted me to monitored visits. He says that I'm the one responsible for poisoning my child with these beliefs."

Now, that's the kind of thing that dominates my perception. It's not a fair view because I only get the worst of it, and I'm not involved in some of the networks and teams that have developed more positive policies.

The other thing that potentially demoralizes me is the fate of many of my mentors and role models. People who I found stimulating and wise and progressive in their thinking, and people from whom I learned and formed many of my own beliefs are financially bankrupt, victims of multimillion dollar lawsuits. Others have left the field because it's not safe. Therapists who are still afloat are dividing their lives into this negative area of self-defense against the risk of being made enemies of the people for what was once their hope of being redeemers of the people.

Now those are grandiose terms, but that's what this field seems to create among some people: either a great deal of idealism or a crashing kind of destruction. I just don't feel that's right.

It's certainly true that everyone has the right to be innocent until proven guilty and everyone has the right to the most effective defense against any kind of accusation. But the very people who provided that kind of constitutional right to people accused of abuse have made a scapegoat of the professionals as the real miscreants in this system. And those people are now developing destructive propaganda and creating a climate of opinion that promotes these devastating lawsuits and humiliating publicity.

That's my view of it as one who was one step away from the trenches, who fell into a position of some national or international recognition, and who wrote a paper once that is now both highly acclaimed and viciously attacked. It's that diametricism, the polarity of beliefs that distresses me. I just hope that within the next century a better kind of reason will prevail.

Dr. Corwin: What are some of the things that you think have gone right?

Dr. Summit: Well, what's certainly gone right is any amount of recognition that we now have for the credibility of children when they express distress, and the right of children to be protected from abuse. The consciousness of child abuse as a phenomenon isn't going to go away, and the institutions of child protection won't be entirely eradicated no matter how individuals may be embarrassed in attempting to protect. And, certainly, a generation or two of people growing up within this climate of understanding can deal with it more rationally rather than emotionally. That is, kids who grow up abused, even if they're not discovered—and I'm talking not only about sexual abuse now but every kind of abuse and neglect—kids who don't get the tools they need to develop in their childhood will have a vastly greater climate of information to draw from rather than blaming themselves for being rotten kids.

So, as the mentality of adequate parenting and open communication becomes basic in society, so will the discussions around abuse and the more bizarre and sickening kinds of abuse. Every piece of that consciousness is positive even though it has two extremes of underside. One extreme is the danger that some kids will exploit their power and use it to make false accusations, or they will misunderstand their own dissociation and create a climate of false accusations. A less menacing parallel is the likelihood that some children who are self-actualized and self-protecting will become kind of a nuisance by screaming out if somebody pinches them too hard, or making a scene at a party demanding that an aunt with halitosis not kiss them.

Part of the public reaction against children's rights is just the nuisance of having to treat children as people worthy of feelings rather than little puppets who have to be grateful for every piece of attention.

The other extreme of child abuse awareness, though, is a kind of reactive retaliation by adults as a group to put children back in their appropriate place and to take things back to a more comfortable time when we didn't have to worry about kids who aren't safe.

I don't think the backlash is fueled so much by its few gurus who articulate issues that emotional allies can rally around. I think it's fueled by our collective discomfort at having to look at a world where we can't always idealize the state of childhood and can't always trust our own memories of happy childhoods. Even if we have a memory of a happy childhood, endorsing the reality of dissociative distortion would force us to wonder if our memory is accurate or not. The inherent uncertainty is just so complex and troubling that it creates a fertile field for driving things back.

So, I'm saying on one hand awareness is wonderful, but there's a price to be paid and work to be done to rationalize and institutionalize that awareness.

Now, where I think we have not gone right with that awareness, and this is a lesson learned with regret, is to define child sexual abuse as a different animal from other kinds of child maltreatment and to define it categorically as a criminal act which requires criminal investigation and demands and deserves criminal prosecution.

That was a stance taken out of existing law. And, after all, we really didn't have laws against and criminal penalties for various kinds of child abuse short of murder and maiming. But we always had laws on the books against any kind of sexual touching of children. And so, there was a criminal prosecution establishment already in place. In the old days, that was a set of laws without much teeth, because children were too easily silenced in their complaints. Once prosecution had the opportunity to really put people in jail on the words of children, they wanted to make up for lost time. And, in our advocacy for the protection of children, we didn't see that there were real hazards to that. Not that we were indifferent to the rights of the accused, but our enthusiasm was for this newfound awareness of children's endangerment.

When we put together multidisciplinary teams where clinical types sat side by side with prosecution types, it created a dissonance of roles that didn't enhance either one. That is, cops and prosecutors who took on social workers' views were stigmatized in their own profession. And certainly social workers who served as criminal investigators were reviled for stepping out of character and doing incompetent work, by police investigative standards.

That wouldn't have been a fatal flaw if it had been developed with more time. But it was a revolutionary experience that happened suddenly in the late 70s into the early 80s. Much of it happened out of a further coalition with clinicians who were providing therapy both for children who were molested and adults who had confessed to molesting children: the whole Parents United Model. The whole Giarettos model of treatment relied on the dual role of the clinical self-help process to provide change for the clients, with the prosecution and the threat of conviction to coerce people into participation long enough for the program to take effect.

That whole process was odious to civil libertarians and allowed for the proposition that these men were confessing not to the truth of their experience, but out of compassion for their family to spare them the ordeal of a courtroom showdown.

So, if I were to put it most simply, I'd just have to say that the issues of incest were much too complicated to fit simply into a crime-and-punishment model and to be subsumed in our conceptual language into a victim/perpetrator model.

I'd have to say that that ambiguity was enhanced by the fact that a lot of this was discovered and exposed and publicized by the women's revolution and by people who were designated feminists who saw child sexual abuse as a pure analog of stranger rape, who argued, reasonably enough, that a child should never be forced to consort with her rapist.

That same argument said that men like that ought to be put in prison, but men like that aren't going to go to prison unless a child can testify. A child can't testify unless there's confrontation with an adversary argument where one well-educated professional's role is to discredit the child. That put children on a firing line that children aren't really capable of taking. I'm not saying that it's wrong to prosecute sexual abuse. I'm not saying that children are not capable ever of testifying. But it became a reality of practice that for every thousand children who are sexually molested, probably five or ten ever testify in court.

So, to put this forth as the law of the land and the priority of the process puts children on the line for a false role. And what I wish I could say more briefly is that clinical people who have skills in talking with children through reporting laws and through being hyped to take this kind of quasi-investigator's role, were then thrust into a potential counter-therapeutic position. The more sensitive they were to the possibility of unreported abuse, and the more they might hope to provide those children with the best intervention and care, the more they were required to be reporters of a crime and to be involved with the children in a potential battle with one of their parents at an adversary courtroom level.

I don't think there's a simple alternative to that, but I have argued repeatedly, and without effect, that we need a different venue from an adversary criminal courtroom in order to evaluate and proceed with these cases.

I think those are questions that don't have an answer but which shouldn't be thrown away without further questioning. We went right down the primrose path in turning child victims into victims of court, and we have been put on the defensive ever since to prove that our methods are worthy for courtroom use. We must either establish guilt beyond reasonable doubt or get out of the courtroom and shut up. Either mental health professionals have consummate skills in assessing children or they have absolutely nothing more than the lay person and should not be allowed access to questioning a child suspected of being molested.

Long ago I began writing and illustrating the fallacy of that expert witness presumption argument without realizing how profound the paradox was. And that is, that anything we learn about the real guts of childhood victimization is not learned from eyewitness participation. It's not learned from candid confession by the people who are doing it. It's not learned from professional clinical training. It's learned from its survivors. They are the very experts who are bound to be discredited as being either immature and fantastic or confused and mentally ill.

So the very fact that if we illustrate and convince the world that child sexual abuse really damages people, and if we oversell the idea that it's the basis of a variety of mental illnesses, then every survivor can be silenced by the charge that they are mentally ill and not worthy of credibility.

What I didn't anticipate in that issue about the children and the mentally ill was kill-the-messenger phenomenon. Because that's where the ambiguity has its greatest obfuscatory power now, and it's a double-edged sword. It is saying both that survivors aren't capable of knowing their own experience and that therapists are incapable of restraint or ethics in dealing with survivors, and therefore they deserve to be punished for creating a false sense of abuse in their clients.

And, furthermore, as an active effort of some of these newer groups, mental health patients are solicited and advertised for and gathered in to check whether or not they are capable of being retractors and whether they will turn on their former therapists, recant their experience, and sue their therapists for bad therapy. There's where the organized resistance can exploit the vulnerability of survivors in a way I never fully anticipated.

The other concern I have for the survivor movement is its disparity. The tendency of survivors to fight among themselves according to what they believe in and whom they believe is most deserving. Women don't necessarily welcome men as survivors. People who claim to be survivors of ritual abuse demand retribution against the powers of Satan. Most other survivors don't identify with those extremes.

As I think I may have tried to illustrate in these conversations, a given survivor has an episodic sense of history which can swing widely from a sense of not being abused at all to being abused by one other person into being abused by the whole community, into being abused by the therapist to believe that any of this was true. And, therefore, to assume a community of survivors is to miss the point that this is a community of people in extreme levels of transition that are not yet capable of reasonable coalescence. They may be and are forced to, doomed to, discover a piece of what I was just decrying: That the credibility of children and mental patients is not necessarily equal with the credibility of regular people, and that the dissociation process itself creates gaps and distortions of memory that allow survivors to war against one another in a dysphasic belief system.

So, I don't presume to believe all of the stories and every piece of the story of a given survivor, even of recognizable abuse. And I realize that it's impossible for the world at large to endorse the experience of all of survivors or to resist the compelling argument that's advanced by the legalists, that if one part of the story isn't true, then you shouldn't believe any part of the story. If one group of survivors is misguided, why should we listen to the others?

There's just such a historic and perfect record of silencing these two groups of people, child victims and adult survivors, and even creating institutional prejudice to keep them silent, that at this point I'll hold my optimism for continuing growth of this field until I see what happens in the next ten years. I think the decade is crucial.

I'll still be alive to watch it but I promise I won't be in there to lead it or to be a commentator on it. I leave it to you to lead and others to make sure that we don't allow this whole thing to just get beaten down into its origins.

What's different at the end of this century than existed the end of the last century? So much that it's probably simplistic to draw any comparison at all. And yet, it's kind of striking how so much of this emerged in the last 15 years and seems to be at risk of fading in the next ten.

What's different is that the voice accorded to this issue is much more intense and more widely disseminated. We look to the Freudian debate in the Vienna Society for Neurology and Psychiatry as if it were a big deal. Yet, it was unknown to the 19th-century world. It was a microcosm of erudition arguing a theoretical point. For all of Freud's power later, that discussion in 1896 didn't have the capacity to create a worldwide conflict or discussion. This one apparently does. At least, it does now, partly because media influence can be so pervasive and individuals are so dependent on what they learn from mass media, much more than they learn from professional journals.

So, what's different is we have a public issue now in the control of the mass media as opposed to one that was arcane. That makes it more unpredictable, I think. The only thing that is solidly predictable is the cyclic nature of this debate, that the backlash is creating the seeds of its own discrediting by its excesses. Backlash theorists are creating conspiracy theories that are even less likely than the ones that they've attacked. So, reasonable people are at least indifferent to this garbage and may be more inclined to pick up reasonable inquiry again.

Reasonable people, the average person on the street, acknowledge that child abuse is a reality. Most everybody will recognize at least that sexual abuse is a reality in proportions greater than used to be believed. Child sexual abuse is a phenomenon that people accept as a generality and attack in particular. We can believe that children are abused. We can believe that children in general are at risk of sexual abuse. We just can't believe that our neighbor is doing it. We can't believe that our lover is doing it. We can't believe that we, as a child, were subjected to it. At the individual level, we push it away.

So, there is a public acknowledgment that sexual abuse is real and serious, and that's more than used to be true.

I'm always in something of a dialectic, representing as best I can the voice of the people and the voice of some sort of human experience that wasn't necessarily available to the study of psychiatry and mental illness. Most everything I've ever done in my life has been addressed to nonpsychiatrists. Some of my work has been picked up within psychiatry and some if it has been rejected. I'll leave it on that note—that as much as I may have been wounded for the failure of the major professions to incorporate the knowledge of trauma, and as much as there's been a perturbation and a kind of an ebb and flow of endorsement of these things, probably the sane and scientifically reasonable thrust is going to be more or less in favor of understanding, and less gullible to the propaganda that's been thrown into this, from the extremists on both sides. I really don't mean to characterize the backlash as the bad guys, and everybody else in our field as the enlightened ones.

We have stumbled in the dark toward a better understanding of something that's never been fully understood before. And in the midst of our stumblings we are passing a torch to a larger number of people who will take a less emotional view of it and turn it into common knowledge.

2

Prosecution of Child Sexual Abuse in the United States

JOHN E. B. MYERS, SUSAN E. DIEDRICH,
DEVON LEE, KELLY FINCHER,
AND RACHEL M. STERN

Tracing the history of child sexual abuse prosecution in the United States, this chapter is divided into five sections. Section One describes child sexual abuse and rape prosecution prior to the 20th century. Section Two discusses 20th-century professional writing on child sexual abuse and rape. Professional writing provides insight into the intellectual and social context in which judges and prosecutors operated over the course of the 20th century. Section Three analyzes child sexual abuse prosecution from 1900 to 1950. Section Four discusses the modern era, beginning roughly in 1980, during which efforts were made to reform the criminal justice system to facilitate prosecution and accommodate children in court. Section Five offers conclusions about child sexual abuse prosecutions in the 20th century.

AUTHORS' NOTE: Portions of this chapter were published in "Professional Writing on Child Sexual Abuse from 1900 to 1975: Dominant Themes and Impact on Prosecution," by J. E. B. Myers, S. Diedrich, D. Lee, K. McClanahan Fincher, and R. Stern, 1999, *Child Maltreatment, 4,* pp. 201-216. Copyright © 1999 by Sage Publications. Adapted with permission.

SECTION ONE

Prosecution Prior
to the 20th Century

Forcible rape is common throughout history (Brownmiller, 1975), and prosecution of rape is nearly as old as the offense itself (Brundage, 1987). Thus, rape is dealt with harshly in the Code of Hammurabi, the Bible, Greek and Roman law, and the Visigothic Code (Drapkin, 1989; Phipps, 1997). In England, rape was prosecuted long before William crossed the Channel in 1066. "Rape was from time immemorial a felony" (Neville, 1957, p. 223). Modest numbers of rape prosecutions occurred throughout English history (Carter, 1985; Hale, 1736/1971; Pollock & Maitland, 1968). Laws against forcible rape applied to children as well as adults.

Laws designed specifically to protect children from sexual abuse appeared by the end of the Middle Ages. These laws stipulated that children lack capacity to consent to sex. "Consensual" intercourse with an underage girl was rape (Laiou, 1993, p. 125). Phipps (1997) writes,

> The first significant discussion of sexual crimes against children occurred during the maturation of canon law [i.e., church law] in the Middle Ages. Teachers of canon law taught that sexual intercourse with a girl who was under the age of consent to marry was rape even if the girl consented and failed to protest the intercourse. . . . Canon law from the fourteenth to fifteenth centuries continued to prohibit sexual intercourse with children. (p. 8)

In England, two influential acts of Parliament dealt with sex offenses against children. First, in 1275, the Statute of Westminster I provided, "The King prohibiteth that none do ravish, nor take away by force, any Maiden within Age, neither by her own consent, nor without." Ravish meant rape. "Within age" meant girls under 12, which was the "age of consent to marriage" (Coke, 1671/1979, p. 163).

The second important child protection law was enacted in 1576. The Statute 18 Elizabeth provided, "If any person shall unlawfully and carnally know any woman child under the age of ten years, every such unlawful and carnal knowledge shall be felony."

On this side of the Atlantic, American law always prohibited forcible rape. In addition to laws against forcible rape, American law prohibited statutory rape. Early statutory rape laws were based on England's Statute 18 Elizabeth. For example, an 1828 New York law forbade "carnally and unlawfully knowing any female child under the age of ten years" (Lewis, 1847, p. 557). Similarly, a Massachusetts statute punished with death anyone who "shall unlawfully and carnally know and abuse any female child, under the age of ten years" (Lewis, 1847).

Turning from legislation to the courts, prosecution for forcible rape of children occurred during the colonial period (Chapin, 1983; Williams, 1993) and the 19th century (e.g., *Brauer v. State*, 1870; *State v. Gray*, 1860). Statutory rape prosecutions occurred as well (e.g., *People v. Benson*, 1856; *People v. Castro*, 1882).

A useful way to study 19th-century prosecution of child sexual abuse is with books on criminal law. Joel Bishop (1814-1901) was one of America's leading 19th-century commentators on criminal law. The first edition of Bishop's influential treatise titled *The Criminal Law* was published in 1856. It thoroughly analyzed forcible rape, citing numerous court decisions, some involving child victims. In addition to forcible rape, Bishop's first edition discussed statutory rape. The entire discussion of child sexual abuse, however, appeared under the heading of rape; it did not discuss child sexual abuse that did not qualify as rape. By the third edition of Bishop's treatise in 1865, the author included a new section titled "Carnal Abuse of Children" (§ 1088). Interestingly, however, in 1865, Bishop wrote that there were very few court decisions on "carnal abuse of children."

During the 19th century, American law clearly prohibited forcible and statutory rape of children. Prosecution of these crimes occurred at a modest pace. In most 19th-century prosecutions for forcible and statutory rape, the accused was a stranger or an acquaintance. Prosecution of incest occurred, but was not common.

SECTION TWO

The Intellectual and Social Context of 20th-Century Prosecution: Professional Writing About Child Sexual Abuse

Prosecution occurs in an intellectual and social context, and historical examination of the criminal justice response to child sexual abuse benefits from analysis of the context in which judges, prosecutors, and legislators function. Professional writing in journals and books forms part of the intellectual context influencing prosecution. It is useful, therefore, to review 20th-century professional writing on child sexual abuse.

Psychological, Psychiatric, Medical, and Sociological Literature Prior to 1975

Throughout the first six decades of the 20th century, relatively little was written about child sexual abuse in psychiatric, psychological, medical, and sociological journals. In 1969, Vincent De Francis described with prescient accuracy the prevalence and effects of child sexual abuse. Sadly, society was not ready for De Francis's revelations. The first edition of Helfer and Kempe's famous book *The Battered Child* (1968) did not discuss child sexual abuse. In 1975, Walters wrote that "[v]irtually no literature exists on the sexual abuse of children" (p. 111). As late as 1977, Henry Kempe gave a speech to the American Academy of Pediatrics in which he described child sexual abuse as a "hidden pediatric problem and a neglected area" (1978, p. 382; see also McKerrow, 1973; O'Brien, 1980).

Prior to the mid-1970s, much of the professional writing about sexual abuse reflected four themes: (a) children are responsible for their own molestation, (b) mothers are to blame, (c) child sexual abuse is rare, and (d) sexual abuse does no harm (Reid, 1995). A few examples from professional journals of the time illustrate these themes.

Children are responsible for their own molestation. A common theme in pre-1975 writing on child sexual abuse—particularly incest—is that children are responsible for the molestation (Guarnieri, 1998; Weiss, Rogers, Darwin, & Dutton, 1955). Finkelhor (1979) writes,

> In the field of "victimology," there is a tradition of theories . . . that try to understand the ways in which victims contribute to their own victimization. The process is usually called "victim precipitation," and it highlights the fact that victims frequently contribute to their own murders—by striking a first blow or hurling an insult—or to their own robberies—by leaving doors unlocked and valuable possessions in plain sight.
>
> What is unusual in the case of sexual abuse of children is the degree of importance that the victim precipitation analysis has assumed. The idea that murder victims bring on their own demise developed fairly late in the field and had a moderate effect on our understanding of homicide. In contrast, the idea that children are responsible for their own seduction has been at the center of almost all writing on sexual abuse since the topic was first broached. (p. 23)

In 1937, Bender and Blau described their work with 5- to 12-year-old incest victims:

> The few studies that have been made of this subject have been contented to consider it an example of adult sex perversion from which innocent children must be protected by proper legal measures. Although this attitude may be correct in some cases, certain features in our material would indicate that the children may not resist and often play an active or even initializing role. . . . The history of the relationship in our cases usually suggested at least some cooperation of the child in the activity, and in some cases the child assumed an active role in initiating the relationship. . . . It is true that the child often rationalized with excuses of fear of physical harm or the enticement of gifts, but these were obviously secondary reasons. Even in the cases in which physical force may have been applied by the adult, this did not wholly account for the frequent repetition of the practice. (p. 513)

A 1975 textbook on psychiatry stated that "[t]he daughters collude in the incestuous liaison and play an active and even initiating role in establishing the pattern" (Henderson, 1975, p. 1536). Kinsey, Pomeroy, Martin, & Gebhard wrote in 1953 that "in many instances, [incestuous experiences] were repeated because the children had become interested in the sexual activity and had more or less actively sought repetitions of their experience" (p. 118). In 1927, Abraham wrote that "in a great number of cases the trauma was desired by the child unconsciously" (p. 48).

Abraham continued by saying that "in all [cases of sexual abuse] the trauma could have been prevented. The children could have called for help, run away, or offered resistance instead of yielding to the seduction" (p. 50). Thus, in pre-1975 professional writing on incest, children were often blamed for the abuse.

Mothers are to blame. In pre-1975 writing, children were not the only ones responsible for sexual abuse. Mothers shared the blame (Weiss et al., 1955). Salter (1988) writes that "the literature on child sexual abuse in this century has often held victims and their mothers responsible for the sexual abuse, particularly in cases of incest, frequently with little mention of the role of the offender" (p. 25). Reid (1995) reviewed the early literature and concluded, "Mother-blaming is as common as victim-blaming in the psychological and sociological literature. Mothers of incest victims are routinely referred to as frigid, hostile, unloving women. As women who are so cold and rejecting that they cause their husbands to seek sexual satisfaction elsewhere" (p. 13; see also Herman, 1992).

Child sexual abuse is rare. Some early writers claimed that child sexual abuse is rare. A sociologist wrote that "[t]he problem of incest is peculiar in several respects. Statistically its occurrence is negligible. Because of this infrequency the extent of its disruptive effect on human group life is minor" (Blumer, 1969).

Sexual abuse does no harm. In addition to claiming that sexual abuse is uncommon, contributors to the pre-1975 professional literature sometimes asserted that abuse does little harm. Salter (1995) writes,

> Did anyone ever assume that child sexual abuse would be harmless? Well, actually, yes. A number of older studies did. The belief that child sexual abuse was not traumatic was entwined with the belief that it was, in actuality, not a trauma visited on the child but a form of acting out by the child. (p. 161)

In 1952, Bender and Grugett wrote, "In contrast to the harsh social taboos surrounding such relationships, there exists no scientific proof that there are any resulting deleterious effects" (p. 827). In 1953, Kinsey et al. advanced the theory that sexual abuse is not inherently harmful:

> It is difficult to understand why a child, except for its cultural conditioning, should be disturbed at having its genitalia touched, or disturbed at

seeing the genitalia of other persons, or disturbed at even more specific sexual contacts. . . . Some of the more experienced students of juvenile problems have come to believe that the emotional reactions of parents, police officers, and other adults who discover that a child has had such contact, may disturb the child more seriously than the sexual contacts themselves. (p. 121)

For indefatigable criticism of Kinsey's methods and motives, see Reisman (1998).

In 1964, Brunhold wrote, "Lasting psychological injury as a result of sexual assaults suffered in infancy is not very common" (p. 8). In 1976, Pomeroy stated, "When we examine a cross-section of the population as we did in the Kinsey Report we find many beautiful and mutually satisfying relationships between fathers and daughters. These may be transient or ongoing, but they have no harmful effects" (p. 13).

SUMMARY

Prior to the mid-1970s, much of the psychiatric, psychological, medical, and sociological writing on child sexual abuse downplayed the seriousness of the problem. Herman (1981) reviewed the early literature and discovered "a vastly elaborated intellectual tradition which served the purpose of suppressing the truth about incest, a tradition which, like so many others, originates in the works of Freud" (p. 9; see also Masson, 1984; Olafson, Corwin, & Summit, 1993).

The Legal Literature

Unless you are an attorney, you may not realize that law libraries are filled with thousands of articles written by law professors and law students. These articles are contained in journals called law reviews. Hundreds of law review articles appear yearly.

Judges use law review articles as research tools and as support for legal analysis (Richardson, 1983). Although law review articles exert a relatively minor influence on judicial decision making, no one disputes that law reviews occasionally sway judges' thinking. Interestingly, a study of court decisions from 1989 to 1991 found that the most frequently cited law review article during that period was an article on expert testimony in child sexual abuse cases (Merritt & Putnam, 1996).

We examined law review articles on child sexual abuse back to the late 1880s. Articles were located through the *Index to Legal Periodicals and Books* (1997), which is the legal profession's equivalent of *Index Medicus* or *Psychological Abstracts*. The *Index to Legal Periodicals and Books* lists law review articles by subject and year. The *Index* began publication in 1888 (Jones, 1888). Today, the *Index* has a subject heading for child sexual abuse. This was not always the case, however. Child sexual abuse was not added as a separate subject until 1991. Prior to 1991, sexual abuse was listed under "child abuse." The subject heading "child abuse" first appeared in 1970. Prior to 1970, physical child abuse was listed under the crime of "assault and battery." Articles on child sexual abuse were listed under "rape." Thus, to locate articles on child sexual abuse prior to the 1970s, it was necessary to use the subject heading "rape." As it turns out, it was useful to read law review articles on rape of adults as well as articles on child sexual abuse. The attitude of pre-1975 law review authors toward adult rape victims was nearly identical to the attitude toward child victims.

Perhaps the most surprising finding from our examination of pre-1975 law review articles on rape and child sexual abuse is the dearth of writing on the subject. In the nearly 90 years from 1888 to 1975, very few law review articles address rape of adult women. Even fewer discuss child sexual abuse. Of the few articles on child sexual abuse, most deal with statutory rape. Almost nothing was written about incest. We were genuinely surprised that out of the hundreds of law review articles published annually, only a handful each year discussed rape or sexual abuse. By contrast, early law reviews published many articles on theft, murder, and other crimes. In the mountainous law review literature before 1975, that so few pages were devoted to sexual assault speaks volumes. The pre-1975 silence of legal scholars is evidence of society's "blind spot" for sexual abuse (Summit, 1988).

Interestingly, of the few pre-1975 law review articles on rape or sexual abuse, most were written by law students, not professors. Prior to roughly 1975, law professors practically ignored rape and sexual abuse as topics worthy of scholarly research and writing.

Reading the relatively few pre-1975 law review articles on rape and sexual abuse, one is struck by the skepticism of women and girls (sexual abuse of boys was rarely discussed). Throughout these law review articles, the level of disbelief is truly remarkable. The best way to understand this pervasive skepticism is to let the authors speak for themselves. Four themes dominate much of the pre-1975 legal writing on rape and sexual abuse: (a) fear of fabricated allegations, (b) fear of "crazy women," (c) preoccupation with consent ("no" really means "yes"), and (d) corroboration of the victim's testimony.

FEAR OF FABRICATED ALLEGATIONS

Sir Matthew Hale lived from 1609 to 1676. Hale served as Chief Justice of the Court of King's Bench, England's most important trial court, from 1671 until his death. Hale's influential treatise titled *The History of the Pleas of the Crown* was published posthumously in 1736. Chapter 58 of Hale's book provides detailed treatment of the law on rape, and it is here that Hale penned his famous remark, "It must be remembered, that [rape] is an accusation easily to be made and hard to be proved, and harder to be defended by the party accused, though never so innocent" (p. 635). Over the years, Hale's words were repeated by countless judges and attorneys (e.g., *People v. Benson*, 1856; *People v. Gammage*, 1992; *People v. Jones*, 1954; *People v. Schott*, 1991; *State v. Nelson*, 1991). Indeed, as late as 1997, we find the Supreme Court of South Dakota writing that "allegations of sexual misconduct are easy to allege and difficult to disprove" (*State v. Chamley*, p. 615).

Law review authors doted on Hale's warning. In 1925, for example, Puttkammer wrote,

> In its very nature rape is a crime which is peculiarly open to false accusations and is difficult of defense. For generations, judges have been repeating Lord Hale's statement that "it is an accusation easily to be made and hard to be proved, and harder to be defended by the party to be accused though never so innocent." (p. 421)

Today, Lord Hale is the object of a good deal of criticism (e.g., Brownmiller, 1975). In fairness to the Chief Justice, however, Hale was no apologist for sex offenders. Hale viewed rape as a despicable crime that "ought severely and impartially to be punished with death" (1736/1971, p. 635). Hale's famous caution does not appear to spring from exaggerated skepticism about women. Rather, Hale's concern arose from his experience as a judge. Hale describes several cases of apparently false allegations of rape, one in which an old man was accused despite overwhelming evidence that he was physically incapable of the crime. Hale wrote,

> I only mention these instances, that we may be the more cautious upon trials of offenses of this nature, wherein the court and jury may with so much ease be imposed upon without great care and vigilance; the heinousness of the offense many times transporting the judge and jury with so much indignation, that they are over hastily carried to the conviction of the person accused thereof by the confident testimony, sometimes of malicious and false witnesses. (p. 636)

Many pre-1975 law review articles are less balanced than Lord Hale. Indeed, law reviews are rife with fear of fabricated claims of rape or sexual abuse. Ploscowe, a law professor, cautioned in 1960 that "[p]rosecuting attorneys must *continually* be on guard for the charge of sex offenses brought by the spurned female that has as its underlying basis a desire for revenge, or a blackmail or shakedown scheme" (p. 233). A 1938 law student article stated that "the rape statute affords promising fields for extortion and malicious prosecutions" ("Statutory Rape," 1938, p. 338). In 1970, a law student wrote,

> The incidence of false accusations and the potential for unjust convictions are perhaps greatest with sexual offenses. Women often falsely accuse men of sexual attacks to extort money, to force marriage, to satisfy a childish desire for notoriety, or to attain personal revenge. Their motives include hatred, a sense of shame after consenting to illicit intercourse, especially when pregnancy results, and delusion. ("The Corroboration Rule," 1970, p. 460)

In 1952, a law student warned that "the sexual nature of the crime is conducive to false accusations" ("Forcible and Statutory Rape," 1952, p. 56). The student author continued,

False reports may also stem from other sources. A rape accusation is so potent a weapon against a man that a woman may deliberately and maliciously distort her report of the sexual encounter to secure for herself money, marriage, or revenge. (p. 69)

FEAR OF "CRAZY WOMEN"

Related to concern about fabricated allegations was fear of "crazy women." Ploscowe wrote,

Complaints of sex offenses are easily made. They spring from a variety of motives and reasons. The psychiatrist and the psychoanalyst would have a field day were he to examine all complaints of rape, sexual tampering with children, incest, homosexual behavior with young boys, deviant sex behavior, etc., in any given community. He could find that complaints are too often made of sexual misbehavior that has occurred only in the over-ripe fantasies of the so-called victims. Frequently, the more or less unconscious wish for the sexual experience is converted into the experience itself. (1960, pp. 222-223)

In 1952, a law student wrote that "[m]ore serious [than the deliberate fabrication] is the problem of the psychopathic woman. She may completely fabricate a forceful sexual act yet be unaware of the fanciful origin of her complaint" ("Forcible and Statutory Rape," 1952, p. 69). In 1966, another law student stated,

Masochistic tendencies seem to lead many women to seek men who will ill-treat them sexually. The problem becomes even greater when one recognizes the existence of a so-called "riddance mechanism." This is a phenomenon where a woman who fears rape unconsciously sets up the rape to rid herself of the fear and to "get it over with." ("The Resistance Standard," 1966, p. 682)

PREOCCUPATION WITH CONSENT

Pre-1975 law review articles on forcible rape were preoccupied with the issue of consent. Several authors discuss the idea that "no" really means "yes." In 1966, a law student made his point by quoting from Slovenko (1965),

Although a woman may desire sexual intercourse, it is customary for her to say, "no, no, no" (although meaning "yes, yes, yes") and to expect the male to be the aggressor. . . . It is always difficult in rape cases to determine whether the female really meant "no." ("The Resistance Standard," 1966, p. 682)

Another student author stated,

Many women, for example, require as a part of preliminary "love play" aggressive overtures by the man. Often their erotic pleasure may be enhanced by, or even depend upon, an accompanying physical struggle.

[A] woman's need for sexual satisfaction may lead to the unconscious desire for forceful penetration, the coercion serving neatly to avoid the guilt feelings which might arise after willing participation.

The feminine wish to be subjected to a sexual attack may become the subject of an hallucination.

Despite the prevalent taboo on aggressive sexuality, many "normal" men and women may unconsciously desire copulation coupled with brute force. ("Forcible and Statutory Rape," 1952, pp. 66-67, 69, 73)

A 1954 student article reported that "resistance during preliminary love-making greatly increases the sexual pleasure of some women" ("Rape and Battery," 1954, p. 728).

Consent was a frequent issue in court. Prior to adoption of rape shield laws in the 1970s, defense attorneys frequently put rape victims "on trial" by offering evidence of the woman's lack of "chastity" (Berger, 1977). As one court put it, "The underlying thought here is that it is more probable that an unchaste woman would assent . . . than a virtuous woman" (People v. Collins, 1962). Another court remarked that "common experience teaches us that the woman who has once departed from the paths of virtue is far more apt to consent to another lapse than is the one who has never stepped aside from that path" (State v. Wood, 1942, p. 418). A third court wrote, "No impartial mind can resist the conclusion that a female who had been in the recent habit of illicit intercourse with others will not be so likely to resist as one who is spotless and pure" (Lee v. State, 1915, p. 145).

Although unchastity affected female credibility, the same was apparently not the case for men. In State v. Sibley (1895), the court stated,

It is a matter of common knowledge that the bad character of a man for chastity does not even in the remotest degree affect his character for truth,

. . . while it does that of a woman. . . . What destroys the standing of the [woman] in all the walks of life has no effect whatever on the standing for truth of the [man]. (p. 171)

Pre-1975 law review articles on rape reflect nearly unanimous support for the defense strategy of highlighting the woman's lack of "chastity." A 1938 law student article stated that "[i]t is everywhere conceded that in a prosecution for rape by force and against the will of a female, her previous unchastity may be shown as rendering it more probable that she consented to the act" ("Statutory Rape," 1938, p. 336). Even in statutory rape cases, in which the victim is a child, and where consent is legally irrelevant, law review authors favored evidence of unchastity. Ploscowe (1960) wrote that

It is imperative that the lack of chastity of the young woman be deemed a defense to a charge of statutory rape. It is ridiculous for the police to charge with rape every male who may have had sexual contact with a promiscuous young woman or a young prostitute. (p. 222)

In the same year, another article stated that "[i]t is not always justifiable to punish a male as a felon for succumbing to the lures of an immoral, underage female" ("Statutory Rape: Previous Chaste," 1960, p. 213; see also "Forcible and Statutory Rape," 1952; "Statutory Rape," 1938; Tonry, 1965).

CORROBORATION OF THE VICTIM'S TESTIMONY

For most crimes—from pocket picking to assault—the uncorroborated testimony of the victim is sufficient evidence to support a verdict of guilt. In other words, a jury may convict entirely on the uncorroborated testimony of the victim. In sex offense cases, however, suspicion of victims was high, and during much of the 20th century, some courts ruled that guilt of a sex offense could not be predicated on a victim's uncorroborated testimony if the victim's testimony was "inherently improbable, or so indefinite, contradictory, or unreliable that it would be unsafe to rest a conviction thereon" ("Rape—Assault," 1939, p. 264). During the 1970s, most courts abandoned the corroboration requirement (Myers,

1997). Pre-1975 law review articles generally favored the corroboration requirement.

Switching from law review articles to books about law, one treatise stands out. John H. Wigmore was one of America's most influential legal scholars. Wigmore was a law professor at Harvard, and in 1904 he published the first edition of his monumental 12-volume treatise on the law of evidence. Although Wigmore was brilliant, his thinking about sex offense victims was remarkably negative. Yet, because Wigmore was so influential among judges and attorneys, he contributed mightily to the tradition of skepticism. Wigmore wrote,

> Modern psychiatrists have amply studied the behavior of errant young girls and women coming before the courts in all sorts of cases. Their psychic complexes are multifarious, distorted partly by inherent defects, partly by diseased derangements or abnormal instincts, partly by bad social environments, partly by temporary physiological or emotional conditions. One form taken by these complexes is that of contriving false charges of sexual offenses by men. The unchaste mentally (let us call it) finds incidental but direct expression in the narration of imaginary sex incidents of which the narrator is the heroine or the victim. On the surface the narration is straight-forward and convincing. The real victim, however, too often in such cases is the innocent man. . . . No judge should ever let a sex offense charge go to the jury unless the female complainant's social history and mental makeup have been examined and testified to by a qualified physician. It is time that the courts awakened to the sinister possibilities of injustice that lurk in believing such a witness without careful psychiatric scrutiny. (1904/1970, pp. 736-737, 740)

Wigmore was tremendously influential, and his belief that women and girls should be psychiatrically examined influenced judges and attorneys (see *Burton v. State*, 1953; *People v. Spigno*, 1957; *Wedmore v. State*, 1957; *Yessen v. State*, 1950). In 1937, a committee of the American Bar Association recommended,

> Today it is unanimously held (and we say "unanimously" advisedly) by experienced psychiatrists that the complainant woman in a sex offense should *always* be examined by competent experts to ascertain whether she suffers from some mental or moral delusion or tendency, frequently found especially in young girls, causing distortion of the imagination in sex cases. . . . The warnings of the psychiatric profession, supported as they are by thousands of observed cases, should be heeded by our profession. (quoted in Wigmore, 1904/1970, Vol. 3A, § 924a)

Lesser legal luminaries than Wigmore and the American Bar Association agreed. A 1950 student law review article stated, "Recognizing that false sex charges may stem from the psychic complexes of a female who appears normal to the layman, courts have permitted psychiatrists to expose mental defects, hysteria, and pathological lying in sex prosecutrices" ("Psychiatric Evaluation," 1950, p. 1338).

Summary

During the first six decades of the 20th century, the legal, mental health, and medical literatures contributed to a legacy of skepticism about allegations of rape and child sexual abuse. Then, quite suddenly, in the middle of the 1970s, professional writing changed dramatically. Before discussing this change, however, we want briefly to describe our concern about the skepticism of the pre-1975 literature. Our misgivings are not that authors were skeptical of women and children. We have no quarrel with skepticism qua skepticism. Indeed, we believe a healthy measure of skepticism is important to any inquiry. Our concern with the pre-1975 literature is not the skepticism, but the level of skepticism, a level that was exaggerated and inaccurate. Skepticism, like most things, is useful in moderation. When taken to extremes, however, skepticism can be dangerous. We believe the skepticism of the pre-1975 literature on rape and child sexual abuse abandoned moderation and crossed the line into dangerous demagoguery.

1975—The Continental Divide in Professional Writing

As far as professional writing about child sexual abuse is concerned, 1975 is the continental divide. Prior to that year, professional writing, although not monolithic, was largely skeptical. Beginning in approximately 1975, however, there was a virtual explosion of writing that was more sympathetic to victims. What caused this dramatic shift in professional writing? The feminist movement of the 1960s and 1970s was largely responsible.

In law review articles, the more positive post-1975 tone can be attributed to authorship. Law students and law professors write most law review articles. It was not until the 1970s that substantial numbers of women began studying law and entering the ranks of law teaching. Prior to that time, the vast majority of law students and law professors were men. Female law students and professors, as well as male students and professors with feminist leanings, have written much of the post-1975 legal literature on rape and child sexual abuse. One of the ground-breaking post-1975 law review articles, for example, was Vivian Berger's article "Man's Trial, Woman's Tribulation: Rape Cases in the Courtroom," in which she wrote that "the singularity of the law of rape stems from a deep distrust of the female accuser" (1977, p. 10; see also Giles, 1976; LeGrand, 1973; McDermott, 1975; "The Rape Corroboration," 1972; Welch, 1976; Wesolowski, 1976; Wood, 1973).

The women's movement was not the only factor that influenced writing on child sexual abuse. The modern era of child protection, which coincided with the women's movement, got seriously under way in the mid-1960s and was firmly entrenched by 1975. In addition, the 1970s witnessed the birth of the victims' rights movement and important scientific efforts to uncover the prevalence and harmful effects of child sexual abuse (Finkelhor, 1979; Russell, 1983, 1986).

Despite impressive gains during the 1970s and 1980s, the long tradition of skepticism continues to influence the thinking of some judges, attorneys, journalists, doctors, and mental health professionals. Indeed, throughout the United States and Europe, the level of skepticism may once again be on the rise (Beckett, 1996; Myers, 1994, 1995).

SECTION THREE

Prosecution of Child Sexual Abuse from 1900 to 1950

Little is known about child sexual abuse prosecution in the United States during the first half of the 20th century. There is no doubt that prosecution occurred. In her elegant history of the Massachusetts Society for the Prevention of Cruelty to Children (MSPCC), Gordon (1988) writes that early in the 20th century, incest "cases were common in family-violence case records . . . , constituting about 10 percent of the caseload" (p. 207). Although "[t]he MSPCC considered incest cases 'too revolting to publish,'" employees of the MSPCC used the courts to protect children.

In 1939, a New York citizens committee reported on 1,395 sex offense victims. "The average age is thirteen years, eight months. They range from two to sixty-eight years. Seventy-three are under six [5%]; 260 between six and ten [19%]; 655 between ten and sixteen [47%]" (Citizens Committee, 1939, quoted in Karpman, 1954, p. 66). In this study, 71% of the sex offense victims were children.

A 1950 study determined that 76.9% of sex offense victims were between 10 and 15 years of age (Karpman, 1954, p. 66). From 1945 to 1951, in Kings County, New York, 73% of rape indictments leading to conviction were for statutory rape ("Forcible and Statutory Rape," 1952).

Although prosecution of child sexual abuse occurred during the first half of the 20th century, we are unaware of any systematic research describing the scope of prosecution and the nature of the cases. In an effort to begin filling this vacuum, we analyzed 463 criminal child sexual abuse cases decided by American appellate courts between 1900 and 1950.

In the United States, a person who is convicted of a serious crime such as child sexual abuse has the right to appeal the conviction to an appellate court. Although rates of appeal differ somewhat from state to state, "the total number of appeals to the intermediate appeals court is likely to amount to less than 10% of all convictions entered by the state's general trial court" (LaFave, Israel, & King, 2000, p. 25). Appellate court judges review cases and either affirm or reverse convictions. A conviction is reversed if serious legal errors occurred during the trial. With most reversals, the prosecutor has the option to retry the defendant.

Based on our review of pre-1975 professional literature and scattered appellate court decisions, we formulated the following predictions:

1. Given the level of skepticism in professional writing regarding victims, relatively few child sexual abuse cases were prosecuted during the first half of the 20th century. In particular, few incest cases were prosecuted.

2. Appellate court decisions from 1900 to 1950 reflected a high level of skepticism regarding child victims.

3. Appellate court decisions from 1900 to 1950 frequently invoked the rule that victims of child sexual abuse should be psychiatrically examined.

4. Appellate court decisions from 1900 to 1950 frequently invoked the rule that corroboration is needed to support a child's testimony.

Method of Locating
Appellate Court Decisions

We analyzed 463 state appellate court decisions in criminal child sexual abuse cases from 1900 to 1950. We did not examine decisions in civil child sexual abuse cases (e.g., juvenile court). Decisions by federal appellate courts were not analyzed because, prior to the 1980s, very few child sexual abuse prosecutions occurred in federal court. During the first half of the 20th century, and today, the vast majority of child sexual abuse prosecution occurs in state court.

Our research is limited to decisions by appellate courts. We did not examine decisions by trial courts. Limiting research to appellate courts occurred because, with very few exceptions, decisions by state trial judges are not published. Nor are trial court decisions indexed in a way that makes them accessible. As a result, there is no national database of state trial court decisions. By contrast, appellate court decisions are indexed and published as described below.

In the United States, decisions by appellate courts set legal precedent, whereas trial court decisions do not. Appellate courts not only adjudicate individual cases, they establish precedent that binds trial judges in future cases in that state. In other words, appellate courts make law. Law created by appellate courts is called "common law." Studying appellate court decisions informs us of the state of the law at given periods, and allows us to discern trends in the law.

There are drawbacks to using appellate court decisions as windows on history. The work of appellate judges provides limited insight into the day-to-day operation of the criminal justice system. For example, appellate decisions tell us very little about decision making by the police and prosecutors. Despite the limitations of appellate court decisions, there is no denying the importance of appellate law. Moreover, appellate decisions are readily available for study, whereas records of the police, prosecutors, and trial judges are often difficult or impossible to examine. Thus, although we acknowledge the shortcomings of appellate cases as historical data, we believe the work of appellate courts constitutes an important piece of the historical puzzle.

The 20th-century decisions of state appellate courts are compiled and published by the West Publishing Company of St. Paul, Minnesota. On a continuous basis, West Publishing collects and publishes appellate court decisions from all state and federal appellate courts. The decisions are published in books that comprise the *West Reporter System*. West's *Reporter System* is the nation's only comprehensive compilation of state and federal appellate court decisions.

Beginning in 1975, West Publishing supplemented the books of its *Reporter System* with an online computer database containing appellate court decisions from all state and federal appellate courts. The online system is called Westlaw (see also Lexis).

Throughout the 20th-century, West Publishing compiled appellate court decisions from its *Reporter System* into an index called *The Decennial Digest: A Complete Digest of All Decisions of the State and Federal Courts as Reported in the National Reporter System and State Reports*. The index is updated regularly. Every ten years, a decennial digest is compiled. We used the appropriate *Decennial Digests* to locate appellate court decisions from 1900 to 1945.

Within the *Decennial Digest*, appellate court decisions are indexed according to subject (e.g., criminal law, divorce, contract, property). Until recently, there was no subject specifically devoted to child sexual abuse. Therefore, to locate decisions on child sexual abuse, we examined the following subject headings: rape, attempted rape, sodomy (often called the "crime against nature"), sexual assault, assault, attempted sexual assault, incest, molestation, carnal knowledge, lewd and lascivious behavior, taking indecent liberties with a child, and contributing to the delinquency of a minor.

To gather decisions from 1945 to 1950, we used the Westlaw computer database. Although Westlaw did not come online until 1975, the Westlaw database contains appellate decisions from 1945 to the present. In Westlaw, we used subject headings similar to the headings used to examine the *Decennial Digest*. As stated above, our research in the *Decennial Digest* and Westlaw disclosed 463 criminal appellate court decisions on child sexual abuse from 1900 to 1950.

In conducting our research in the *Decennial Digest* and Westlaw, we worried that we might fail to locate a significant number of appellate court decisions. As a cross-check on our case-finding method, we examined a leading legal encyclopedia, *Corpus Juris*, published in 1929. In *Corpus Juris*, we reviewed the article titled "Rape." This article describes legal principles and cites numerous appellate court decisions prior to 1929. There is a significant degree of overlap between the decisions we found in the *Decennial Digest*/Westlaw search and the cases cited in *Corpus Juris*. Our study of *Corpus Juris*, nonetheless, did add a small number of cases to our sample.

We did not find every criminal appellate court decision on child sexual abuse from 1900 to 1950.[1] We believe, however, that we located a sufficient percentage of the decisions to allow us to draw tentative conclusions about prosecution from 1900 to 1950.

Characteristics Examined in Decisions

We examined appellate court decisions involving sexual offenses against children. As stated earlier, our research is limited to criminal cases. We did not examine civil cases, such as cases in juvenile or family court.

We defined "child" as a female or male younger than 18 years of age. In our sample of 463 appellate court decisions, many of the decisions reported the child's age in years. In some decisions, however, the child's precise age is not mentioned in the appellate court decision. Instead, the decision makes a statement such as, "This is a prosecution for carnal knowledge of a minor under age fourteen."

In this research, each appellate court decision was read by one of the authors. The reader documented the following case information:

- Age of child
- Gender of child
- Relationship of perpetrator to child—extrafamilial versus intrafamilial (Intrafamilial was defined as biological parent, stepparent,

adoptive parent, uncle, or other blood relative. Extrafamilial was defined as stranger, mother's boyfriend, or acquaintance.)

- Whether corroboration was required of the child's trial testimony
- Whether a psychological evaluation was ordered of the child
- Whether convictions were reversed or affirmed by the appellate court (Only guilty verdicts result in appeals. If a defendant is acquitted at trial, the prosecution cannot appeal the acquittal.)
- Punishments given to convicted perpetrators

In addition to the foregoing objective information, we sought to determine whether appellate court decisions written between 1900 and 1950 reveal the kind of skepticism about women and girls that is so flagrant in professional writing of the time. Admittedly, assessing judicial decisions for evidence of skepticism is a subjective process, a process that required us to read between the lines as well as on the surface. Nevertheless, we were keenly interested to see whether the rampant skepticism of the literature was afoot in judicial decisions. Thus, we examined decisions for evidence of blatant or subtle skepticism about victims.

Results

Here we describe the results of our examination of 463 criminal appellate court decisions decided between 1900 and 1950.

VOLUME OF APPELLATE
DECISIONS OVER TIME

The volume of child sexual abuse prosecution increased at a fairly steady pace from 1900 to 1950. During the first decade of the 20th century, we found only four appellate court decisions on child sexual abuse. We should quickly add, however, that there were more than four appellate court decisions from 1900 to 1910.[2] We simply did not find them with our research methodology. Moreover, only a fraction of convictions are appealed. Thus, without question, there were many more than four prosecutions during the first decade of the 20th century. Nevertheless, the small number of appellate court decisions that we succeeded in locating suggests that prosecution of child sexual abuse was far from common from 1900 to 1910.

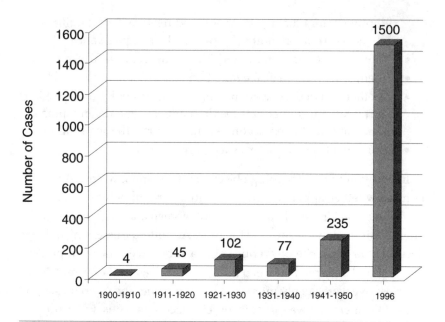

Figure 2.1. Criminal Appellate Court Decisions on Child Sexual Abuse from 1900 to 1950 (plus 1996 for comparison)
NOTE: This figure does not represent all decisions from 1900 to 1950.

Figure 2.1 indicates that the rate of prosecution increased gradually over the course of the first half of the century. The last column of Figure 2.1 allows one to compare the rate of appellate court decisions prior to 1950 with the rate in the recent past. Using a sample of 2 months in 1996, we estimate (roughly) that there were approximately 1,500 appellate court decisions on child sexual abuse in 1996.

It should be noted regarding Figure 2.1 that over the course of the 20th century, the total volume of criminal litigation for all crimes increased significantly. Figure 2.1 does not take this overall increase into account.

GENDER OF VICTIMS

Most, but not all, decisions reported the gender of the victim. In the decisions we examined from 1900 to 1950, we found that 90% of victims were female. The years 1931 to 1940 varied slightly from this figure, with 81.8% of the victims female and 18.2% male.

Table 2.1   Characteristics of Child Victims

	1900-1910	1911-1920	1921-1930	1931-1940	1941-1950
Total Cases	4	45	102	77	235
Females	4(100%)	41(97.6%)	88(88.9%)	63(81.8%)	221(94%)
Males	0	1(2.4%)	11(11.1%)	14(18.2%)	14(6%)
Age					
Under 6	0	1	1	5	8
6-14	1	25	55	52	75
15-18	1	13	14	9	31
Relationship					
Intrafamilial	2(50%)	17(51.5%)	17(25.4%)	5(6.8%)	40(26.1%)
Extrafamilial	2(50%)	16(48.5%)	50(74.6%)	68(93.2%)	113(73.9%)

NOTE: Not all of the cases surveyed reported the age of the victim, the sex of the victim, or the relationship between the victim and the offender.

AGE OF VICTIMS

Of decisions reporting the child's age, 5.2% of victims were younger than age 6, 71.4% of victims were between the ages of 6 and 14, and 23.4% of victims were between the ages of 15 and 18 (see Table 2.1). Of the decisions reporting the age of the victim, the mean age of the child at the time of the offense was 12.1 years.

EXTRAFAMILIAL
VERSUS INTRAFAMILIAL

Approximately 75% of the decisions involved extrafamilial abuse (see Table 2.1).

CHARACTERISTICS OF
CRIMES CHARGED

The breakdown of crimes charged in the 463 appellate court decisions is presented in Table 2.2.

Table 2.2   Characteristics of Crimes Charged

Crime Charged	1900-1910	1911-1920	1921-1930	1931-1940	1941-1950
Lewd Act	0	8	27	31	53
Rape	2	12	22	7	58
Attempted Rape	0	0	3	2	18
Statutory Rape	1	9	12	0	22
Sodomy	0	0	2	2	8
Incest	1	10	5	1	4
Carnal Knowledge	0	5	11	8	30
Assault	0	0	1	3	4
Indecent Liberties	0	0	15	9	26
Other	0	3	5	14	9

Rape was charged in 21.8% of decisions. A lewd act was the offense in 25.7% of decisions. Overall, 93.3% of the charges involved some type of physical contact abuse. The remaining 6.7% of the charges involved crimes such as enticement and indecent exposure.

It is difficult to draw meaningful conclusions from the crimes charged because states differ somewhat in terminology, and because the crime charged does not always correspond with the type of abuse inflicted.

MOST CONVICTIONS WERE AFFIRMED

Of the 463 decisions reviewed in this research, 72.5% of the guilty verdicts were affirmed on appeal (i.e., upheld on appeal). Appellate courts reversed 27.5% of the guilty verdicts.

In a large portion of reversals in this research, the appellate court reversed because the trial judge allowed the prosecutor to introduce evidence that the accused person committed other crimes—crimes for which the accused was not then on trial. Very few reversals were based on concerns about a child's testimony.

Table 2.3   Issues on Appeal

	1900-1910	1911-1920	1921-1930	1931-1940	1941-1950
Outcome					
Affirmed	1(25%)	31(68.9%)	72(70.6%)	53(68.9%)	179(76.1%)
Reversed	3(75%)	14(31.1%)	30(29.4%)	24(31.1%)	56(23.9%)
Hearsay[a]					
Allowed	0	16	13	4	51
Not Allowed	1	1	2	1	20
Child's Testimony[b]					
Allowed	4	40	65	57	190
Corroboration Required	0	1	6	6	9
Competency Questioned	1	0	8	7	10
Credibility Questioned	0	3	0	0	1
Sanity Questioned	0	1	0	1	0
Psych Exam Ordered	0	0	0	0	1
Sentencing					
Prison	4	15	15	3	27
Death	0	0	5	0	1

NOTE: a. Cases reporting hearsay evidence at issue on appeal
b. Cases reporting child's testimony at issue on appeal

CHILDREN TESTIFIED IN MOST CASES

Of the 463 decisions reviewed in this research, children testified in 76.9% of the cases (see Table 2.3).

CORROBORATION OF THE CHILD'S TESTIMONY

In the 463 appellate court decisions examined in this project, corroboration of the child's testimony was an issue on appeal in only 22 cases (4.7%) (see Table 2.3).

COMPETENCE TO TESTIFY

Children's testimonial competence was an issue on appeal in only 26 of the 463 appellate court decisions (5.6%) (see Table 2.3).

COURT-ORDERED PSYCHOLOGICAL EXAMINATION OF THE CHILD

We found only one case in the 463 reviewed in which an appellate court ordered a psychological examination of a child (see Table 2.3).

SENTENCING OF CONVICTED OFFENDERS

Only 64 of the 463 decisions examined (13.3%) reported the sentence given to the offender (see Table 2.3). Sentences varied somewhat from state to state. As expected, more severe sentences were given for more serious types of abuse. Offenders who committed rape or incest received the harshest punishments, ranging from 25 to 99 years imprisonment. In the decisions reviewed in this research, appellate courts did not discuss treatment or rehabilitation of offenders.

The death penalty was available as punishment for rape in 18 states in 1925 (Bye, 1926). Johnson (1957) found 124 death sentences for rape in North Carolina alone from 1909 to 1954. In 1965, 15 states provided the death penalty for "carnal knowledge" of a child (Bedau, 1982). In our research of child sexual abuse cases from 1900 to 1950, we found six instances in which the death penalty was imposed (see Table 2.3). The U.S. Supreme Court ruled in *Coker v. Georgia* (1977) that the death penalty for rape of an adult woman is unconstitutional as a violation of the cruel and unusual punishment clause of the Eighth Amendment to the U.S. Constitution.

Discussion

Before we began our review of criminal appellate court decisions from the first half of the 20th century, we made four predictions. First, we projected that relatively few child sexual abuse cases were prosecuted from 1900 to 1950. Second, we hypothesized that appellate court decisions during the first half of the 20th century reflected a high level of skepticism regarding allegations of child sexual abuse. Third, we predicted that early appellate court judges often invoked the rule that children should be psychiatrically examined. Finally, we assumed that appellate courts from 1900 to 1950 frequently required corroboration of the victim's testimony. For the most part, our predictions were refuted.

Prosecution occurred at a steady, although modest, pace. From 1900 onward, the volume of prosecution increased at a modest pace. By late 20th-century standards, the volume of prosecution during the first half of the century was modest. Nevertheless, American criminal courts routinely adjudicated allegations of child sexual abuse. The American legal system did not ignore sexual abuse of children. At the same time, however, the low rate of prosecution during the first half of the 20th century supports the conclusion that Americans were not ready to acknowledge the prevalence of child sexual abuse.

Open skepticism is uncommon in appellate court decisions. We were pleasantly surprised to find that appellate court decisions from 1900 to 1950 contain very little open skepticism of allegations of child sexual abuse. By and large, appellate court judges handled child sexual abuse cases in the same professional manner they handled other crimes: methodically reviewing the evidence and applying the law. As with other crimes, most child sexual abuse convictions were upheld on appeal.

Appellate court judges during the first half of the 20th century were certainly aware of skepticism concerning allegations of rape and sexual abuse. Judges read the newspaper, and they perused law books, law reviews, and professional journals. No doubt, quite a few early 20th-century judges shared the skepticism expressed in the literature. Why, then, does so little of this skepticism show up in judicial decisions? We believe there are two reasons.

First, judges take their responsibility seriously. The function of an appellate court judge is to review the outcome of a trial, not to stand on a soapbox and pontificate about divisive social issues. Throughout American history, judges have an admirable, if imperfect, record of sticking to the law and avoiding sociopolitical entanglements. Thus, although quite a few early 20th-century judges probably shared the skepticism of their day, they held their skepticism in check when they penned their decisions.

The second reason we find little open skepticism in appellate court decisions from the first half of the 20th century relates, we believe, to the strength of the evidence in the cases. Then as now, the prosecution's most important witness was the child, and, in many of the cases we reviewed, children provided powerful evidence. The famous English judge William Blackstone observed long ago that children "often give the clearest and truest testimony" (1769, p. 214). Judges see the reality of child sexual abuse at close range.

Appellate courts did not routinely order psychiatric examination of children. Wigmore opined that "no judge should ever let a sex offense charge go to the jury unless the female complainant's social history and mental makeup have been examined and testified to by a qualified physician" (1904/1970, p. 740). Despite the admonition of this influential legal scholar, very few appellate court decisions from 1900 to 1950 required psychiatric examination of children or even discussed the issue. To be sure, such examinations occurred at the trial level, but appellate judges were not preoccupied with psychiatric assessment.

Appellate courts did not routinely insist on corroboration of children's testimony. Although quite a few states had some version of the corroboration requirement, appellate court decisions from 1900 to 1950 devoted little attention to corroboration. Moreover, appellate courts routinely affirmed convictions based on the uncorroborated testimony of children.

The rate of reversal on appeal from 1900 to 1950 appears to be somewhat higher than the reversal rate today. In our study of 463 appellate court decisions between 1900 and 1950, courts reversed 27.5% of the guilty verdicts. How does the reversal rate from 1900 to 1950 for child sexual abuse compare to the reversal rate during that period for other crimes (e.g., murder)? To approximate an answer to this question, we examined reversal rates for nonsexual crimes in 1920, 1930, and 1940. We examined 210 cases for each of these years. For 1920, the reversal rate for nonsexual crimes was 34%. In 1930, 26% of the nonsexual crimes were reversed on appeal. In 1940, the reversal rate for nonsexual crimes was 32%. The average reversal rate for nonsexual crimes was 31%. Recall that the reversal rate for child sexual abuse from 1900 to 1950 was 27.5%. This figure is in the same parameters as the reversal rate for nonsexual crimes.

Turning our attention to the 1990s, Myers and his colleagues (1999) examined 43 child sexual abuse cases; 35% of the cases were reversed. Statistics exist on reversal rates in criminal cases in federal court. Unfortunately, the federal statistics refer to all crimes, not just child sexual abuse. During the 12-month period ending June 30, 1998, the reversal rate for criminal cases in federal court was 10.2% (Administrative Office of the United States Courts, 1998, p. 11, Table B-5). In 1999, LaFave, Israel, and King estimated a reversal rate in state courts for all crimes between 5% and 10% (Vol. 1, p. 148).

Children continue to carry the burden of proof. In decisions from 1900 to 1950, children testified in 76.9% of cases. The capacity to prosecute child sexual abuse was dependent on children's ability to testify in court. The same is true today. During the 1980s and 1990s, children testified in most child sexual abuse trials. Myers, Redlich, Goodman, Prizmich, & Imwinkelreid (1999) examined 42 child sexual abuse trials decided after 1995. Children testified in every case.

Fortunately, research and experience indicate that when children are prepared for testifying, and when they receive emotional support before, during, and after the experience, most are able to testify reasonably well (Dezwirek-Sas, Wolfe, & Gowdey, 1996). Moreover, children who are prepared and emotionally supported generally do not suffer long-term psychological harm from testifying (Flin, Bull, Boon, & Knox, 1993; Goodman et al., 1992; Henry, 1997; Lipovsky, 1994; Oates, Lynch, Stern, O'Toole, & Cooney, 1995; Runyan, Everson, Edelsohn, Hunter, & Coulter, 1988; Whitcomb, Goodman, Runyan, & Hoak, 1994).

Prosecutors did not use expert mental health testimony. In appellate court decisions from 1900 to 1950, we found no cases in which prosecutors relied on expert testimony from mental health professionals to help prove child sexual abuse.

Summary. We sought to determine how American appellate courts from 1900 to 1950 handled cases of child sexual abuse. Our research indicates that appellate court judges administered the law fairly and impartially. The judicial system, like all human systems, makes errors, and falls prey to bias and stereotypes. Nevertheless, early American courts acquitted themselves well in these difficult matters.

Skepticism in today's appellate court decisions. Reviewing appellate court decisions from 1900 to 1950, we found very little of the exaggerated skepticism that was rampant in professional writing of the time. Is the same true of appellate court decisions today? The first author has devoted much of the past 16 years to reading appellate court decisions in child abuse cases. During that decade and a half, no evidence was found of inflated skepticism about child sexual abuse. Beginning in the 1990s, appellate court judges became increasingly concerned about children's suggestibility and about the questioning techniques employed during interviews of some children. Such concern was realistic, however, given the emergence of new psychological research on suggestibility and strong evidence of defective interviewing in some cases. Although American judges are concerned about the credibility of children, the concern remains tempered and balanced. Nothing in today's appellate case law indicates an exaggerated level of skepticism about children's credibility or about allegations of sexual abuse.

SECTION FOUR

The Modern Era—1980 to the Present: Reforming the Criminal Justice System to Facilitate Prosecution and Accommodate Children

As the prevalence of child sexual abuse was brought to public attention in the late 1970s and early 1980s ("Cover Story," 1983; Finkelhor, 1994), prosecution increased dramatically (Myers, 1997). Along with increased prosecution came calls to reform the legal system to accommodate the increasing number of children testifying in court (Libai, 1969; Parker, 1981/1982). This section briefly describes three areas of reform: (a) altering the courtroom to accommodate young witnesses, (b) allowing certain children to testify via closed-circuit television, and (c) expert testimony from mental health professionals. For in-depth discussions of legal reforms, see Bottoms and Goodman (1996), McGough (1994), and Myers (1996, 1997).

Alerting the Courtroom to Accommodate Children

The courtroom is a forbidding place to children. During the 1980s and 1990s, steps were taken to accommodate little witnesses. Without sacrificing the rights of defendants, judges altered time-honored practices to accommodate children in court. As the Alaska Supreme Court observed, "the rules of evidence were not developed to handle the problems presented by the child witness. Therefore our courts must be free to adapt these rules, where appropriate, to accommodate these unique cases" (*In re T.P.*, 1992, p. 1241). Illustrative of permissible accommodations, the witness chair may be turned slightly away from the accused (*United States v. Williams*, 1993). A prosecutor may be positioned in the courtroom so that a young child does not have to look directly at the accused while answering the prosecutor's questions (*People v. Sharp*, 1994). The judge may prohibit spectators from entering or leaving the courtroom during a child's testimony (Connecticut General Statutes, 1997, § 54-86G(b)(1)). In limited circumstances, the judge may close the courtroom to spectators (Myers, 1997). The judge may instruct attorneys not to raise their voices in a way that could frighten a young witness. A child may be allowed regular breaks during testimony (California Penal Code, 2000, § 868.8(d)). The judge may relocate people in the courtroom to make testifying easier for a child. The judge has authority to control questioning so children comprehend what is asked (Federal Rules of Evidence, 1975, 611(a)). One of the most important reforms is allowing children to be accompanied in court by a supportive adult. Emotional support is not only humane, it is effective. Goodman and her colleagues (1992) found that the presence of a supportive adult helps some children testify more completely. Modest reforms to accommodate children are an important accomplishment.

Testimony Via Closed-Circuit Television

In the United States, the courtroom reform that generated the greatest controversy is permitting selected children to testify via closed-circuit television, outside the physical presence of the accused. Closed-circuit testimony is controversial because the U. S. Constitution guarantees the accused a right to face-to-face confrontation with the witnesses against him. In *Maryland v. Craig* (1990), the U.S. Supreme Court ruled that although the right to face-to-face confrontation is important, the right is not absolute. Face-to-face confrontation sometimes gives way to the government's interest in protecting children from the psychological harm of a face-to-face encounter.

Testimony via closed-circuit television generated a flurry of litigation and law review commentary (e.g., Montoya, 1992, 1995). In the final analysis, however, the controversy over video testimony is a tempest in a teapot. Although closed-circuit is used routinely in England and Scotland (Davies & Noon, 1991; Murray, 1995), closed-circuit is rare in the United States, where the defendant's constitutional right of face-to-face confrontation looms large. Moreover, American prosecutors generally prefer children to testify in court, where the jury can see a "real child" rather than a TV image. In the United States, the high-tech (and constitutionally tricky) reform of closed-circuit television is much less important than the decidedly low-tech (and constitutionally tame) reform of allowing children to be accompanied to the witness stand by a trusted adult.

Expert Testimony from Mental Health Professionals: The Use and Abuse of Child Sexual Abuse Accommodation Syndrome

Child sexual abuse is often difficult to prove in court. The child is usually the only eyewitness. In *Pennsylvania v. Ritchie* (1987), the U.S. Supreme Court noted that "[c]hild abuse is one of the most difficult crimes to detect and prosecute, in large part because there often are no witnesses except the victim" (p. 60). Although most children are competent witnesses, some are too young or too frightened to testify effectively or at all. The problems of ineffective child testimony and lack of eyewitnesses are compounded by the paucity of medical evidence in most child sexual abuse cases. Because evidence to prove child sexual abuse is sparse, prosecutors during the 1980s turned for the first time to mental health professionals for expert testimony.

Expert testimony from mental health professionals is a complex subject, the details of which are beyond the scope of this chapter. Given the purpose of this book, however—to honor the work of Dr. Roland Summit—it is appropriate to analyze one aspect of expert mental health testimony: the role of Summit's child sexual abuse accommodation syndrome (CSAAS) in child sexual abuse prosecution.

CSAAS appeared in the literature in 1983. The first appellate court decision referring to CSAAS was handed down in 1985 (*People v. Payan*). Since 1985, CSAAS has been cited in dozens of appellate court decisions. Today, 18 years after CSAAS appeared in print, the syndrome plays a valuable role in some child sexual abuse cases, particularly criminal jury trials (e.g., *People v. Bowker*, 1988; *People v. Gray*, 1986; State v. DeCosta, 2001; Chapman v. State, 2001). During CSAAS's early sojourns to court in the 1980s, however, some judges, attorneys, and expert witnesses misunderstood the syndrome. Some professionals erroneously concluded that CSAAS is a device to diagnose or detect sexual abuse. Of course, CSAAS is nothing of the sort. Summit reminds us that CSAAS "is neither an illness nor a diagnosis, and it can't be used to measure whether or not a child has been sexually abused" (Meinig, 1991, p. 6). Despite this admonition, a number of lawyers misconstrued CSAAS as proof of sexual abuse (e.g., Myers, 1987). Abetted by a small cadre of equally confused mental health professionals, these lawyers offered expert testimony on CSAAS to prove that children had been sexually abused. In effect, the experts testified that children were abused *because* the children had CSAAS (e.g., *Westbrook v. State*, 1988). Offering CSAAS to prove sexual abuse seriously distorts the syndrome. As judges noticed the distortion, they grew increasingly skeptical of CSAAS.

WHY DID SOME LAWYERS
MISUNDERSTAND AND MISUSE CSAAS?

To understand why some lawyers—primarily prosecutors—misunderstood and misused CSAAS, recall that child sexual abuse is often difficult to prove. During the 1980s, prosecutors turned increasingly to social workers, psychologists, and psychiatrists for testimony that children were sexually abused or had symptoms consistent with sexual abuse. Increased reliance on testimony from mental health professionals coincided with publication of CSAAS, and the confluence of these events— publication of CSAAS and increased reliance on expert testimony—set the stage for misuse of CSAAS.

But what caused prosecutors to misunderstand CSAAS? The source of the misunderstanding lies *not* so much in Summit's 1983 article describing CSAAS but in an article published 11 years earlier. In 1962, Kempe and his colleagues published their landmark article titled "The Battered Child Syndrome." Expert testimony on battered child syndrome quickly found its way into court to prove that physical injuries were not accidental. Battered child syndrome provides strong evidence of non-accidental injury, and judges routinely approve battered child syndrome in physical abuse cases. Thus, beginning in the 1960s, prosecutors became accustomed to using syndromes in child abuse cases.

Turning from physical abuse to sexual abuse, prosecution of sexual abuse occurred at a modest pace through the first seven decades of the 20th century. Beginning in the 1980s, however, sexual abuse prosecution increased dramatically, and prosecutors—many of whom were new to sexual abuse—scrambled to prove the crime. Accustomed as they were to proving *physical* abuse with battered child syndrome, some prosecutors turned to CSAAS to prove *sexual* abuse. The reasoning behind this approach was that battered child syndrome proves physical abuse, and judges regularly approve battered child syndrome in physical abuse cases. Thus, syndromes can be used to prove child abuse. Just as battered child syndrome proves physical abuse, so CSAAS, which, after all, is just another syndrome, must prove sexual abuse. In other words, CSAAS is to sexual abuse what battered child syndrome is to physical abuse. Put another way, CSAAS is the sexual abuse analogue of battered children syndrome. Therefore, CSAAS proves sexual abuse (see *People v. Payan,* 1985).

The error of this reasoning is clear: Battered child syndrome *does* prove physical abuse. CSAAS, however, does *not* prove sexual abuse. Battered child syndrome is a diagnostic syndrome (Myers, 1993). With battered child syndrome, the physician reasons backward from the type of injuries to the etiology of the injuries. CSAAS, by contrast, is a nondiagnostic syndrome. With CSAAS, one cannot reason backward from the behaviors comprising CSAAS (e.g., delayed reporting, recantation) to the etiology of those behaviors. Thus, unlike battered child syndrome, which *is* probative of physical abuse, CSAAS is *not* probative of sexual abuse. Prosecutors fell into error because they were accustomed to using battered child syndrome and because they mistakenly equated CSAAS with battered child syndrome. Appellate courts occasionally drew the same erroneous equation.

Perhaps it is not surprising that lawyers were confused about CSAAS. Lawyers, after all, are not schooled in the medical and psychological literatures. But why would some mental health professionals serving as expert witnesses fall into similar confusion? Three factors contributed to the confusion. The first source of confusion relates to the process by which mental health professionals evaluate children for possible sexual abuse. The evaluator considers a broad range of information, including the child's statements describing abuse, medical evidence, psychological symptoms, and reports by police, child protective services, and others. Although CSAAS does not contribute directly to the assessment process because CSAAS does not detect abuse, the syndrome does play a subsidiary role in assessment. Once a professional concludes abuse is likely, CSAAS helps explain delayed reporting, ambivalence, inconsistency, and recantation. Thus, CSAAS *is* involved in assessment, and mental health professionals providing expert testimony on whether abuse occurred may have occasion to mention CSAAS. Once CSAAS becomes part of an expert's testimony, however, it is relatively easy to confuse the CSAAS label with the expert's opinion that abuse occurred (see *In re Sara M.*, 1987).

The second reason for confusion among mental health professionals also relates to the assessment process. As mentioned above, when evaluating possible abuse, mental health professionals consider behavioral symptoms. Some professionals think these symptoms comprise a syndrome (e.g., *In re E.M.*, 1987). Call it "child abuse syndrome" if you like. The clear consensus among experts, however, is that there is no psychological syndrome that diagnoses sexual abuse (Kendall-Tackett, Williams, & Finkelhor, 1993; Myers et al., 1989). Nevertheless, some professionals persist in using "syndrome" terminology, and some court opinions reflect this flawed reasoning (e.g., *In re E.M.*, 1987; *In re Nicole V.*, 1987;

Jimmerson v. State, 1989; *State v. McCoy,* 1987; *Ward v. State,* 1988). It is a simple matter to confuse child sexual abuse syndrome with child sexual abuse accommodation syndrome.

The third source of confusion about CSAAS derives from the simple fact that some mental health professionals made the same mistake the lawyers made: They erroneously concluded that CSAAS does detect or diagnose child sexual abuse. A professional laboring under this misperception would testify that a child was sexually abused because the child has CSAAS.

GETTING IT RIGHT:
JUDGES CLARIFY THE ROLE OF CSAAS

A number of appellate courts fell prey to the confusion generated by the misapplication of CSAAS (e.g., *Allison v. State,* 1986; *Keri v. State,* 1986). Indeed, a modicum of confusion persists to this day (see *Hadden v. State,* 1997). To their credit, however, judges quickly distinguished legitimate from illegitimate uses of CSAAS (see *Hall v. State,* 1993; *In re Sara M.,* 1987; *Lantrip v. Commonwealth,* 1986; *People v. Beckley,* 1990; *People v. Bowker,* 1988; *State v. J.Q.,* 1993; *Steward v. State,* 1995; *Yarborough v. State,* 1987). The Wyoming Supreme Court described the consensus of judicial opinion in *Frenzel v. State* (1993):

> CSAAS is not intended as a means of detecting the existence of abuse. . . .
> Because CSAAS is not diagnostic, the majority of courts dealing with
> CSAAS testimony have limited its admissibility. . . . Several jurisdictions
> admit CSAAS testimony solely to rehabilitate the victim's credibility. . . .
> Generally, limits placed on the admissibility of CSAAS are intended to ad-
> dress its shortcomings due to its limited purpose. Therefore, these courts
> have fashioned the admission of CSAAS so as to avoid its being relied
> upon by the prosecution or the jury as proof that the abuse actually oc-
> curred. . . . CSAAS testimony is restricted because it offers no help to the
> jury of proof that abuse occurred. There is general agreement on the notion
> that CSAAS is unreliable for determining whether abuse actually oc-
> curred. . . . However, we also find that CSAAS evidence is relevant and ad-
> missible to dispel myths the public might hold concerning a child sexual
> abuse victim's post-abuse behavior if that behavior is an issue in the case.
> . . . Qualified experts on child sexual abuse may, therefore, use evidence of
> CSAAS characteristics of sexually abused children for the sole purpose of
> explaining a victim's specific behavior which might be incorrectly con-

strued as inconsistent with an abuse victim or to rebut an attack on the victim's credibility. (pp. 747-749)

When properly understood, child sexual abuse accommodation syndrome plays a useful role in protecting children from sexual abuse, and CSAAS is an important "legal" feather in Dr. Summit's cap.

SECTION FIVE

Conclusion

Child sexual abuse was prosecuted throughout the 20th century. By late 20th-century standards, the volume of prosecution during the first half of the century was modest. Yet, despite skeptical railings in professional journals and law reviews, judges and attorneys soldiered away, protecting children and punishing perpetrators. In this new century, it is important not to lose sight of the accomplishments of the early days.

Those who labor in the field of child protection today may erroneously believe prosecution is a new idea. It is tempting to be smug and self-congratulatory, with thoughts like, "Of course, you know, it is we 'moderns' who first realized the importance of prosecution."

The lesson of history should keep our egos in check. There is no denying that prosecution increased significantly in the 1980s and 1990s, and that today's legal system is more accommodating of victims than the system of old. Yet, despite the tremendous strides of the late 20th century, the first half of the century saw real progress. Indeed, it took markedly more courage to prosecute child sexual abuse in 1938—when skepticism was rampant—than it does in 2001—when skepticism is relatively low and when society understands the seriousness of sexual abuse. We should tip our 21st-century hats to the pioneers who went before us in the difficult days from 1900 to 1975.

Notes

1. The first author located twelve California Supreme Court decisions handed down between 1900 and 1910 in which the victim of rape was a minor.
2. See Note 1.

References

Abraham, K. (1927). The experiencing of sexual traumas as a form of sexual activity. In K. Abraham (Ed.), *Selected papers* (pp. 47-62). London: Hogarth.

Administrative Office of the United States Courts. (1998). *Statistical tables for the federal judiciary.* Washington, DC: Government Printing Office.

Allison v. State, 346 S.E.2d 380 (Ga. Ct. App. 1986).

American Bar Association. (1937/1938). *Committee on the improvement of the law of evidence.* Chicago: American Bar Association.

Beckett, K. (1996). Culture and the politics of signification: The case of child sexual abuse. *Social Problems, 43*(1), 57-76.

Bedau, H. A. (1982). *The death penalty in America* (3rd ed). New York: Oxford University Press.

Bender, L., & Blau, A. (1937). The reactions of children to sexual relations with adults. *American Journal of Orthopsychiatry, 7,* 500-518.

Bender, L., & Grugett, A. E. (1952). A follow-up report on children who had atypical sexual experience. *American Journal of Orthopsychiatry, 22,* 825-837.

Berger, V. (1977). Man's trial, woman's tribulation: Rape cases in the courtroom. *Columbia Law Review, 77,* 1-100.

Bishop, J. P. (1856). *The criminal law* (1st ed.)[Microfilm]. Boston: Little, Brown.

Bishop, J. P. (1865). *The criminal law* (3rd ed.)[Microfilm]. Boston: Little, Brown.

Blackstone, W. (1769). *Commentaries on the law of England.* London.

Blumer, H. (1969). Social movements. In B. McLaughlin (Ed.), *Studies in social movements: A sociological perspective* (pp. 8-29). New York: Free Press.

Bottoms, B. L., & Goodman, G. S. (Eds.). (1996). *International perspectives on child abuse and children's testimony: Psychological research and law.* Thousand Oaks, CA: Sage.

Brauer v. State, 25 Wis. 413 (1870).

Brownmiller, S. (1975). *Against our will: Men, women and rape.* New York: Simon & Schuster.

Brundage, J. A. (1987). *Law, sex, and Christian society in medieval Europe.* Chicago: University of Chicago Press.

Brunhold, H. (1964). Observations after sexual trauma suffered in childhood. *Excerpta Criminologica, 11,* 5-8.

Burton v. State, 111 N.E.2d 892 (Ind. 1953).

Bye, R. T. (1926). Recent history and present status of capital punishment in the United States. *Journal of the American Institute of Criminal Law and Criminology, 17,* 234-245.

California Penal Code. (2000). St. Paul, MN: West Publishing.

Carter, J. M. (1985). *Rape in medieval England: A historical and sociological study.* New York: University Press of America.

Chapin, B. (1983). *Criminal justice in colonial America, 1606-1660.* Athens: University of Georgia Press.

Chapman v. State, 18P. 3d 1164 (Wyo. 2001).

Coke, E. (1979). *The second part of the institutes of the laws of England* (D. S. Berkowitz & S. E. Thorne, Eds.). New York: Garland. (Original work published 1671)

Coker v. Georgia, 433 U.S. 584 (1977).

Connecticut General Statutes. (1997).

Corpus juris: Being a complete and systematic statement of the whole body of the law as embodied in and developed by all reported decisions. (1929). London: The American Law Book Co.

The corroboration rule and crimes accompanying a rape. (1970). *University of Pennsylvania Law Review, 118*, 458-472.

"Cover Story." (1983, September 5). *Time Magazine, 122*(10).

Davies, G., & Noon, E. (1991). *An evaluation of the live link for child witnesses*. London: The Home Office.

Decennial Digests. (1910). St. Paul, MN: West.

Decennial Digests. (1920). St. Paul, MN: West.

Decennial Digests. (1930). St. Paul, MN: West.

Decennial Digests. (1940). St. Paul, MN: West.

Decennial Digests. (1950). St. Paul, MN: West.

De Francis, V. (1969). Protecting the child victim of sexual crimes committed by adults. A research project conducted under child welfare research grant R-222 for the U.S. Children's Bureau. Denver: American Humane Association.

Dezwirek-Sas, L., Wolfe, D. A., & Gowdey, K. (1996). Children and the courts in Canada. In B. L. Bottoms & G. S. Goodman (Eds.), *International perspectives on child abuse and children's testimony: Psychological research and law* (pp. 77-95). Thousand Oaks, CA: Sage.

Drapkin, I. (1989). *Crime and punishment in the ancient world*. Lexington, MA: Lexington Books.

18 Elizabeth, c. 7, 4 Statutes of the Realm 618.

Federal Rules of Evidence. (1975).

Finkelhor, D. (1979). *Sexually victimized children*. New York: Free Press.

Finkelhor, D. (1994). Current information on the scope and nature of child sexual abuse. *The Future of Children, 4*(2), 31-53.

Flin, R., Bull, R., Boon, J., & Knox, A. (1993). Child witnesses in Scottish criminal trials. *International Review of Victimology, 2*, 309-329.

Forcible and statutory rape: An exploration of the operation and objective of the consent standard. (1952). *Yale Law Journal, 62*, 55-83.

Frenzel v. State, 849 P.2d 741 (Wyo. 1993).

Giles, L. E. (1976). The admissibility of a rape-complainant's previous sexual conduct: The need for legislative reform. *New England Law Review, 11*, 497-507.

Goodman, G. S., Taub, E. P., Jones, D. P. H., England, P., Port, L. K., Rudy, L., & Prado, L. (1992). Testifying in criminal court. *Monographs of the Society for Research in Child Development, 57*(5), 1-141.

Gordon, L. (1988). *Heroes of their own lives: The politics and history of family violence*. New York: Penguin Books.

Guarnieri, P. (1998). "Dangerous girls," family secrets, and incest, 1861-1930. *International Journal of Law and Psychiatry, 21*, 369-383.

Hadden v. State, 690 So.2d 573 (Fla. 1997).

Hale, M. (1971). *The history of the pleas of the crown* (C. M. Gray, Ed.). Chicago: University of Chicago Press. (Original work published 1736)

Hall v. State, 611 So.2d 915 (Miss. 1993).

Helfer, R. E., & Kempe, C. H. (1968). *The battered child*. Chicago: University of Chicago Press.

Henderson, D. J. (1975). Incest. In A. M. Freedman, H. I. Kaplan, & B. J. Sadock (Eds.), *Comprehensive textbook of psychiatry* (2nd ed). Baltimore: Williams and Wilkins.

Henry, J. (1997). System intervention trauma to child sexual abuse victims following disclosure. *Journal of Interpersonal Violence, 12,* 499-512.

Herman, J. L. (1981). *Father-daughter incest.* Cambridge, MA: Harvard University Press.

Herman, J. L. (1992). *Trauma and recovery.* New York: Basic Books.

Hunter, R. J., Ralph, P. H., & Marquart, J. (1993). The death sentencing of rapists in pre-*Furman* Texas (1942-1971): The racial dimension. *American Journal of Criminal Law, 20,* 313-337.

In re E. M., 520 N.Y.S.2d 327 (Family Ct. 1987).

In re Nicole V., 510 N.Y.S.2d 567 (App. Div. 1987).

In re Sarah M., 239 Cal. Rptr. 605 (Ct. App. 1987).

In re T. P., 838 P.2d 1236 (Alaska 1992).

Index to Legal Periodicals & Books. (1997). Bronx, NY: H.W. Wilson.

Jimmerson v. State, 380 S.E.2d 65 (Ga. Ct. App. 1989).

Johnson, E. (1957). Selective factors in capital punishment. *Social Forces, 36,* 165-169.

Jones, L. A. (1888). *An index to legal periodical literature.* Boston: Boston Books.

Karpman, B. (1954). *The sexual offender and his offenses: Etiology, pathology, psychodynamics and treatment.* New York: Julian Press.

Kempe, C. H. (1978). Sexual abuse, another hidden pediatric problem: The 1977 C. Anderson Aldrich lecture. *Pediatrics, 62,* 382-389.

Kempe, C. H., Silverman, F. N., Steele, B. F., Droegemuller, W., & Silver, A. K. (1962). The battered child syndrome. *Journal of the American Medical Association, 187*(3), 17-24.

Kendall-Tackett, K. A., Williams, L. M., & Finkelhor, D. (1993). Impact of sexual abuse on children: A review and synthesis of recent empirical studies. *Psychological Bulletin, 113,* 164-180.

Keri v. State, 347 S.E.2d 236 (Ga. Ct. App. 1986).

Kinsey, A.C., Pomeroy, W. B., Martin, C. E., & Gebhard, P. H. (1953). *Sexual behavior in the human female.* Philadelphia: W. B. Saunders.

LaFave, W. R., Israel, J. H., & King, N. J. (1999). *Criminal procedure* (2nd ed., Vols. 1-6). St. Paul, MN: West Publishing.

LaFave, W. R., Israel, J. H., & King, N. J. (2000). *Criminal procedure* (3rd ed., Vols. 1-6). St. Paul, MN: West Publishing.

Laiou, A. E. (1993). *Consent and coercion to sex and marriage in ancient and medieval societies.* Washington, DC: Dumbarton Oaks Research Library and Collection.

Lantrip v. Commonwealth, 713 S.W.2d 816 (Ky. 1986).

Lee v. State, 179 S.W. 145 (Tenn. 1915).

LeGrand, C. E. (1973). Rape and rape laws: Sexism in society and law. *California Law Review, 61,* 919-941.

Lewis, E. (1847). *An abridgment of the criminal law of the United States.* Philadelphia: Thomas, Cowperthwait.

Lexis. Available: www.lawschool.lexis.com

Libai, D. (1969). The protection of the child victim of a sexual offense in the criminal justice system. *Wayne Law Review, 15,* 977-1032.

Lipovsky, J. A. (1994). The impact of court on children: Research findings and practical recommendations. *Journal of Interpersonal Violence, 9,* 238-257.

Maryland v. Craig, 497 U.S. 836 (1990).

Masson, J. M. (1984). *The assault on truth: Freud's suppression of the seduction theory.* New York: Farrar, Straus & Giroux.

McDermott, T. E. (1975). California rape evidence reform: An analysis of Senate Bill 1678. *Hastings Law Journal, 26,* 1551-1573.

McGough, L. S. (1994). *Child witnesses: Fragile voices in the American legal system.* New Haven, CT: Yale University Press.

McKerrow, W. D. (1973). Protecting the sexually abused child. Paper presented at the Second National Symposium on Child Abuse, American Humane Association, Children's Division, Denver, CO.

Meinig, M. B. (1991). Profile of Roland Summit. *Violence Update, 1*(9), 6.

Merritt, D. J., & Putnam, M. (1996). Judges and scholars: Do courts and scholarly journals cite the same law review articles? *Chicago-Kent Law Review, 71,* 871-908.

Montoya, J. (1992). On truth and shielding in child abuse trials. *Hastings Law Journal, 43,* 1259-1319.

Montoya, J. (1995). Lessons from *Akiki* and *Michaels* on shielding child witnesses. *Psychology, Public Policy, and Law, 1,* 340-369.

Murray, K. (1995). *Live television link: An evaluation of its use by child witnesses in Scottish criminal trials.* Edinburgh: The Scottish Office.

Myers, J. E. B. (1987). *Child witness law and practice.* New York: John Wiley.

Myers, J. E. B. (1993). Expert testimony describing psychological syndromes. *Pacific Law Journal, 24,* 1449-1464.

Myers, J. E. B. (Ed.). (1994). *The backlash: Child protection under fire.* Thousand Oaks, CA: Sage.

Myers, J. E. B. (1995). New era of skepticism regarding children's credibility. *Psychology, Public Policy, and Law, 1,* 387-398.

Myers, J. E. B. (1996). A decade of international legal reform regarding child abuse investigation and litigation: Steps toward a child witness code. *Pacific Law Journal, 28,* 169-241.

Myers, J. E. B. (1997). *Evidence in child abuse and neglect cases* (3rd ed.). New York: John Wiley.

Myers, J. E. B., Bays, J., Becker, J., Berliner, L., Corwin, D. L., & Saywitz, K. J. (1989). Expert testimony in child sexual abuse litigation. *Nebraska Law Review, 68*(1-2), 1-145.

Myers, J. E. B., Redlich, A. D., Goodman, G. S., Prizmich, L. P., & Imwinkelreid, E. (1999). Jurors' perceptions of hearsay in child sexual abuse cases. *Psychology, Public Policy, and Law, 5,* 388-419.

Neville, D. G. (1957). Rape in early English law. *Justice of the Peace and Local Government Review, 121,* 223-224.

Oates, R. K., Lynch, D. L., Stearn, A. E., O'Toole, B. I., & Cooney, G. (1995). The criminal justice system and the sexually abused child: Help or hinderance? *Medical Journal of Australia, 70,* 435-445.

O'Brien, S. (1980). *Child abuse: A crying shame.* Provo, UT: Brigham Young University Press.

Olafson, E., Corwin, D. L., & Summit, R. C. (1993). Modern history of child sexual abuse awareness: Cycles of discovery and suppression. *Child Abuse & Neglect, 17*(1), 7-24.

Parker, J. Y. (1981/1982). Rights of child witnesses: Is the court a protector or perpetrator? *New England Law Review,* 643-717.

Pennsylvania v. Ritchie, 480 U.S. 39 (1987).

People v. Beckley, 456 N.W.2d 391 (Mich. 1990).

People v. Benson, 6 Cal. 221 (1856).

People v. Bowker, 249 Cal. Rptr. 886 (Ct. App. 1988).

People v. Castro, 60 Cal. 118 (1882).

People v. Collins, 186 N.E.2d 30 (Ill. 1962).

People v. Gammage, 828 P.2d 682 (Cal. 1992).

People v. Gray, 231 Cal. Rptr. 659 (Ct. App. 1986).

People v. Jones, 266 P.2d 38 (Cal. 1954).

People v. Payan, 220 Cal. Rptr. 126 (Ct. App. 1985) (ordered not published).

People v. Schott, 582 N.E.2d 690 (Ill. Ct. App. 1991).

People v. Sharp, 36 Cal. Rptr. 2d 117 (Ct. App. 1994).

People v. Spigno, 319 P.2d 458 (Cal. Ct. App. 1957).

Phipps, C. A. (1997). Children, adults, sex and the criminal law: In search of reason. *Seton Hall Legislative Journal, 22*(1), 1-141.

Ploscowe, M. (1960). Sex offenses: The American legal context. *Law and Contemporary Problems, 25*, 217-224.

Pollock, F., & Maitland, F. W. (1968). *The history of English law.* Cambridge, UK: Cambridge University Press.

Pomeroy, W. B. (1976, November). A new look at incest. *Forum,* pp. 9-13.

Psychiatric evaluation of the mentally abnormal witness. (1950). *Yale Law Journal, 59*, 1324-1341.

Puttkammer, E. W. (1925). Consent in rape. *Illinois Law Review, 19*, 410-428.

Rape and battery between husband and wife. (1954). *Stanford Law Review, 6*, 719-728.

Rape—assault with intent to commit—necessity of corroborating evidence—prosecutrix. (1939). *Oregon Law Review, 18*, 264-265.

The rape corroboration requirement: Repeal not reform. (1972). *Yale Law Journal, 81*, 1365-1391.

Reid, T. (1995). *Father-daughter incest in contemporary fiction.* Unpublished manuscript.

Reisman, J. A. (1998). *Kinsey: Crimes & consequences.* Arlington, VA: Institute for Media Education.

The resistance standard in rape legislation. (1966). *Stanford Law Review, 18*, 680-689.

Richardson, F. K. (1983). Law reviews and the courts. *Whittier Law Review, 5*, 385-393.

Runyan, D. K., Everson, M. D., Edelsohn, G. A., Hunter, W. M., & Coulter, M. L. (1988). Impact of legal intervention on sexually abused children. *Journal of Pediatrics, 113*, 647-653.

Russell, D. E. H. (1983). The incidence and prevalence of intrafamilial and extrafamilial sexual abuse of female children. *Child Abuse & Neglect, 7*, 133-146.

Russell, D. E. H. (1986). *The secret trauma: Incest in the lives of girls and women.* New York: Basic Books.

Salter, A. C. (1988). *Treating child sex offenders and victims.* Newbury Park, CA: Sage.

Salter, A. C. (1995). *Transforming trauma: A guide to understanding and treating adult survivors of child sexual abuse.* Thousand Oaks, CA: Sage.

Slovenko, R. (1965). A panoramic overview: Sexual behavior and the law. In R. Slovenko (Ed.). *Sexual behavior and the law.* Springfield, IL: Thomas.

State v. Chamley, 568 N.W.2d 607 (S.D. 1997).

State v. DeCosta, 772 A. 2d 340 (N.H. 2001).

State v. Gray, 53 N.C. 130 (Jones 1860).

State v. J. Q., 617 A.2d 1196 (N.J. 1993).

State v. McCoy, 400 N.W.2d 807 (Minn. Ct. App. 1987).

State v. Nelson, 818 S.W.2d 285 (Mo. Ct. App. 1991).

State v. Sibley, 33 S.W. 167 (Mo. 1895).

State v. Wood, 122 P.2d 416 (Ariz. 1942).

Statutory rape—desirability of evidence that female was previously unchaste or married in mitigation of punishment. (1938). *Virginia Law Review, 24,* 335-341.

Statutory rape: Previous chaste character in Florida. (1960). *University of Florida Law Review, 13,* 201-214.

Steward v. State, 652 N.E.2d 490 (Ind. 1995).

Summit, R. C. (1983). The child sexual abuse accommodation syndrome. *Child Abuse & Neglect, 7,* 177-193.

Summit, R. C. (1988). Hidden victims, hidden pain: Societal avoidance of child sexual abuse. In G. E. Wyatt & G. J. Powell (Eds.), *Lasting effects of child sexual abuse* (pp. 39-60). Newbury Park, CA: Sage.

Tonry, R. A. (1965). Statutory rape: A critique. *Louisiana Law Review, 26*(1), 105-117.

United States v. Williams, 37 M.J. 289 (C.M.A. 1993).

Walters, D. R. (1975). *Physical and sexual abuse of children: Causes and treatment.* Bloomington: Indiana University Press.

Ward v. State, 519 So.2d 1082 (Fla. Ct. App. 1988).

Wedmore v. State, 143 N.E.2d 649 (Ind. 1957).

Weiss, J., Rogers, E., Darwin, M. R., & Dutton, C. E. (1955). A study of girl sex victims. *Psychiatric Quarterly, 29,* 1-28.

Welch, D. (1976). Criminal procedure—instruction to jury that rape is easy to charge and difficult to disprove is no longer to be given. *State v. Feddersen,* 230 N.W.2d 510 (Iowa 1975). *Texas Tech Law Review, 7,* 732-737.

Wesolowski, J. J. (1976). Indicia of consent? A proposal for change to the common law rule admitting evidence of a rape victim's character for chastity. *Loyola University Law Journal, 7*(1), 118-140.

Westbrook v. State, 368 S.E.2d 131 (Ga. Ct. App. 1988).

Westlaw. Available: www.lawschool.westlaw.com

Whitcomb, D., Goodman, G. S., Runyan, D. K., & Hoak, S. (1994, April). *The emotional effects of testifying on sexually abused children.* Washington, DC: National Institute of Justice, Research in Brief, U.S. Department of Justice.

Wigmore, J. H. (1970). *Evidence in trials at common law* (Vols. 1-11). Boston: Little, Brown. (Original work published 1904)

Williams, D. (1993). The gratification of that corrupt and lawless passion: Character types and themes in early New England rape narratives. In F. Shuffelton (Ed.), *A mixed race: Ethnicity in early America.* New York: Oxford University Press.

Wood, P. L. (1973). The victim in a forcible rape case: A feminist view. *American Criminal Law Review, 11,* 335-354.

Yarborough v. State, 514 So.2d 1215 (Miss. 1987).

Yessen v. State, 92 N.E.2d 621 (Ind. 1950).

3

When Paradigms Collide

Roland Summit and the
Rediscovery of Child Sexual Abuse

ERNA OLAFSON

> We observe according to preset categories and often cannot
> "see" what stares us in the face.
>
> *Stephen Jay Gould (1989, p. 189)*

> To speak publicly about one's knowledge of atrocities is to invite
> the stigma that attaches to victims.
>
> *J. L. Herman (1992, p. 2)*

As we review the career of psychiatrist Roland Summit in the 1990s context of a powerful double backlash against the "True Believers" of the
child abuse "sect" (Pendergrast, 1995) and the "fanatic feminists" (Faludi,
1991; Gardner, 1991, p. 121), it may be useful to remind ourselves of the
world into which Summit and others dared to introduce the idea that the

sexual abuse of children was a major public health problem as well as a moral issue. What was believed about the sexual abuse of children 25 years ago? How did Summit and a number of others in the 1970s challenge these beliefs? Why did they succeed in stimulating a fundamental shift in modern attitudes about child sexual abuse when their predecessors had failed? Do the same social, intellectual, and political forces that explained away child sexual abuse for a century after its 19th-century discovery by French and American physicians, British feminists, and a lone Viennese psychiatrist, Sigmund Freud, now fuel the backlash and threaten to bury this issue yet again? The focus here will be on child sexual abuse, but issues of gender, hierarchy, professionalism, and power will be addressed as they affect the modern rediscovery of child sexual abuse and the intense negative reaction that followed it.

The Rediscovery of Child Sexual Abuse

In the 1970s, a number of individuals came independently to examine the issue of child sexual abuse, and then they came together to foster a fundamental shift in social and professional attitudes about child sexual abuse, and by implication, about psychiatric diagnosis, about the family, about gender identity, and about childhood sexuality. The publications, speak-outs, and activism of the emergent woman's liberation movement of the time catalyzed and politically supported this shift in attitudes about child sexual abuse (Herman, 1992), but there were also professionals in a number of fields who contributed. Summit was one of the few psychiatrists among these pioneers. In his 1996 interviews with psychiatrist David Corwin, his friend and one-time student, Summit describes this early period of "stumbling in the dark toward a fuller understanding of something that's never been fully understood before" (Summit, 1996, August 13, p. 20).

The critics of this early period seem to forget just how revolutionary this attempt to come to grips with child sexual abuse really was and just how unsettling such scientific revolutions can be (Nathan & Snedeker, 1995). Our modern understanding of child sexual abuse is a historical rarity, something genuinely new in the medical and moral history of humanity. It took a paradigm shift (Kuhn, 1970), a shattering of assumptions (Janoff-Bulman, 1992), to reach this understanding. A long-forgotten paper in 1896 by Sigmund Freud was the first to describe the psychological effects of child sex abuse, and it was almost a century later that rigorous research in this area began to appear (Olafson, Corwin, & Summit, 1993). Summit has long been clear about the scope of this discovery and the power of the forces that would resuppress it. He wrote, for example, in 1988,

> Drawing on observations of current controversies, historical precedents, and the experiences of present-day adult survivors of sexual abuse, it will be illustrated that it is all of society, not just those immediately affected, that protects the secret of child sexual abuse. We have overlooked or outrageously trivialized this subject, not because it is peripheral to major social interests, but because it is so central that we have not yet dared to conceptualize its scope. (p. 41)

Although it has been argued that from the mid-19th century until the present awareness of child sexual abuse has repeatedly emerged and been resuppressed, suppression never reached the point of complete historical amnesia (Masson, 1984; Olafson et al., 1993; Summit, 1988). Once the French pathologist Alphonse Tardieu had, in 1867, published his findings that child sexual abuse was more common than previously known, and Freud in 1896 had described its psychological costs, the issue was never really forgotten (Masson, 1984). Child sexual abuse had entered professional discourse, and it remained there for much of the 20th century, often discussed, explained, and for the most part, explained away. By the 1970s, when Summit and others began their challenge to this discourse, professional beliefs and attitudes about child sexual abuse included the following propositions:

- incest hardly ever happens, perhaps in one or two among a million people (Henderson, 1975; Weinberg, 1955)
- when child sexual abuse does take place, it does not generally seem to hurt the child, and there is no reason that it should; indeed, the experience of incest can create attractive and erotically competent young people (Bender & Blau, 1937; Kinsey, Pomeroy, Martin, & Gebhard, 1953; Yates, 1978)
- children often invite and participate in sexual abuse, even initiating it in a seductive and aggressive manner to satisfy their uncon-

scious sexual impulses (Abraham, 1927; Bender & Blau, 1937; Revitch & Weiss, 1962; Weiss, Rogers, Darwin, & Dutton, 1955)

- children and women who make accusations of sexual assault are often lying, fantasizing, or mentally disturbed (Masson, 1984; Wigmore, 1978)

- those men who do commit sexual crimes are for the most part deviant drifters who are mentally ill and in need of compassion and treatment, certainly not respectable fathers of families; we should not overreact to them or punish them too severely (Freedman, 1987)

- women who focus on sexual crimes by men are castrators, "latent" lesbians, prudes, or otherwise sexually abnormal; they hate men and take pleasure in humiliating them by making such accusations (Gardner, 1987, 1991; Jeffreys, 1985; Kinsey et al., 1953; Rush, 1980)

- the sexual problems in America today arise from sexual repressiveness and the remnants of Puritanism and Victorianism, not from sexual freedom and full sexual self-expression; we must put an end to "Sexual McCarthyism" (Jones, 1997; Robinson, 1976; Yates, 1978)

- when incest does take place, it is the mother's fault, whether because of collusion, neglect, or because she facilitates incest between her passive husband and her seductive daughter, in order to express maternal hostility against the girl and satisfy her own latent homosexual longing for her daughter (Lustig, Dresser, Spellman, & Murray, 1966; Salter, 1988)

- there are many societies reported by anthropologists in which children engage freely in sex with each other and with adults and are sexually healthier than the inhibited and sexually pathetic Americans (Bender & Blau, 1937; Yates, 1978)

Does this list read oddly now? It is possible that for many readers outside of the child abuse field it does not, except perhaps for the data on the rarity of incest or the convoluted argument about the latent homosexuality of mothers in incestuous homes. The challenge to these ideas came first from the feminist grassroots, and a revised discourse about the prevalence and effects of child sexual abuse soon found its way into some professional journals. Although subsequent research findings have confirmed much that Summit and his collegues argued in the 1970s and early 1980s, and daytime television has sensationalized this discourse by offering confessional incest survivor accounts as popular entertainment, this modest scientific revolution has not convincingly transformed discourse about child sexual abuse in the mainstream institutions of health, mental health, and the law. In professional organizations, journals, and textbooks, many old ideas persist, generally joined by new "backlash" attitudes about child sexual abuse and memory (Myers, 1994; Olafson et al., 1993; Pope & Brown, 1996). The grassroots sources and popular media elaboration of these new ideas about child sexual abuse may explain, at least in part, the minimal enthusiasm with which they have been received by the mainstream in mental health and medicine, even when they have had research support.

What were these new ideas? How did Summit and his colleagues challenge the conventional scientific wisdom about child sexual abuse? Their innovations included the following propositions:

- child sexual abuse and incest are not rare, and the perpetrators are generally not strangers but are known and trusted adults in the child's life (Finkelhor, 1979a; Russell, 1983, 1986)

- child sexual abuse damages children both medically and psychologically, and the damages can be long-lasting (Herman, 1981)

- sexually abused children who seem to be consenting or participating are instead submitting to the superior power of adults (Summit, 1983)

- children's silence about ongoing sexual abuse does not imply consent but rather accommodation (Summit, 1983)

- when they are questioned, child witnesses are more trustworthy than previously believed (Goodman & Clarke-Stewart, 1991)

- even when children assent and do not appear to be damaged, child sexual abuse is wrong because children cannot consent (Finkelhor, 1979b; Herman, 1981; Summit, 1983)

- perpetrators of child sexual abuse can be respectable, churchgoing fathers of families who appear to be psychologically normal (Herman, 1981; Salter, 1988, 1995)

- maternal collusion is far from universal in incest families, and when it occurs, it may be a measure of maternal powerlessness; the mothers in such homes are often disabled or are themselves victimized by the fathers (Herman, 1981)

As often happens in the history of science, these innovations came largely (but not entirely) from outside established institutions (Butterfield, 1957; Woloch, 1982). Their proponents founded abuse-focused societies and journals to develop them, a step that was essential to their development, just as earlier scientific revolutionaries had created scientific societies, journals, and even new universities when the established churches and universities would have none of their paradigm-shattering and hierarchy-threatening discoveries (Butterfield, 1957; Halévy, 1955; Olafson et al., 1993; Woloch, 1982). For example, Summit's 1983 paper on the child sexual abuse accommodation syndrome, which was recently ranked by child abuse professionals as second in influence only to the 1962 paper on the battered child syndrome by Henry Kempe and his colleagues (Kempe, Silverman, Steele, Droegmueller, & Silver, 1962), was first rejected by the venerable *Journal of Orthopsychiatry* before being published in one of the newly founded journals *Child Abuse and Neglect* (Oates & Donnelly, 1997; Summit, 1996, June 21, pp. 48-49).

Indeed, as Summit stated in his Corwin interviews, most of those who were making gains in this field were outside of psychiatry and often outside of the mental health professions altogether, from feminists and sociologists to police and vice officers, and many of them knew each other (1996, June 21, p. 16). Early epithets applied to the emergent child sexual abuse field, such as "cottage industry," or "self-styled experts," referred disparagingly to the multidisciplinary and improvisational nature of this scientific revolution. We should remember, however, as even a cursory glance at the history of science reveals, that major changes in scientific thinking quite often take place outside of the conservative constraints of established institutions and are then gradually—and often only after great resistance—legitimized within the mainstream.

Grassroots organizations and individuals provided both political support and information about abuse to the emergent child abuse network. Summit described to Corwin one early grassroots contact in 1970 with Jolly K., a child sexual abuse survivor and founder of Parents Anonymous, an organization for which Summit became the first board member. Jolly K., in a "verbal knock-down-drag-out fight" educated Summit, "the bright young psychiatrist," that child sexual abuse was integral to child abuse, and she commissioned his first paper on the subject (Summit, 1996, June 21, p. 8). By listening to feminists and child abuse survivors, Summit and his fellow pioneers explored outside the boundaries of professionalized knowledge, thus making them vulnerable to criticism, just as Freud had been chastised nearly a century before for heeding the "old wives' tales" and "paranoid drivel" of alleged victims (Masson, 1984, p. 135).

In summary, to the extent that they succeeded, these pioneers did so for a number of reasons. They listened as feminists, child abuse survivors, and patients bore witness, and they took these witnesses seriously and learned from them. Their contacts with the grassroots also gave them political support and influence (Herman, 1992). In alliance with contemporaries who were investigating the impact of many kinds of traumas on children and adults, they were institutionally creative, so that when established organizations and publications did not offer forums for their theoretical formulations and research findings, they created their own (Olafson et al., 1993). From the earliest days, they set about to conduct careful comparative and retrospective research, the first time in human history that child sexual abuse was rigorously studied (Olafson et al., 1993).

They also networked extensively. Unlike Sigmund Freud in 1896 and Sandor Ferenczi in 1932, the child sexual abuse pathfinders of the 1970s were not alone. Herman writes, "To speak publicly about one's knowledge of atrocities is to invite the stigma that attaches to victims" (1992, p. 2). As the backlash emerged to stigmatize the child abuse pioneers for speaking publicly about the atrocity of child sexual abuse, they did not face their critics in isolation as Freud had done (Herman, 1992; Masson, 1984). Summit noted that they telephoned and corresponded and met at early conferences, and, as he observed, they needed each other, for child sexual abuse was the "stepchild" of mental health (Summit, 1996, June 21, p. 15). Summit told Corwin, "But if it hadn't been for that intensity of discovery and interpersonal support, nobody would have emerged with any expressed ideas because there was no audience for these ideas at the time. We were each other's audience, really" (1996, June 21, p. 1). As

Herman reminds us, advances in knowledge are seldom "Promethean acts of solitary male genius" (Herman, 1992, p. 18). They depend on a supportive social and political context. The intense networking Summit describes was crucial to sustaining the rediscovery of child sexual abuse.

Professionalized Knowledge and the Origins of the Backlash

In examining the many sources of the child sexual abuse backlash, the issue of legitimacy cannot be ignored. The child sexual abuse pioneers appeared to be challenging not only the dominant paradigms in the mental health fields about diagnostic etiology, the family, sexuality, and related issues, but also—by absorbing meanings from patients and lay activists and by functioning largely outside of older professional channels—these interlopers challenged the reality-defining monopolies claimed by the legitimate, established mental health professions (Larson, 1977; Olafson et al., 1993). The resistance of professional monopolies of competence to lay challengers of dubious provenance contributed to the backlash. But there were many other forces as well. These will be described briefly, and then one of them, the influence of sexual modernism, a factor that is often given short shrift in analyses of the backlash, will be explored at greater length.

Class, Gender, and Age Bias

When Brown University professor Ross Cheit began to consider bringing legal action against the San Francisco Boys Chorus for the sexual abuse he had suffered as a child in that organization, he was reportedly told by several people, "You'll be believed because you're a man," a statement he found reassuring until he began to consider its implications for women (Freyd, 1996, p. 184). The diminished credibility of women and children as witnesses, especially when they report sexual assaults on themselves by respectable and powerful men, has a long worldwide history (Bell & Offen, 1983; Olafson et al., 1993). Although it is well beyond the scope of this paper to demonstrate the nature and extent of these biases, the following passage from Shakespeare testifies to their antiquity. In *Measure for Measure,* Angelo, an official in the court of a duke, tells Isabella that unless she "yields up" her body to his will, he intends to kill her imprisoned brother. When she answers that she will "tell the world aloud what man thou art," Angelo replies,

> Who will believe thee, Isabel? My unsoil'd name, th' austereness of my life, my vouch against you, and my place I' th' state, will so your accusation overweigh that you shall stifle in your own report and smell of calumny.... Say what you can: my false o'erweighs your true. (Shakespeare, 1958, pp. 268-269)

Angelo's reputation, power, class, and gender would protect him from a woman's sexual accusation.

The current atmosphere of political correctness has driven blatant expressions of class and gender prejudices largely underground, but evidence of their persistence surfaces in current state Bar Association studies of gender bias in American courts (Czapanskiy, 1993), references in the child abuse backlash literature to "witch hunts" and "mass hysteria," and a contemporary focus on memory research "utilized to cast doubt on accuser memory alone" (Grand, quoted in Brown, Scheflin, & Hammond, 1998, p. 14). Class bias is also evident in newsletter descriptions of the respectability, normality, good clothes, and pleasant demeanor of those who attend meetings of the False Memory Syndrome Foundation, an advocacy group made up of parents accused of child sexual abuse and their advisors in the scientific community (Brown, 1996a, p. 349; Pope & Brown, 1996, p. 76). Paul McHugh, chief of psychiatry at Johns Hopkins University and a member of the FMSF Scientific Advisory Board, invokes respectability when he writes, "But now I'm seeing all these men with fine records, stable lives, marriages intact, their children with fine school records, and they are being accused of the most horrible and violent acts" (quoted in Brown et al., 1998, p. 17). As for gender bias, Kristiansen, Felton, and Hovdestad summarize the literature and their own research findings as follows: "Like other social and mental health issues pertaining to women . . . people's beliefs about recovered memories and other aspects of child abuse appear to be more closely tied to autocratic misogynism than they are to social values or science" (1996,

p. 56). Family values discourse has been described as disguised antifeminist rhetoric (Briere, Henschel, & Smiljanich, 1992). Enns and her colleagues have pointed out that the very idea of a "false memory syndrome" presupposes a traditional feminine stereotype of women as gullible, conforming, passive, narcissistic, and masochistic (Enns, McNeilly, Corkery, & Gilbert, 1995).

The FMSF literature has also expressed explicit concerns about feminism, concerns that feminist psychologist Laura Brown describes as "at a deep level, accurate" (1996a, p. 350). As Brown further writes,

> This feminist viewpoint says that the disruption of families by an accusation of sexual abuse that is true is painful and yet healing and necessary; it states that sexual abuse, because it is an element of patriarchy, can be found everywhere in patriarchy. (1996b, p. 16)

The feminists who identified incest as a problem in families called for a restructuring of the family toward greater equity in order to reduce the risks of this form of patriarchal oppression (Armstrong, 1978; Herman, 1981; Luepnitz, 1988). Brown reminds us that the child abuse field has largely forgotten this early political component and calls for an effort to "find our ways back to making the connections between psychotherapy and working for social justice" (1996b, p. 16).

Other Social and Political
Sources in Favor of Suppression

Although the challenges to the credibility of children and adults who state they have been sexually abused have paralleled a shift to the right in American political attitudes, these challenges have by no means been confined to patriarchal, family-values, right-wing publications, as any media survey can attest (Stanton, 1997). Information about the prevalence and impact of sexual abuse has constituted unwelcome news among many constituencies. The spectacle of child witnesses betraying their adult protectors to state authorities discomfits liberals as well as conservatives; it evokes the totalitarian excesses when Hitler Youth members or Vietcong children were taught to inform on their parents

(Koonz, 1987, p. 287; Mydans, 1998). Indeed, the civil liberties concerns about state intrusion into the private sphere raised by the issue of protecting children from abusive parents remain unresolved (Olafson et al., 1993).

The timing and context of this issue's emergence in a 20th-century context of only intermittent social commitment to children's issues also played a role in the rapid emergence of a backlash. The rediscovery of child sexual abuse does not fully belong where it is so often placed, that is, with the constellation of events in the 1960s when Henry Kempe first wrote about the battered child syndrome. The battered child became known during the decade when President Johnson's Great Society legislation was focusing, among many other social reforms, on reducing child poverty, abuse, and neglect. Knowledge about the battered child in the 1960s came from physicians who were treating victimized children. The engine of change came from adult men and some women who were credentialed professional meaning makers and legislators working *on behalf of children*. The parents targeted for child abuse reporting and possible loss of parental rights generally belonged to social classes without much in the way of economic resources, political power, or access to the media.

The situation was very different with child sexual abuse, which was rediscovered more than a decade later and emerged in the context of the gender wars and the sexual revolutions of the 1970s. For child sexual abuse, issues of memory were central from the outset in a way that they were never central for the battered child syndrome. The rediscovery of sexual abuse was initially sparked, not by the sight of bruised babies in emergency departments, but by the voices of adult women describing abuses that they said had taken place decades before they spoke out. Concern about the sexual victimization of children was thus out of step chronologically and thematically with other major programs on behalf of children, and it came at a time when American birth rates were dropping and societal interest in children's issues was waning.

Indeed, by the time child sexual abuse emerged fully into American public consciousness in the early 1980s, the defunding of programs designed to aid children was everywhere evident, whereas the reporting requirements for child abuse remained in place, leaving social service agencies underfunded, understaffed, and overwhelmed. It was inevitable in a context of large case loads and rapid personnel turnover in social service agencies that errors would follow, quite apart from the missteps that the scientists in the field might be committing as they explored this new area. Governmental intrusion into the home is problematic in any free society, and when those mandated to intrude were sometimes young, ill-trained, underpaid, and overburdened, the problem intensified, especially when the homes so entered were inhabited by upper-middle-class adults with the money, power, and influence to fight back.

Timeless Attitudes Toward Victims

In addition to the historical reasons behind the backlash, there exist the timeless attitudes toward victimization described by Summit when he chose Jean Goodwin's felicitous phrase, "shared negative hallucination," to describe societal avoidance of child sexual abuse (Goodwin, 1985; Summit, 1988, p. 40). Summit wrote that all of our systems of justice, reason, and power have been adjusted to ignore the existence of such a "fatal flaw," and asked rhetorically, "What if the instruments of the social scientists have been calibrated to filter out the insistent static of posttraumatic pain that is central to the origins of violence and emotional disturbance?" (1988, p. 51). Even adult survivors, Summit wrote, "do not usually present their shameful credentials for inspection," nor do perpetrators of sexual assaults willingly confess to them. "We have avoided confronting child sexual abuse not only through protective disbelief among the outsiders but through dedicated hiding by the insiders," Summit wrote. "We should understand by now that most people will overlook clues, blame victims, and stigmatize victim families as sick rather than consider that trusted friends could be sexual predators" (1988, p. 43). As Olafson, Corwin, and Summit concluded in 1993,

> If we were really to take into account the role sexual coercion and violence play in shaping human culture and personal identity, fundamental structures of thought could well be shaken and changed. Such great shifts in world view unsettle even those whose privileges and self-images are not directly threatened by them. (1993, p. 19)

These timeless attitudes about victimization have also been high-lighted in two important volumes published in 1992. In *Shattered Assumptions*, psychologist Ronnie Janoff-Bulman quoted the research of Lerner's "just world theory" about societal attitudes to victims. According to Lerner's studies, we generally protect our illusions about a just world and our personal safety and control by assuming that people get what they deserve and deserve what they get (Janoff-Bulman, 1992, pp. 9-10). Lerner's research revealed that individuals thus devalue and blame victims of even random and uncontrollable events. Janoff-Bulman added that cross-culturally and transhistorically,

> Within the population of survivors who have been victimized by another person, there is one group that is particularly blamed by other people: female victims of sexual violence. Women who have been raped, molested, or sexually assaulted are deemed particularly blameworthy. (Janoff-Bulman, 1992, p. 152)

Judith Herman's *Trauma and Recovery* framed this timeless issue politically. When traumatic events are caused by humans, she wrote, "Those who bear witness are caught in the conflict between victim and perpetrator," and it is tempting to take the side of the perpetrator and do nothing rather than to share the burden of pain and the stigmatization that alliance with the victim can bring (1992, p. 7). Herman added,

> The systematic study of psychological trauma therefore depends on the support of a political movement. Indeed, whether such study can be pursued or discussed in public is itself a political question. The study of war trauma becomes legitimate only in a context that challenges the sacrifice of young men in war. The study of trauma in sexual and domestic life becomes legitimate only in a context that challenges the subordination of women and children. Advances in the field occur only when they are supported by a political movement powerful enough to legitimate an alliance between investigators and patients to counteract the ordinary social processes of silencing and denial. (1992, p. 9)

In summary, the forces that suppressed the issue of child sexual abuse for centuries and have fed the rapid backlash were cognitive rigidity in the professionalized knowledge of the organized health professions, the defense of the patriarchal family, societal assumptions about social class and deviant sexuality, gender bias, wavering public commitments to children's issues, civil liberties concerns about the sanctity of the home, the fragmenting of the organized feminist movement that had politically empowered survivors and their advocates, and timeless prejudices against victims of all disasters, especially interpersonal ones.

Olafson and colleagues also made reference to the 20th-century sexual revolutions when they wrote, "Proponents of sexual modernism, with their progressive and optimistic outlook regarding individual liberation and sexual self expression, could well find the new research findings about the coercive, compulsive, and cruel aspects of human sexuality especially difficult to accept" (Olafson et al., 1993, p. 19). The modern sexual revolutions have contributed both to the long suppression of the realities of child sexual abuse and to the backlash, but this contribution has often been minimized or even omitted in accounts of these phenomena (Brown, 1996a; Myers, 1994).

The Modernization of Sex and the Rediscovery of Child Sexual Abuse

It has been said that child advocate "extremists" argue that "pedophiles and pedophile protectors" fuel the backlash (Brown et al., 1998, p. 1). Although there is some merit to the argument that attorneys defending alleged perpetrators can influence public attitudes about child sexual abuse through skillful media manipulation on behalf of their clients, there are also historical attitudes about childhood sexuality and adult-child sexual contacts that are not confined to the media spins of the Defense Bar or the pedophile press. These more mainstream attitudes have influenced the debate about child sexual abuse from the beginnings of this century into the current controversies. Summit's eloquent challenges to these attitudes are among his greatest achievements. As we shall see, Summit took on not only pedophiles and pedophile protectors but also the very mainstream of psychiatry and sexology.

It has become something of an article of faith by the end of the 20th century that children are naturally sexual. This belief has emerged gradually in Western consciousness for well over a century. It has its roots in

Victorianism, a Victorianism far more complex than its dominant stereo-type suggests. When a group of women scholars at Stanford's Center for Research on Women set out to gather the material for *Victorian women* (Hellerstein, Hume, & Offen, 1981) in the years between 1975 and 1980, we brought to our project the received wisdom of the time that the Victo-rians were asexual or sexually repressed, that Freud had discovered childhood sexuality, and so on. We found a very different reality. The Victorians did not fit the stereotype constructed by the crusaders of the 20th-century sexual revolutions. Although the Victorians were indeed peculiar in some of the things they had to say about sex (and so may the moderns be), they appear to have been almost obsessed by the subject (Foucault, 1978; Gay, 1984). We have learned since that the much ma-ligned Queen Victoria, for whom the prudishness of the age was named, very much enjoyed her marital intimacies with her Albert and wondered how she would do without them after his death from typhoid fever (Weintraub, 1987, 1997). It was not sex Queen Victoria deplored, but its consequences, the "so very animal and unecstatic" realities of pregnancy and childbirth (Hellerstein et al., 1981, p. 209). Sex was very much on the minds of the Victorians, a reality that comes clear when we study their dress and postures, the exaggerated secondary sexual characteristics displayed by the corseted women of the time with their protruding bus-tled rumps and uplifted breasts, and their bearded men.

The Victorians also knew that children could be sexual. All over Europe in the 19th century (in *Victorian Women* we argued, to the distress of at least one French reviewer, that "Victorianism" was not confined to England), there was a concern about childhood masturbation that in-cluded horrific devices invented to prevent it (Hare, 1962). This worry, which dated back to the middle years of the 18th century, reflected a keen awareness that if left to themselves, girls as well as boys could and would masturbate. That is to say, fundamental assumptions about child-hood sexuality were undergoing seismic shifts before Freud crystallized the issue in his classic formulations about the normality of infant and childhood sexuality at the end of more than a century of European medi-cal and moral discussion of child and infant sexuality (Olafson et al., 1993). Eroticized children were also prominent in late Victorian poetry and art (Dijkstra, 1986; Fussell, 1975). This was a true paradigm shift in social attitudes, and as the French historians of *mentalités* remind us, such changes are often measured in generations rather than in decades (Hunt, 1989).

Much of the long 20th-century campaign for the modernization of sex has explicitly repudiated Victorianism, or has repudiated what those who hoped to escape it (or to avoid being accused of it) imagined Victorianism to be. Historian Paul Robinson (1976) dated the modernization of sex to the years between 1890 and 1910 and named Havelock Ellis rather than Sigmund Freud as the true founding father of modernist sexual theory. Robinson stated that "the modernists were sexual enthusiasts" who saw sex as a worthwhile human activity and not a danger to moral character or physical health (1976, pp. 2-3). Among their other goals, Robinson wrote, the sexual modernists sought to broaden the range of acceptable sexual behavior and to destigmatize behaviors that had been defined as deviant. In massive studies published between 1897 and 1910, Ellis began the project of sexual modernization that was carried forward by Alfred Kinsey and his colleagues at mid-century and William Masters and Virginia Johnson a generation later.

The idea that children were naturally and normally sexual was central to this century-long sexual revolution. The Victorians had recognized childhood sexuality and expressed caution; a child's masturbation could cause health problems, insanity, and even death (Hare, 1962; MacDonald, 1967; Neumann, 1975). Freud and Ellis, building on a good deal of contemporary research and clinical work, normalized the sexual child. Ellis quoted Freud on children as follows: "In reality, the new-born infant brings sexuality with it into the world, sexual sensations accompany it through the days of lactation and childhood, and very few children fail to experience sexual activities and feelings before the period of puberty" (Ellis, 1936, Vol. 2, Part 3, p. 36).

But Freud did more than normalize childhood sexuality. Let us look again at one well-known passage in his 1905 case study of Dora. When Dora was 14, Herr K, a friend of her father, one day

> suddenly clasped the girl to him and pressed a kiss upon her lips. This was surely just the situation to call up a distinct feeling of sexual excitement in a girl of fourteen who had never before been approached. But Dora had at that moment a violent feeling of disgust. (1905/1963, p. 43)

Freud wrote that Dora did not tell anyone about this incident for years, but she avoided being alone with the older man. Eventually Herr K propositioned Dora again, sent her flowers daily for a year, gave her valuable presents, and followed her on the street. Did the adolescent Dora's disgust and fear when confronted with the unexpected sexual advances, trickery, and stalking by a man her father's age need explanation? It did to Freud.

> In this scene . . . the behavior of this child of fourteen was almost entirely and completely hysterical. I should without question consider a person hysterical in whom an occasion for sexual excitement elicited feelings that were preponderantly or exclusively unpleasurable. (p. 44)

As Freud interpreted this case, he also argued that the slap Dora gave Herr K when the man propositioned her again "by no means signified a final 'No' on her part" (p. 131), and that she was secretly in love with Herr K. Dora, as we know, rejected Freud's line of reasoning and left treatment abruptly.

But Freud's message lingered on. For a child of 14 *not* to respond sexually when approached by a man her father's age was abnormal. Childhood sexuality, at least for the later stages of childhood, was not only normal but normative.

Freud's student, Karl Abraham, in "The Experiencing of Sexual Trauma as a Form of Sexual Activity," published in 1907 and often quoted in subsequent psychiatric literature, argued that in many cases sexual trauma was desired unconsciously by the child. Abraham's evidence was that the children did not run, call for help, or offer resistance; instead, they succumbed to the adults who were assaulting them sexually. In the case example he gave of a 9-year-old girl nearly raped by a neighbor who coaxed her into the woods with him, he argued that the child had "allowed herself to be seduced" and implied that this was the reason for the girl's subsequent secrecy about what had happened to her (p. 52).

In a widely quoted paper to which Summit also refers, Loretta Bender (the Bender who created the Bender-Gestalt, a respected psychological instrument that is still widely used) and Abram Blau presented findings in 1937 of 16 cases (11 boys and 5 girls) who had had sexual relations with adult men (and, in one case, a woman). Some of the children suffered from sexually transmitted diseases, but Bender and Blau did not find them for the most part to be psychologically disturbed. The authors argued that the "emotional placidity" of most of these children would seem to indicate that they derived some fundamental satisfaction from the relationship.

> These children rarely acted as injured parties and often did not show any evidence of guilt, anxiety or shame. Any emotional disturbance they presented could be attributed to external restraint rather than to internal guilt. Finally, a most striking feature was that these children were distinguished as unusually charming and attractive in their outward personalities. Thus, it is not remarkable that frequently we considered the possibility that the child might have been the actual seducer rather than the one innocently seduced. (Bender & Blau, 1937, p. 514)

About these children, who ranged in age from 5 to 12, Bender and Blau concluded, "This study seems to indicate that these children undoubtedly do not deserve completely the cloak of innocence with which they have been endowed by moralists, social reformers and legislators," and "It is true that the child often rationalized with excuses of fear of physical harm or the enticement of gifts, but these were obviously secondary reasons" (p. 514). Bender and Blau do not state how they knew that fears of being physically hurt by the adults who were sexually assaulting them were "secondary" for these children. Indeed, Bender and Blau refer to the children's offenses and make reference to their sex delinquency, rather than to the criminal assaults upon them by adults.

The Bender and Blau article also contains a significantly sexual modernist passage, citing cross-cultural anthropological studies by Malinowski, Briffault, and Rene Guyon, as well as the *Memoirs* of Casanova to show that sexual activity among children is recognized as normal in many cultures. They concluded their brief anthropological survey by stating,

> It is unnecessary to discuss the psychological motivations at the basis of these [parent-child incest] taboos, but their significance is implied by the fact that there is a complete lack of scientific proof of any possible deleterious eugenic or other effects, despite popular belief to the contrary. (p. 515)

In 1942, Sloane and Karpinski cited Bender and Blau to state, "The view that sexual relations with adults (including incest) among children are not basically destructive is confirmed by the observations of Rasmussen and of Bender and Blau" (p. 666). They also quoted Abraham that sexual traumas cannot be regarded as the cause of mental disease, but merely exercise an influence on the form taken by it, and they added, "The 'traumatic' aspect furthermore loses some of its significance when it is realized the child itself often unconsciously desires the sexual activity and becomes a more or less willing partner in the act" (p. 666). Sloane and Karpinski did find that the girls in their cases, who were adolescent rather than the prepubertal youngsters in Bender and Blau's study, showed serious repercussions, although "the severity of the taboos which society has erected against incest has undoubtedly contributed to the nature of the reaction" (1942, p. 673).

The stage was set for Alfred Kinsey, who would argue that adult-child sex could cause problems for children, but only because of the nature of our modern Western culture. Kinsey, in a tradition that dates back at least to Jean-Jacques Rousseau, set out to restore to us what could be called our "noble savage" humanity, in Kinsey's case our "natural" sexual natures, uncorrupted by the shackles of Victorianism and the Judeo-Christian heritage. Social taboos or external constraints caused children whatever problems they faced following sex with adults; it was time to rid ourselves of these taboos. In their natural state, children were sexual.

Robinson's assessment of Kinsey, written before the rediscovery of child sexual abuse had become widely known, and well before the revelations about Kinsey in James H. Jones's 1997 biography of Kinsey (which Robinson described on the book jacket as "massively researched and judiciously argued"), included the following passage:

> Ultimately one's judgment of Kinsey depends on how one evaluates the human sexual condition (or, less grandly, the American sexual condition) at mid-twentieth century. If, on the one hand, one is convinced that we still live in the shadow of Victorianism, that ignorance and prejudice in sexual matters continue to create unacceptable levels of anxiety, then Kinsey will earn our admiration as a person who did as much as any intellectual can to make sexual life less painful, freer, and perhaps even happier. If, however, one believes that, in the process of demystification, sex has become

trivialized, that in eliminating the anxiety we have also eliminated the ec-
stasy, then Kinsey, while not to be despised, must be regretted. (Robinson,
1976, p. 119)

The third alternative, that there were sexual contacts—those between
adults and children, even when the children "consented" and even
when the sexual stimulation afforded the children some pleasure—that
could be toxically damaging to the young, was not one Robinson considered, nor was this alternative yet available in the mid-1970s when he
published his history of sexual modernism.

Dora was upset when Herr K grabbed her and kissed her; Freud
thought a normal girl would not have been. Thus, when Kinsey wrote in
passages that have been often quoted that the fears reported by women
who had been sexually approached by adult men during childhood
were inappropriate because it is difficult to understand why a child
should be disturbed at having its genitalia touched or even at more specific sexual contacts, he was speaking for an inherited tradition to which
he added great authority with his influential studies (Kinsey et al., 1953,
p. 121). That his stance of scientific neutrality and objectivity about all
forms of sexual deviance masked a position of sexual libertarian advocacy has long been suspected, not only because of the above passage, but
in long sections about man-boy sexual contacts based, as Jones now
informs us, on information received from practicing pedophiles, and
not, as some have suspected, on experiments conducted by the Kinsey
team on male children (Kinsey, Pomeroy, & Martin, 1948; Reisman,
Eichel, Court, & Muir, 1990). As Jones writes, "Kinsey's deep-seated ani-
mosity to traditional morality led him to take a benign view of child molestation and incest" (Jones, 1997, p. 620).

Kinsey's advocacy of the benefits of sexual "outlets" for the young is
explicit in material that has only recently come to light in the Jones biography. Jones cites a letter Kinsey received from a man whose wife mas-
turbated the couple's 9-year-old nephew to orgasm two or three times
per night at the boy's reported request and asked for Kinsey's advice
about whether he and his wife were pursuing the proper course. Kinsey
wrote back that they should continue the practice:

Apparently the small boy is erotically responsive and it looks as if he is already so conditioned to the sort of contact that he has had that the chances

of his getting along without a regular sexual outlet are now reduced. If he were to be forced to go without any outlet of any sort, it is probable that he would be nervously disturbed and might be difficult to handle socially. . . . We do not consider that complete cessation of the activity is a practical alternative for reasons I have already mentioned. (Jones, 1997, pp. 620-621)

However, Jones noted that Kinsey was not very optimistic about incest, although Kinsey did not believe that such cases had to end badly; he thought that the legal and social difficulties probably complicated the issue more than the actual relationships themselves (p. 621).

Kinsey had data on orgasm in 604 preadolescent boys, one of whom, at the age of 10, had been brought to orgasm 14 times in a 24-hour period, and one 5-month-old baby boy who had had three orgasms, although the time required to achieve this was not specified. Kinsey stated that he obtained this data from nine adult male subjects, "who, with their adult backgrounds, are able to recognize and interpret the boys' experiences" (Kinsey et al., 1948, p. 177). His pedophile informants told him that there are some preadolescent boys who fail to reach climax "even under prolonged and varied and repeated stimulation." Kinsey theorized that this probably represented psychological blockage more often than physiological incapacity (1948, p. 178). Kinsey saw these data on the sexual activities of younger males as "important substantiation of the Freudian view of sexuality as a component that is present in the human animal from earliest infancy" (1948, p. 180). He concluded,

In the population as a whole, a much smaller percentage of the boys experience orgasm at any early age, because few of them find themselves in circumstances that test their capacities; but the positive record on these boys who did have the opportunity makes it certain that many infant males and younger boys are capable of orgasm, and it is probable that half or more of the boys in an uninhibited society could reach climax by the time they were three or four years of age. (1948, p. 178)

Kinsey's descriptions of the orgasms of these boys included the following passages:

A gradual, and sometimes prolonged, build-up to orgasm, which involves still more violent convulsions of the whole body; heavy breathing, groaning, sobbing, or more violent cries, sometimes with an abundance of tears (especially with the younger children) . . . culminating in extreme trembling, collapse, loss of color, and sometimes fainting of subject. Sometimes happens only in the boy's first experience. . . . Pained or frightened at approach of orgasm. The genitalia of many adult males become hypersensitive immediately at and after orgasm, and some males suffer excruciating pain and may scream if movement is continued or the penis even touched. The males in the present group become similarly hypersensitive before the arrival of actual orgasm, will fight away from the partner and may make violent attempts to avoid climax, *although they derive definite pleasure from the situation* [italics added]. Such individuals quickly return to complete the experience, or to have a second experience if the first was complete. About 8 percent of the younger boys are involved here, but it is a smaller percentage of older boys and adults which continues these reactions throughout life. (Kinsey et al., 1948, p. 161)

The "partners" who provided this information to Kinsey, including the data about the "definite pleasure" the boys derived from the situation while fighting away from their partners, were, as Jones informs us, pedophiles, one of whom, Mr. X, had had sexual relations with 600 preadolescent males and 200 preadolescent females (Jones, 1997, p. 507). As the conservative critics Reisman and her colleagues comment, "Looking to sexual molesters for information about childhood sexuality is like drawing conclusions on the sexuality of adult females from the testimony of rapists" (1990, p. 33). Kinsey described in detail these graphic accounts of children who were frightened, sobbing, fighting away, screaming, crying, and fainting during sex with their pedophile partners, and he saw only substantiation of Freud's theory that children were naturally sexual.

In this and in numerous other papers in the mainstream professional journals, including a study commissioned by the state of California from San Francisco's Langley-Porter Institute (Weiss et al., 1955), adult-child sexual contacts were seen as victimless crimes, if indeed they were crimes at all, and the child victims were described as "participating" and even as the aggressive seducers of "entirely harmless" pedophiles (for a succinct summary of this literature, see Salter, 1988, pp. 25-42). Thus, psychiatrist Alayne Yates was heir to a long tradition in psychiatry and sexology (although one that was nearing its end) when she published *Sex Without Shame* in 1978 and headed her chapter on incest with the Guyon Society slogan, "Sex before eight or else it's too late" (Yates, 1978, p. 112). Yates wrote that the girls she had evaluated "who were young, uncoerced, and initially pleased with the relationship remain emotionally unscathed, even after protracted incest. They are fully orgasmic, sexually competent, attractive, and sometimes seductive" (p. 120). Yates added that when the outcome for girls from incestuous homes is foster placement,

> [T]he transition may require the relinquishment of pleasure. Society expects its children to be asexual and the foster home may be totally unprepared for a sensuous child. . . . In an understanding, unruffled placement the girls usually do adjust, temporarily inhibiting their eroticism as convention dictates. (pp. 120-121)

Yates concluded,

> There is an important lesson to be learned from non-coercive father-daughter incest. Early erotic pleasure by itself does not damage the child. It can produce sexually competent and notably erotic young women. Childhood is the best time to learn, although parents may not always be the best teachers. (p. 121)

The normative edge of sexual modernism is evident in much of what Yates had to say, as in her chapter about the child from age seven to puberty, "If the child is not yet masturbating, he should be. . . . Brothers and sisters may experiment with each other" (p. 211). Yates expressed concern that parents were continuing to "inhibit and distort" the sexual drives of children, just as she felt her own sexuality had been inhibited in her family of origin (p. 30).

Reading back into all of these accounts with what Summit and others have taught us, we can recognize the distress and helplessness of these child victims—the young Dora repelled by Herr K's advances, the little girl Abraham described who was almost raped and kept it secret, the children who told Bender and Blau that they had been threatened and bribed, and the little boys in the Kinsey studies who fought away from their molesters and screamed and cried. If we can see the suffering of these children, why did these caring and competent professionals not see it? Among other factors, they were blinded by the revolutionary discovery of childhood sexuality, inherited from Freud and increasingly dominant across multiple disciplines. We also know from the Jones biography of Kinsey and from passages in Yates's *Sex Without Shame* that both Kinsey and Yates felt personally stifled by their own parents' inhibiting attitudes about sexuality, and they hoped to create a healthier sexual climate for future children.

Until the very recent past, then, it was not extremists who argued that adult-child sex might be benign. It was respected professionals who could even be classed as moderates, and whose mission was sexual enlightenment and sexual liberation to free our society from the repressive constraints of Victorianism in the name of sexual health. It was not pedophiles and pedophile protectors who, in some cases well into the 1980s, argued that adult-child sex could be benign if the child was consenting and the relationship "non-coercive," and it was not only the pedophile press who used cross-cultural and animal studies to make this liberationist point. Indeed, it is interesting that David Finkelhor found it necessary to protest in 1979 that it was *not* "Victorian" to be concerned about the sexual abuse of children, and that this concern was compatible with the most progressive attitude toward sexuality being voiced at the time, in which consent was the sole standard by which the legitimacy of sexual acts be evaluated (1979b, p. 697).

It was perhaps Summit's greatest gift to children that he, who knew Alayne Yates and had read the crucial passages in Kinsey, Freud, Bender and Blau, and all the others who had written on this subject, was able to transcend his training and look freshly at the "consenting" or "participating" child victim. In a manner rare for adults, Summit got inside the mind of the "consenting" child and made us pay attention. He wrote that when intruders—fathers, stepfathers, mother's boyfriends—come in the night and the children awaken to find hands or mouth exploring their bodies,

> The normal reaction is to "play possum." . . . Small creatures simply do not call on force to deal with overwhelming threat. When there is no place to run, they have no choice but to try to hide. Children generally learn to cope silently with terrors in the night. (Summit, 1983, p. 183)

As if speaking directly to his eminent predecessors, to Abraham, Bender, Blau, and Kinsey, Summit responded that children who seem to be consenting are submitting, and that even in those cases where the child acquiesces, children cannot consent. He explained why children do not fight and resist, why they do not tell, and why they often retract after they have disclosed. On these issues, his insights have been supported in subsequent research, to an even greater extent than he imagined when he wrote the accommodation paper (Lawson & Chaffin, 1992; Sorenson & Snow, 1991; Summit, 1996, June 21, p. 51).

Summit also addressed the empathy gap between adults and children, a gulf that Abraham, Bender, Blau, and other predecessors had somehow missed. He recognized that adults find it almost impossible to imagine themselves back into the intrinsic helplessness and dependency of the childhood condition, back into the reality that children, especially young children, are attached to their caretakers and want to please them. About childhood, Summit wrote,

> The intrinsic helplessness of a child clashes with the cherished adult sense of free will. . . . Adults have spent years repressing and distancing themselves from that horror. . . . Adults must be reminded that the wordless action or gesture of a parent is an absolutely compelling force for a dependent child and the threat of loss of love or loss of family security is more frightening to the child than any threat of violence. (Summit, 1983, p. 183)

Children's dependent, repeated compliance with the sexual demands of caretakers was not the sexual seductiveness, participation, and consent that Abraham, Bender, Kinsey, and others had imagined it to be (Summit, 1983).

Summit wrote movingly about the invisibility and silence that had heretofore hidden the victims of child sexual abuse atrocities and hidden their pain, the "shared negative hallucination" about the realities of child sexual abuse (Goodwin, 1985; Summit, 1983, 1988). Skeptics asked at the time, and the backlash still insistently asks, how is it possible that this plague is all around us and is yet not noticed? The victims are supposedly right there, under everyone's noses, damaged, traumatized, and yet somehow not seen. Are there perhaps not so many of them, or are they perhaps not really so very damaged? Summit offered an answer in the self-camouflage children adopted as they accommodate to abuse. He wrote,

The mythology and protective denial surrounding sexual abuse can be seen as a natural consequence both of the stereotypic coping mechanisms of the child victim and the need of almost all adults to insulate themselves from the painful realities of childhood victimization. (1983, p. 179)

He wrote that as victims mature, many learn to hide their stigmatizing sexual traumas from exposure. Victims, perpetrators, and bystanders prefer not to speak of these things, and so societal denial persists.

Ethics and the Issue of Consent

Periods of paradigm shift can lead to wild and rudderless times in which anything seems possible. The 1970s constituted such a time in American history, during which the rediscovery of child sexual abuse was a relatively minor episode. In social terms, the sexual revolutions were the big story. At the end of the 1970s, David Finkelhor wrote that ethical clarity on the issue of child sexual abuse was important for the benefit of society as a whole because of the increasingly confused sexual ethics in America at the time. "Taboos have fallen by the wayside," Finkelhor wrote,

and new standards have not been articulated to replace the old. A sense of polarization exists; many people have the impression that one is either broadly in favor of sexual expression or broadly opposed. Moral confusion about sex is in part responsible for the occurrence of sexual abuse, as some people interpret the current sexual revolution as an exhortation that "all is permitted." (1979b, p. 697)

But even "participating victims" cannot be said to have consented when the victim is a child, Finkelhor argued, because children do not have the freedom to say no, and because children cannot understand to what they are consenting. Herman put it this way:

Children are essentially a captive population, totally dependent upon their parents or other adults for their basic needs. Thus they will do whatever they perceive to be necessary to preserve a relationship with their caretakers. If an adult insists upon a sexual relationship with a dependent child, the child will comply. Given this reality, it makes no sense to invoke the idea of consent. (1981, p. 27)

In 1983, Summit expanded on the ethical issues Finkelhor and Herman raised:

A corollary to the expectation of self-protection is the general assumption that uncomplaining children are acting in a consenting relationship. This expectation is dubious even for the mythic seductive adolescent. Given the assumption that an adolescent can be sexually attractive, seductive, and even deliberately provocative, it should be clear that no child has equal power to say no to a parental figure or to anticipate the consequences of sexual involvement with an adult caretaker. Ordinary ethics demand that the adult in such a mismatch bear sole responsibility for any clandestine sexual activity with a minor. (p. 182)

Summary of Sexual
Modernization and Sex Abuse

How could Summit's predecessors have missed what he saw so clearly? Is there something about sex that blinded them? Possibly so, but conceptual blinders and unconscious biases that preclude accurate observation are known to be common in the history of science. There have been many other "shared negative hallucinations." Although the history of physics provides numerous examples, a contemporary example from the history of paleontology brings this point home especially well. When Stephen Jay Gould wrote, in the quotation that heads this chapter, that we observe according to preset categories and often cannot "see" what stares us in the face, he was referring to scientific study of fossil specimens from Canada's Burgess Shale that had been misclassified since their discovery by Charles Walcott in 1909 (Gould, 1989). To see them as they were would have radically undermined fundamental early 20th-century assumptions about the orderly and progressive course of evolution. Conceptual blinders not only prevented accurate observation of these specimens but also caused Walcott, who was head of the Smithsonian, to "see" things in the fossils that were not there and even to retouch photographs to fit his preconceptions. Interestingly, paleontologist Harry

Whittington's reclassification of the fossils (and the consequent radical revision of our understanding of the nature and course of evolution) took place in the paradigm-shattering period between 1975 and 1978, during almost exactly the same years that Roland Summit and his associates were rediscovering child sexual abuse. Gould argued that Whittington was no iconoclast, but a conservative scientist who did not set out to shatter a paradigm, and even tried to preserve the established evolutionary schema (by misclassifying one specimen as a trilobite, for example) until the evidence became overwhelming.

The professionals who minimized or excused child sexual abuse throughout much of the 20th century were also defending fundamental worldviews. Their errors about children's sexuality have been presented here in the context of the battles these professionals were fighting against what they viewed as Victorianism's toxic heritage of repressive sexual taboos. It would be a distortion to view them as apologists for pedophilia. They saw themselves as agents of enlightenment on behalf of sexual freedom and self-expression for everyone, although the publication of many incest apologias in the popular men's magazines of the 1970s reveal, as many have argued, that sexual modernism had a male bias (Herman, 1981). In any event, just about the time that sexual modernism, which included in its ideology the celebration of childhood sexuality, was triumphing in the 1970s, warning notes sounded. Ann Burgess, Susan Brownmiller, Florence Rush, and many others published works in this decade about rape trauma and child sexual abuse; sociologist Linda Williams set out to study rape at a hospital emergency room and discovered that the victims were not adult women raped by strangers, but in almost half the cases, children sexually assaulted by adults who were generally known to them (Brownmiller, 1975; Burgess, Groth, Holmstrom, & Sgroi, 1978; Burgess & Holmstrom, 1974; Rush, 1980; Williams, 1994). As the paradigm of sexual modernism collided with this new information, Finkelhor, Herman, and Summit grappled with the thorny ethical issues this collision raised, and they concluded that because children cannot consent, sex between adults and children is wrong whether or not it damages the child. Summit also demolished generations of misconceptions about the seductive, participating child victim.

Concluding Comments

> There is a sad, self-preserving irony about a world that cannot see its own cruelty with victims who can't give voice to their pain. After 125 years of discarded enlightenment, we still act as if victims are freaks and as if it is a virtue to be ignorant of sexual victimization.
>
> *Roland Summit (1988, p. 57)*

Two emergent paradigms collided in the 1970s in America—sexual modernism and the rediscovery of child sexual abuse. Just as the triumphant armies of sexual liberation prepared to celebrate their victory against Victorianism, the party was spoiled with new voices warning that sexual activity with the young was dangerous, damaging, and wrong. The issues raised by this collision have not been settled, and the scientific and ethical battles continue. Summit sees the current mood as a kind of war, in which it is

> not a little playing field where everyone can be sort of objective and grow together toward an ultimate truth. It's fox hole warfare, where if you stick your head up it may get shot off. . . . It's that diametricism, the polarity of beliefs that distresses me. I just hope that . . . within the next century a better kind of reason will prevail. (Summit, 1996, August 13, p. 3)

In addition to the many forces that have fed both suppression and backlash, such as the preservation of the patriarchal family, gender bias, victim blaming, and the inherent conservatism of professionalized knowledge, it has been argued in this chapter that the ideology of the 20th-century sexual modernist crusade has made it difficult for many men and women to hear and heed the warning notes sounded about the dangers of adult-child sex. The child sexual abuse discourse has included epithets that "validators" of child abuse hate sex and hate men (Gardner, 1991). It seems evident that many enlightened moderns, whatever their politics, do not wish to be identified as prudish, Puritan, or Victorian (Finkelhor, 1979b; Herman, 1981; Leonard, 1997).

Child sexual abuse as anathema, as an abomination, has no very long history. In a sense, child sexual abuse came to the forefront as a moral issue in the 1970s as an Eleventh Commandment just as the first Ten were under fire. We should recall that this was the time when deconstruction, poststructuralism, and postmodernism spread through the great American universities like computer viruses (Farber & Sherry, 1997). The resultant intellectual mood in the academy and much of the media included a radical moral relativism in which it became nearly impossible to make judgments that certain acts were wrong (Gelernter, 1997). For a time, it even became difficult to assert that certain categories of existence signified by language had reality apart from their signifiers. Thus, "the child" was said to have been invented in the late Middle Ages or the early Renaissance (Ariès, 1962); as a corollary, of course, "child abuse" was also a social construction, if a somewhat more dubious and recent one. Although the postmodern philosophies that speak of the social construction of reality have proven useful to radical resistance movements as they have deconstructed the "objectively" known truths of the dominant culture (such "truths" for example, as that sexual contacts with adults do not really harm children), their ultimate ethical implications appear to be nihilistic. They *de*construct, not *con*struct. We are left within an ethical vacuum. As one critic describes our current dilemma, "The problem is the ethical dissolution of America and Europe, a collapse of any shared value-systems or any way in which we can talk to one another about right and wrong" (Wilson, 1998, p. A31). A relativism far more naive than the imported European philosophies from which it is derived continues to affect media coverage of social issues, some legal theory, and many academic departments where social policy is taught (Taylor, 1989). It bodes ill for the vulnerable.

The late 1960s and the 1970s were also the time when the writings of the Marquis de Sade, with their vivid descriptions of sodomy, sadism, murder, and the sexual corruption of the young, were seriously being promoted as worthy of inclusion in the Western canon (Shattuck, 1996). The introduction to the 1965 Grove Press edition of Sade's works described their publication as a victory against Puritanism and Victorianism (Shattuck, 1996, p. 293). In a chapter about the Sade revival in his book, *Forbidden Knowledge,* cultural historian Roger Shattuck writes, "Anyone who does not register a sense of taboo in reading Sade lacks some element of humanity" (1996, p. 293). Assessing the "perilous theme" of Shattuck's "brave" book on forbidden knowledge, critic Andrew Delbanco writes, "Shattuck knows that by using words such as 'perversion' without irony he marks himself as a fogy who has not given up his old-fashioned sense of norms for postmodern relativism" (1997, p. 4).

Child sexual abuse also emerged as a moral issue in the context of postmodern relativism, but the investigation of its nature and consequences was primarily an area of scientific inquiry. Nevertheless, some critical rhetoric about the child abuse field reads almost as if the rediscovery of child sexual abuse by a sect of zealots resulted in a fixed belief system to which child abuse "cultists" still rigidly and irrationally adhere, instead of a scientific inquiry. As with all areas of science, the child abuse field has made mistakes and has learned from them as well as from continuing research studies. On the ethical issue, however, which is distinct from science, the conviction stands: Sexual contact between adults and children is wrong because children cannot consent. Recent statements, such as, "Children of all classes have been touched sexually by adults, yet a significant minority show no ill effects, and a few report positive outcomes" (Nathan & Snedeker, 1995, p. 250), or a publication in the *Journal of Sex Research* that child sexual abuse is not associated with pervasive harm (Rind & Tromovitch, 1997), have no bearing on this ethical issue because they do not address consent.

Summit concluded his 1988 paper by writing that when we finally open our eyes to children, open our eyes to the societal flaws we have chosen to overlook, and allow a growing recognition of our hidden pain,

> We will be ready to explore the potential of human development freed from fundamental betrayal and abandonment. It is not grandiose to suggest that such a shift in caring might strengthen women, sensitize men, and actually eliminate substantial amounts of heartbreak, alienation, mental disorder, and mayhem. (p. 58)

At the end of the Corwin interviews, after describing the time of discovery in the 1970s and the period of excess, confusion, and emerging backlash in the 1980s, Summit mused,

> We have stumbled in the dark toward a better understanding of something that's never been fully understood before. And in the midst of our

stumbling we are passing a kind of torch to a larger number of people who will take a less emotional view of it and turn it into common knowledge, I think. (Summit, 1996, August 13, p. 20)

References

Abraham, K. (1927). The experiencing of sexual trauma as a form of sexual activity. In K. Abraham (Ed.), *Selected papers* (pp. 47-62). London: Hogarth. (Original work published 1907)

Aries, P. (1962). *Centuries of childhood: A social history of family life* (R. Baldick, Trans.). New York: Knopf.

Armstrong, L. (1978). *Kiss daddy goodnight: A speak-out on incest.* New York: Pocket Books.

Bell, S. G., & Offen, K. M. (Eds.). (1983). *Women, the family, and freedom: The debate in documents* (Vols. 1-2). Stanford, CA: Stanford University Press.

Bender, L., & Blau, A. (1937). The reaction of children to sexual relations with adults. *American Journal of Orthopsychiatry, 7,* 500-518.

Briere, J., Henschel, D., & Smiljanich, K. (1992). Attitudes toward sexual abuse: Sex differences and construct validity. *Journal of Research in Personality, 26,* 398-406.

Brown, D., Scheflin, A. W., & Hammond, D. C. (1998). *Memory, trauma treatment, and the law.* New York: W.W. Norton.

Brown, L. S. (1996a). On the construction of truth and falsity: Whose memory, whose history? In K. Pezdek & W. P. Banks (Eds.), *The recovered memory/false memory debate* (pp. 341-353). San Diego, CA: Academic Press.

Brown, L. S. (1996b). Politics of memory, politics of incest: Doing therapy and politics that really matter. In S. Contratto & J. Gutfreund (Eds.), *A feminist clinician's guide to the memory debate* (pp. 5-18). New York & London: Harrington Park Press.

Brownmiller, S. (1975). *Against our will: Men, women and rape.* New York: Bantam Books.

Burgess, A. W., Groth, A. N., Holmstrom, L. L., & Sgroi, S. M. (1978). *Sexual assault of children and adolescents.* Lexington, MA: Lexington Books.

Burgess, A. W., & Holmstrom, L. L. (1974). *Rape: Victims of crisis.* Bowie, MD: R. J. Brady.

Butterfield, H. (1957). *The origins of modern science* (Rev. ed.). New York: Free Press.

Czapanskiy, K. (1993). Domestic violence, the family, and the lawyering process: Lessons from studies on gender bias in the courts. *Family Law Quarterly, 27,* 247-277.

Delbanco, A. (1997, September 25). The risk of freedom. *The New York Review of Books, 44*(13), pp. 4, 6-7.

Dijkstra, B. (1986). *Idols of perversity: Fantasies of feminine evil in fin-de-siecle culture.* New York & Oxford: Oxford University Press.

Ellis, H. (1936). *Studies in the psychology of sex* (Vols. 1-2). New York: Random House.

Enns, C. Z., McNeilly, C. L, Corkery, J. M., & Gilbert, M. S. (1995). The debate about delayed memories of child sexual abuse: A feminist perspective. *The Counseling Psychologist, 23,* 181-279.

Faludi, S. (1991). *Backlash: The undeclared war against American women.* New York: Crown.

Farber, D. A., & Sherry, S. (1997). *Beyond all reason: The radical assault on truth in American law.* New York & Oxford, UK: Oxford University Press.

Finkelhor, D. (1979a). *Sexually victimized children.* New York: Free Press.

Finkelhor, D. (1979b). What's wrong with sex between adults and children? Ethics and the problem of sexual abuse. *American Journal of Orthopsychiatry, 49,* 693-697.

Foucault, M. (1978). *The history of sexuality: An introduction* (R. Hurley, Trans.). New York: Pantheon.

Freedman, E. B. (1987). Uncontrolled desires: The response to the sexual psychopath, 1920-1960. *Journal of American History, 74*(1), 83-106.

Freud, S. (1963). *Dora: An analysis of a case of hysteria* (P. Rieff, Ed.). New York: Collier. (Original work published 1905)

Freyd, J. (1996). *Betrayal trauma: The logic of forgetting childhood abuse.* Cambridge, MA: Harvard University Press.

Fussell, P. (1975). *The Great War and modern memory.* London: Oxford University Press.

Gardner, R. A. (1987). *The parental alienation syndrome and the differentiation between fabricated and genuine child sex abuse.* Cresskill, NJ: Creative Therapeutics.

Gardner, R. A. (1991). *Sex abuse hysteria: Salem witch trials revisited.* Cresskill, NJ: Creative Therapeutics.

Gay, P. (1984). *The bourgeois experience: Victoria to Freud: Education of the senses.* New York & London: Oxford University Press.

Gelernter, D. H. (1997). *Drawing life: Surviving the Unabomber.* New York: Free Press.

Goodman, G. S., & Clarke-Stewart, A. (1991). Suggestibility in children's testimony: Implications for sexual abuse investigations. In J. Doris (Ed.), *The suggestibility of children's recollections* (pp. 92-105). Washington, DC: American Psychological Association.

Goodwin, J. (1985). Credibility problems in multiple personality disorder patients and abused children. In R. P. Kluft (Ed.), *Childhood antecedents of multiple personality* (pp. 2-19). Washington, DC: American Psychiatric Press.

Gould, S. J. (1989). *Wonderful life: The Burgess Shale and the nature of history.* New York and London: W.W. Norton.

Halévy, E. (1955). *The growth of philosophic radicalism* (M. Morris, Trans.). Boston: Beacon Press.

Hare, E. H. (1962). Masturbatory insanity: The history of an idea. *The Journal of Mental Science, 108,* 1-25.

Hellerstein, E. O., Hume, L. P., & Offen, K. M. (1981). *Victorian women: A documentary account of women's lives in nineteenth century England, France and the United States.* Stanford, CA: Stanford University Press.

Henderson, D. J. (1975). Incest. In A. M. Freedman, H. I. Kaplan, and B. J. Sadock (Eds.), *Comprehensive textbook of psychiatry* (2nd ed.). Baltimore, MD: Williams and Wilkins.

Herman, J. L. (1981). *Father-daughter incest.* Cambridge, MA & London, UK: Harvard University Press.

Herman, J. L. (1992). *Trauma and recovery.* New York: Basic Books.

Hunt, L. (Ed.). (1989). *The new cultural history.* Berkeley, Los Angeles, London: University of California Press.

Janoff-Bulman, R. (1992). *Shattered assumptions: Towards a new psychology of trauma.* New York: Free Press.

Jeffreys, S. (1985). *The spinster and her enemies: Feminism and sexuality, 1880-1930*. London, UK: Pandora Press.

Jones, J. H. (1997). *Alfred C. Kinsey: A public/private life*. New York: W.W. Norton.

Kempe, C. H., Silverman, F. N., Steele, B. F., Droegmueller, W., & Silver, H. K. (1962). The battered child syndrome. *Journal of the American Medical Association, 181*, 17-24.

Kinsey, A. C., Pomeroy, W. B., & Martin, C. E. (1948). *Sexual behavior in the human male*. Philadelphia: W. B. Saunders.

Kinsey, A. C., Pomeroy, W. B., Martin, C. E., & Gebhard, P.H. (1953). *Sexual behavior in the human female*. Philadelphia: W. B. Saunders.

Koonz, C. (1987). *Mothers in the Fatherland: Women, the family, and Nazi politics*. New York: St. Martin's Press.

Kristiansen, C. M., Felton, K. A., & Hovdestad, W. E. (1996). Recovered memories of child abuse: Fact, fantasy, or fancy? In S. Contratto & M. J. Gutfreund (Eds.), *A feminist clinician's guide to the memory debate* (pp. 47-59). New York: Harrington Park Press.

Kuhn, T. S. (1970). *The structure of scientific revolutions* (2nd ed.). Chicago: University of Chicago Press.

Larson, M. S. (1977). *The rise of professionalism: A sociological analysis*. Berkeley: University of California Press.

Lawson, L., & Chaffin, M. (1992). False negatives in sexual abuse disclosure interviews. *Journal of Interpersonal Violence, 7*, 532-542.

Leonard, J. (1997, November 24). The new Puritanism: Who's afraid of Lolita? (We are). *The Nation*, pp. 11-15.

Luepnitz, D. A. (1988). *The family interpreted*. New York: Basic Books.

Lustig, N., Dresser, J., Spellman, S., & Murray, T. (1966). Incest: A family group survival pattern. *Archives of General Psychiatry, 14*, 31-40.

MacDonald, R. H. (1967). The frightful consequences of onanism. Notes on the history of a delusion. *Journal of the History of Ideas, 28*, 423-431.

Masson, J. M. (1984). *The assault on truth: Freud's suppression of the seduction theory*. New York: Farrar, Straus, & Giroux.

Mydans, S. (1998, April 17). Pol Pot, brutal dictator who forced Cambodians to Killing Fields, dies at 73. *New York Times International*, p. A12.

Myers, J. E. B. (Ed.). (1994). *The backlash: Child protection under fire*. Thousand Oaks, CA: Sage.

Nathan, D., & Snedeker, M. (1995). *Satan's silence: Ritual abuse and the making of a modern American witch hunt*. New York: Basic Books.

Neumann, R. P. (1975). Masturbation, madness and the modern concepts of childhood and adolescence. *Journal of Social History, 9*, 1-28.

Oates, R. K., & Donnelly, A. C. (1997). Influential papers in child abuse. *Child Abuse & Neglect, 21*, 319-326.

Olafson, E., Corwin, D. L., & Summit, R. C. (1993). Modern history of child sexual abuse awareness: Cycles of discovery and suppression. *Child Abuse & Neglect, 17*, 7-24.

Pendergrast, M. (1995). *Victims of memory: Incest accusations and shattered lives*. Hinesburg, VT: Upper Access.

Pope, K. S., & Brown, L. S. (1996). *Recovered memories of abuse: Assessment, therapy, forensics*. Washington, DC: American Psychological Association.

Reisman, J. A., Eichel, E., Court, J. H., & Muir, J. G. (Eds.). (1990). *Kinsey, sex and fraud.* Lafayette, LA: Huntington House.

Revitch, E., & Weiss, R. G. (1962). The pedophiliac offender. *Diseases of the Nervous System, 23,* 73-78.

Rind, B., & Tromovitch, P. (1997). A meta-analytic review of findings from national samples on psychological correlates of child sexual abuse. *Journal of Sex Research, 3,* 237-255.

Robinson, P. (1976). *The modernization of sex: Havelock Ellis, Alfred Kinsey, William Masters, and Virginia Johnson.* New York: Harper & Row.

Rush, F. (1980). *The best kept secret: Sexual abuse of children.* New York: McGraw-Hill.

Russell, D. E. H. (1983). The incidence and prevalence of intrafamilial and extrafamilial sexual abuse of female children. *Child Abuse & Neglect, 7,* 133-146.

Russell, D. E. H. (1986). *The secret trauma: Incest in the lives of girls and women.* New York: Basic Books.

Salter, A. (1988). *Treating child sex offenders and victims: A practical guide.* Newbury Park, CA: Sage.

Salter, A. (1995). *Transforming trauma: A guide to understanding and treating adult survivors of child sexual abuse.* Thousand Oaks, CA: Sage.

Shakespeare, W. (1958). *The comedies.* New York: Heritage Press.

Shattuck, R. (1996). *Forbidden knowledge: From Prometheus to pornography.* New York: St. Martin's.

Sloane, P., & Karpinski, E. (1942). Effects of incest on the participants. *American Journal of Orthopsychiatry, 12,* 666-673.

Sorenson, T., & Snow, B. (1991). How children tell: The process of disclosure in child sexual abuse. *Child Welfare, 70,* 1-15.

Stanton, M. (August, 1997). U-turn on memory lane. *Columbia Journalism Review,* 44-49.

Summit, R. C. (1983). The child sexual abuse accommodation syndrome. *Child Abuse & Neglect, 7,* 177-193.

Summit, R. C. (1988). Hidden victims, hidden pain: Society's avoidance of child sexual abuse. In G. E. Wyatt & G. J. Powell (Eds.), *Lasting effects of child sexual abuse* (pp. 39-60). Newbury Park, CA: Sage.

Summit, R. C. (1996, June 21). Interview with David Corwin, M.D., Part I. Unpublished manuscript.

Summit, R. C. (1996, August 13). Interview with David Corwin, M.D., Part II. Unpublished manuscript.

Taylor, C. (1989). *Sources of the self: The making of the modern identity.* Cambridge, MA: Harvard University Press.

Weinberg, K. (1955). *Incest behavior.* New York: Citadel.

Weintraub, S. (1987). *Victoria: An intimate biography.* New York: Truman Talley Books (E. P. Dutton).

Weintraub, S. (1997). *Uncrowned king: The life of Prince Albert.* New York: Free Press.

Weiss, J., Rogers, E., Darwin, M. R., & Dutton, C. E. (1955). A study of girl sex victims. *The Psychiatric Quarterly Supplement, 29*(1), 1-27.

Wigmore, J. H. (1978). *Evidence in trials at common law.* Boston: Little, Brown. (Original work published 1904)

Williams, L. M. (1994). Recall of childhood trauma: A prospective study of women's memories of child sexual abuse. *Journal of Consulting and Clinical Psychology, 62,* 1167-1176.

Wilson, A. N. (1998, June 16). The good book of few answers. *New York Times International,* p. A31.

Woloch, I. (1982). *Eighteenth century Europe: Tradition and progress, 1715-1789.* New York and London: W.W. Norton.

Yates, A. (1978). *Sex without shame.* New York: William Morrow.

4

Scientific Support for Expert Testimony on Child Sexual Abuse Accommodation

THOMAS D. LYON

Roland Summit's article on child sexual abuse accommodation (CSAA) (Summit, 1983) describes sexually abused children's secrecy, helplessness, entrapment, delayed disclosure, and retraction. The paper is both admired and maligned. On the one hand, it has been hailed as one of the most influential papers ever written on child abuse (Oates & Donnelly, 1997). On the other hand, testimony on accommodation is often dismissed as "dangerous pseudoscience" by both commentators and the courts (Summit, 1992).

There are two reasons for this difference of opinion. The first is because of a misunderstanding regarding the relevance of accommodation in diagnosing abuse. The fact that a child exhibits sexual abuse accommodation does not *increase* the likelihood that the child was abused. For example, learning that a child alleging abuse retracted her allegation does not make it *more* likely that her allegation was true. However, it is important for jurors to hear that a surprising number of sexually abused children retract their allegations. Otherwise, they may assume that retractions conclusively prove that abuse did *not* occur. Those who insist that accommodation ought to be diagnostic of child sexual abuse in order to be useful information in court fault accommodation for failing a standard it was never intended to meet.

The second reason CSAA provokes disagreement is because of uncertainty whether it is a "scientific" concept. There is a judicial trend toward insisting that expert testimony be scientifically valid, regardless of whether it is intended to diagnose or to educate. If scientific research does not support the existence of accommodation, then any use of it in court may be challenged.

I will argue that there *is* scientific support for child sexual abuse accommodation, based on both observational and experimental research. Observational research demonstrates that a substantial proportion of abused children either delay reporting or fail to report their abuse. Abused children are afraid and embarrassed to tell. Children who do manage to tell are often not believed, and even when they are believed, are often not identified by social services or the police as abused. Experimental research documents children's tendency to keep secrets for others, particularly when the other is a loved one.

I will also argue that research casting doubt on the existence of accommodation often suffers from a methodological problem attributable to the effects of accommodation on the substantiation of sexual abuse. Because accommodation suppresses convincing reports of abuse, much of the research on abused children underestimates the extent to which accommodation occurs. If a child's secrecy suppresses disclosure, a parent's reluctance to believe suppresses reporting, and a child's reluctance to discuss makes substantiation unlikely, research limiting itself to substantiated cases will paint a skewed picture of the disclosure process. I hope to paint a more complete picture here.

First, I will discuss the most common objection to CSAA: It is not diagnostic of abuse. I will explain why this objection misunderstands the purpose and utility of accommodation. Second, I will consider the claim that CSAA is unscientific. I will show that in part this second claim is merely a restatement of the first objection, but in part a potentially valid criticism. I will discuss recent case law that makes it imperative to address the criticism head on, given the courts' appetite for expert testimony that is "scientific." Third, I will review the observational and experimental research on children's disclosure processes and argue that there is indeed evidence that accommodation occurs among a substantial proportion of abused children. Fourth, I will discuss the methodological problems that create inconsistencies among the research findings, and emphasize that the exact frequency of accommodation symptoms among abused children is unknown. Although Summit (1983) sometimes asserts that *most* abused children exhibit a particular accommodation symptom, it is safer to conclude that *many* abused children do so. As I will argue, however, such a conclusion does not undercut CSAA's usefulness as a means by which jurors can be educated about the dynamics of sexual abuse.

Is the Fact That a Child Has CSAA Evidence That the Child Was Abused?

Child sexual abuse accommodation documents how repeated sexual abuse is initiated and maintained in secrecy. It describes how sexual abuse is initiated through threats to keep the abuse a secret and through exploitation of the helpless and dependent child. It describes how the child's inability to report the first acts of abuse guarantees future victimization, and how attempts to maintain a sense of control and positive feelings for the abuser lead the child to blame herself for the abuse and turn any anger inward. CSAA describes how disclosure, if and when it occurs, is delayed and unconvincing, due to the child's ambivalence about the utility of telling, the child's adjustment problems preceding disclosure (which undermine credibility), and the reluctance of the nonoffending parent to believe the child. Finally, CSAA describes how abused children frequently recant their allegations in response to the negative consequences of disclosure, most notably the rejection by those to whom they turn for support, and their removal from their homes.

One criticism of child sexual abuse accommodation is that it is not proof of abuse. Although true, the criticism is misguided, because it reflects a misunderstanding of what the existence of child sexual abuse accommodation proves (Summit, 1992; see also Kalman, 1998; Lyon & Koehler, 1996; Mosteller, 1996; Myers, 1992). When a child exhibits one or more symptoms of child sexual abuse accommodation (e.g., delayed disclosure), this does not increase the likelihood that the child was abused. There is no reason to believe that true allegations are more likely than false allegations to be delayed. Therefore, it is inappropriate to use accommodation symptoms as "substantive evidence" of abuse. The purpose of accommodation symptoms, however, is to challenge the assumption that children who exhibit accommodation symptoms must *not* have been abused. It is appropriate to tell the jury that accommodation frequently occurs among abused children, in order to disabuse the jury of misconceptions regarding how abused children ought to behave. In legal terms, describing the symptoms of accommodation is an appropriate means by which one may "rebut" attacks on or "rehabilitate" a child's credibility (Myers, 1992). For example, if the defense argues that because the child did not report abuse until long after exposure to the defendant, the abuse did not occur, the prosecution could offer expert testimony that victims of abuse often delay reporting due to guilt and fear.

Critics may have misunderstood the purpose of child sexual abuse accommodation because of Summit's (1983) reference to it as a "syndrome." Using the term "syndrome" invites analogies to battered child syndrome, in which a child's symptoms, taken together, suggest that otherwise innocent injuries are abusive. In contrast, accommodation is not evidence of abuse. Moreover, a child need not show a cluster of accommodation symptoms in order to be accommodating abuse. For example, a child may delay reporting, yet never recant. Summit (1992) states that had he anticipated misunderstanding of child sexual abuse accommodation "syndrome," he would have avoided the term. I have done so in this chapter.

Most courts allow child sexual abuse accommodation testimony to rebut attacks on a child's credibility (Myers, 1992). Although overzealous prosecutors and experts may stray beyond the permissive use of accommodation, and suggest to a jury that a child's symptoms prove abuse (Mason, 1995), courts have the power to exercise control. In California, accommodation testimony is admissible only if the prosecutor specifically identifies the misconception the testimony is designed to rebut (e.g., delay undermines credibility), the expert limits testimony to abused children as a class, and describes how the reactions in question are not inconsistent with abuse (rather than diagnostic of abuse) (*People v. Bowker*, 1988). Restrictions on the scope of accommodation testimony minimize the likelihood that it will be misused by the prosecution or misunderstood by the jury.

The Scientific Basis for CSAA:
Why Does It Matter?

A second criticism of accommodation is that it is not supported by scientific evidence. Most of the time, the criticism is simply an elaborate way of saying that various reactions to abuse are not proof of abuse, and constitutes a misunderstanding of what accommodation includes and what it is intended to accomplish. For example, in disallowing expert testimony on purportedly diagnostic indicators of abuse such as sexualized behavior and sleep disturbances, the Florida Supreme Court held that "Child Sexual Abuse Accommodation Syndrome has not been proven by a preponderance of scientific evidence to be generally accepted by a majority of experts in psychology" *(Hadden v. State,* 1997, p. 575), thus using the word "accommodation" to refer to indicators having nothing to do with accommodation. Similarly, Mason (1995) cites reviews of research that is critical of "clear indicators of sexual abuse" as responsive to "Summit's model" (p. 402), despite the fact that Summit's model neither posits that accommodation is an indicator of sexual abuse nor incorporates the purported indicators. The reviews cited by Mason do not examine the prevalence of accommodation symptoms (such as delayed reporting and recantation) among abused children because they focus on examining differences between abused children and nonabused children (Berliner & Conte, 1993; Kendall-Tackett, Williams, & Finkelhor, 1993).

Commentators who recognize accommodation for what it is, but nevertheless find its scientific foundation lacking, present a more serious challenge. Kovera and Borgida (1997) point to the "absence of well-controlled empirical studies that might support or refute Summit's clinical observations" (p. S112). Ceci and Bruck (1995) argue that there is surprisingly little scientific support for the assertion that abused children who are threatened are reluctant to reveal their abuse. Bradley and Wood (1996) contend that there is a lack of scientific support for the proposition that abused children are reluctant to discuss their abuse, and that they frequently recant.

Whether Summit would aggressively defend the scientific status of child sexual abuse accommodation is unclear. He often emphasizes the extent to which the accommodation is *not* scientific. For example, Summit has stated that "it should be understood without apology that [accommodation] is a clinical opinion, not a scientific instrument" (Summit, 1992, p. 156). He has described the origins of the article on accommodation as "clinical study" (Summit, 1983, p. 179), producing "correlations and observations that have emerged as self-evident within an extended network of child abuse treatment programs and self-help organizations" (p. 180). This point has not been lost on critics, who highlight how Summit's views were derived from "clinical experience" (Mason, 1995, p. 402).

Although once a generally accepted source of wisdom, clinical experience has come under increasing attack. Experimental psychologists argue that clinicians are subject to confirmatory biases, in which they seek out, interpret, and generate information consistent with their prejudices and preconceptions. Experience may not increase knowledge, but only spawn arrogant confidence that one's pet theories are correct (Dawes, 1994). Without research to back them up, claims about what is common or typical among abused children may say more about clinicians' tools for evaluating child abuse cases than about the true nature of abused children (Ceci & Bruck, 1995).

I suspect that Summit went out of his way to deny that CSAA is a "scientific instrument" in order to counter claims that accommodation testimony should satisfy the Frye rule (*Frye v. U.S.,* 1923), which requires that expert testimony based on a novel scientific method of proof be generally accepted in the field in which it belongs. The rule is most often applied to recently developed techniques that produce quantifiable results with little apparent subjective interpretation. Calling CSAA a clinical opinion rather than a scientific instrument makes it less novel and more subjective, and thus potentially less susceptible to exclusion under Frye.

Recently, however, the U.S. Supreme Court held that the Frye rule did not survive the Federal Rules of Evidence (*Daubert v. Merrell-Dow Pharmaceuticals,* 1993). The opinion is binding on all federal courts applying the Federal Rules, and has already influenced a number of state courts, most of which have rules of evidence modeled after the Federal Rules (Mueller & Kirkpatrick, 2000). The Supreme Court held that trial courts should screen out expert testimony that is unscientific by asking several questions: Is the theory or technique testable? Has the theory or technique been subjected to peer review and publication? What is the known or potential rate of error? Are there standards controlling the technique's operation? "General acceptance" is still relevant, but takes a back seat to the courts' own evaluation of the scientific validity of the proffered testimony.

The Court's opinion leaves no doubt that it is enamored of the scientific method, and that it thinks the lower courts should be, too. The strategic value of denying oneself scientific status is, therefore, at best unclear. Some commentators argued that the *Daubert* criteria might apply only to expert testimony that is self-avowedly "scientific" (Mueller & Kirkpatrick, 1999). Because the Federal Rules of Evidence allow for expert testimony based on "scientific, technical, or other specialized knowledge," (2000, Rule 702) clinical judgment might qualify as "specialized" knowledge and be exempt. Such an approach has now been rejected by the Supreme Court, which recently held that no expert testimony is categorically exempt from *Daubert's* requirements (*Kumho Tire Co., Ltd. v. Carmichael,* 1999). Whether state courts will follow *Kumho's* lead and apply *Daubert* criteria to all expert testimony is unknown.

Even before *Kumho,* experts were not always successful in claiming that because their work was unscientific, they were not subject to the requirements of *Frye* or *Daubert.* Consider *State v. Foret* (1993), a case decided by the Louisiana Supreme Court, which applied the *Daubert* criteria to expert testimony regarding behavioral symptoms of sexual abuse. The court adopted the position that only scientific expert testimony was subject to the *Daubert* rules, but then assumed "for the purposes of argument" that the expert's testimony was scientific (*State v. Foret,* 1993, p. 1123, n. 7). The court then rejected the testimony, in part because of admissions that use of CSAA "is partly a science and partly an art form" (p. 1125).

Touting CSAA as more art than science neither prevents courts from applying standards for scientific evidence nor increases the likelihood of acceptance under those standards. Clinicians who call themselves artists in order to avoid scrutiny under *Daubert* risk being hoist by their own petard. If there is scientific support for accommodation, experts ought to say so.

Scientific Support for Accommodation

In court, the most frequently discussed aspects of accommodation are secrecy, delayed disclosure, and retraction. A large body of observational research has examined the prevalence of these characteristics among abused children. Moreover, a fair amount of research has examined children's willingness to keep secrets to protect others. This research provides a basis for assessing the scientific validity of accommodation.

DO CHILD VICTIMS DISCLOSE THE ABUSE?

Summit cited research that "the majority of the victims in retrospective surveys had never told anyone during their childhood" (Summit, 1983, p. 181). Rates of nondisclosure among women run from 33% to 92% (Bagley & Ramsay, 1986 [92% never reported to an adult]; Finkelhor, 1979 [63%]; Finkelhor, Hotaling, Lewis, & Smith, 1990 [33%]; Russell, 1986 [of those for whom information was available regarding reporting, 47%]), and among men from 42% to 85% (Finkelhor, 1979 [73%]; Finkelhor et al., 1990 [42%]; Johnson & Shrier, 1985 [85%]).

These numbers might be exaggerated if respondents are reporting abuse that never occurred. On the other hand, if adults who never revealed their abuse as children continue to deny being abused, these numbers are conservative. For example, Ferguson, Lynskey, and Horwood (1996) found that 87% of respondents who had been sexually abused as children had reported the abuse to at least one other person, a much higher percentage than found in several other surveys. However, because they questioned women who had just turned 18 years of age, they may have missed women who were still concealing their abuse. The authors acknowledge the potential for underreporting when they discuss their prevalence figures, which were lower than those in other surveys. Underreporting would reduce estimates of prevalence and increase the proportion of abuse that had been previously disclosed.

Because most known cases of child sexual abuse are based at least in part on the child's report of abuse, it is difficult to estimate rates of nondisclosure among children. The exception is when a child suffers from a sexually transmitted disease (STD), or presents with clear medical signs of abuse, because in such cases one can be confident that sexual abuse occurred without confirmation from the child. In such cases, 25% to 57% of children fail to disclose when questioned. Dubowitz, Black, and Harrington (1992) found that 25% of children with medical evidence indicative of sexual abuse (e.g., hymenal scarring) failed to disclose when questioned by an interdisciplinary team. Elliot and Briere (1994) discovered that 34% of children with external evidence of abuse (primarily diagnostic medical evidence, a confession, or an eyewitness) failed to disclose abuse at a crisis center interview. Gordon and Jaudes (1996) observed that 36% of children with an STD failed to disclose the name of the perpetrator both in the emergency room interview and at the investigative interview. Lawson and Chaffin (1992) noted that 57% of children with a sexually transmitted disease failed to disclose. Finally, Muram, Speck, and Gold (1991) found that 49% of children with medical evidence diagnostic of sexual abuse failed to disclose. Of course, some of these children may have forgotten their abuse, in which case the numbers exaggerate reluctance to some unknown extent. Nevertheless, the numbers are suggestive that substantial numbers of abused children fail to reveal.

Summit (1983) argued that even when children do reveal, their disclosures are often conflicted and delayed. In Dubowitz et al. (1992), in addition to the 25% who disclosed nothing, another 28% of the children with medical findings indicative of sexual abuse "partially" disclosed, defined as suggestive doll play or an inconclusive account of alleged abuse. Similarly, in Gordon and Jaudes (1996), 21% of the children with an STD initially failed to disclose the name of the perpetrator. Wade and Westcott (1997) questioned children about their experience with investigative interviews, and children often reported that they provided incomplete reports, attributing this

> to the difficulty of talking about their abuse; lack of knowledge about what was happening; anxiety about what the investigation would lead to; concern that what they would say would cause distress to people they cared for; the stress of the interview itself; or their dislike of the interviewer. (p. 58)

Bradley and Wood (1996) observed a lower percentage of reluctance when examining social service records of substantiated cases of abuse, a finding that will be discussed in the section dealing with methodological difficulties.

Studies examining the time at which the abuse occurred find that although large percentages of children report the abuse immediately, a number do so only after substantial delay. In a sample of 248 cases in which an investigative multidisciplinary team concluded that abuse had occurred, Elliot and Briere (1994) discovered that 75% of the subjects failed to disclose the abuse within the year that it first occurred. Sauzier (1989) reported that only 24% of the 156 children evaluated and treated at a family crisis program for sexually abused children reported abuse within a week after it occurred, whereas 17% delayed more than a year, and 39% told no one before the evaluation (their delay was not calculated). Immediate reporting appeared to be less likely when the offender was related to the children, when the abuse was more serious than fondling or attempted touching, and when compliance was obtained through threat or manipulation (rather than aggression).

In Sas and Cunningham's (1995) sample of 524 children whose sexual abuse was prosecuted in criminal court, one-third of the children waited more than one year after the first incident to disclose. Immediate reporting was less likely when the victim and perpetrator were emotionally close and when the perpetrator practiced preabuse grooming (rather than force). Somewhat smaller percentages of delay have been reported in other criminal court samples. Goodman et al. (1992) examined 218 children whose sexual abuse was prosecuted in criminal court, and found that whereas 42% reported their abuse within 48 hours of the last assault, 15% waited more than six months. Whitcomb et al. (1994) examined 431 cases of sexual abuse referred to a prosecutor for potential criminal prosecution, and found that although 52% reported abuse within one week of the last incident, 14% waited more than six months to do so. These numbers may be smaller because of the way in which some researchers define delay; if one measures delay from the last time the abuse occurred, rather than the first time, one understates the delay among children who are abused over time. Sas and Cunningham (1995) noted that if a child did not report abuse within 48 hours of the first time it occurred, there was a 70% chance that he or she would be abused again. In Goodman et al. (1992), abuse lasted longer than six months for

25% of the children. If these children reported abuse shortly after the last time they were abused, they were not counted as delayed reports.

WHY DON'T ABUSED CHILDREN DISCLOSE?

The most commonly mentioned reason for nondisclosure is fear: Abuse victims fear harm to themselves, harm to loved ones, and harm to the perpetrator. "[T]he only consistent and meaningful impression gained by the child is one of danger and fearful outcome based on secrecy" (Summit, 1983, p. 181). Russell (1986) questioned the 44 women in her survey who had been abused but who had never told anyone, in an effort to determine why they kept the abuse a secret. "[T]he two most common reasons were fear of punishment by the perpetrator and/or someone else, including abandonment and rejection and a desire to protect the perpetrator, or fear of hurting someone else" (Russell, 1986, p. 132). Similar fears are reported by children who disclosed for the first time when evaluated at a family crisis center. In Sauzier's (1989) review of 156 abused children seen for evaluation and treatment, initially silent children who were victims of more serious abuse "described the fear of losing the affection and goodwill of the offender; fear of the consequences of telling (being blamed or punished for the abuse by the non-offending parent); fear of being harmed; and fear of retaliation against someone in their family" (p. 460; see also Finkelhor, 1980, in which some female college students who did not reveal childhood abuse "were afraid of retaliation by the older partner, and did not believe parents or other authorities could adequately defend them" [p. 267]; Johnson & Shrier, 1985, noting that adolescent males revealing abuse for the first time explain "that they wanted to forget about the incident, wanted to protect the assailant, or were afraid of the reactions of their peers and family members" [p. 374]); and Palmer, Brown, Rae-Grant, & Loughlin, 1999, documenting a community sample who had not disclosed sexual, physical, emotional abuse, or all three, mentioned "fear of the abuser (85%), fear of negative reactions from other family members (80%), fear that no one would believe them (72%)" (p. 269). Similar disincentives were discovered by Sas and Cunningham (1995) in their review of criminal cases:

> Many powerful factors work to prevent immediate disclosure: the adult/child power imbalance, the child's training to defer to elders, the existence of a trust and/or dependency relationship, admonishments to keep the secret, implied or imagined negative consequences of telling, and feelings of guilt, self-blame, stigmatization and isolation. (p. 87)

Victims of abuse are frequently threatened by the abuser. Most of Herman's (1981) sample of 40 women who were outpatients in psychotherapy and who had suffered incest as children

> were warned not to tell anyone about the sexual episodes. They were threatened with the most dreadful consequences if they told: their mothers would have a nervous breakdown, their parents would divorce, their fathers would be put in jail, or they themselves would be punished and sent away from home. (p. 88)

Children in forensic samples also report having been threatened. In Smith and Elstein's (1993) nationwide survey of 954 criminal cases of child sexual abuse, 27% of the children reported having been specifically warned not to reveal the abuse. Furthermore,

> [t]hese warnings ranged from pleas that the abuser would get into trouble if the child told (or that the abuser would be sent away and the child would never see them again—a powerful message to a young child whose abuser is also a "beloved" parent), to threats that the child would be blamed for the abuse (especially troubling were children who were told that the defendant's intimate—the child's mother—would blame the child for "having sex" with the defendant and would thus turn against him or her), to ominous warnings that the defendant would hurt or kill the child (or someone he or she loved) if they revealed the abuse. (p. 93)

Sas and Cunningham (1995) found that children who delayed reporting were more likely to have been warned not to tell than children who reported immediately. Among children who reported abuse within the first 48 hours, 15% were warned not to tell. On the other hand,

> About half of delayed disclosers reported that the abusers never made an overt request that the child not tell. One fifth said there had been a threat of physical harm or death with the child or a family member as the intended victim. Among the remainder of cases, the most common admonishments not to tell were a simple statement that it is a secret or that they should not

tell, a warning that the child would be in trouble, a warning that the abuser would be in trouble, a threat of withdrawing privileges, a warning that it would hurt the mother to know, and a promise of money for not telling. (p. 122)

In her sample of 390 child victims in criminal sexual abuse cases, Gray (1993) found that 33% of the children had been threatened not to tell. Threats were not related to whether children told before being asked; Gray did not examine whether threats increased delay.

The lack of a specific warning not to tell does not mean that a child is unafraid to reveal. It is not always necessary for the offender to threaten the child for the child to recognize the dangers of revealing the abuse. Herman (1981) reports that "[t]hose who remembered no warnings simply intuited that guarding the incest secret was part of their obligation to keep the family together" (p. 88). Sas and Cunningham (1995) found that immediate disclosure was less likely when the abuser had physically abused the child, the child's mother, or both; they concluded that "overt threats were not necessary if the man had a history of violence within the home" (p. 122).

Often, abuse victims believe that they are at least partially responsible for the abuse, and are therefore ashamed to reveal (Summit, 1983). As noted above, Sauzier (1989) and Sas and Cunningham (1995) found that children sometimes mention their fears of being blamed for the abuse (see also Finkelhor, 1980, regarding female college students who never revealed abuse, that "many feared that they would be blamed themselves for what had happened" [p. 267]; and Russell, 1986, who notes that "self-blame made [some victims] feel too ashamed or guilty to tell. Some expressed fear of being blamed or of not being believed" [p. 132]). Several studies have reported self-blame among sexual abuse victims, and self-blame appears to be related to the extent to which the non-offending parent blames the child (Hazzard, Celano, Gould, Lawry, & Webb, 1995; Moore, McPhee, & Trought, 1986).

That many threatened children nevertheless reveal their abuse might lead one to argue that threats do not deter disclosure. However, this fact only justifies the conclusion that threats do not completely deter disclosure, not that they fail to reduce the likelihood that disclosure occurs. Moreover, cases in which threats are effective will be underrepresented in studies of children known to be abused, because an effective threat will suppress disclosure, and children who fail to disclose will rarely appear in research on abused children. Therefore, studies of cases in which children ultimately revealed abuse exclude the very children for whom threats are most effective.

IS THERE EXPERIMENTAL EVIDENCE
THAT CHILDREN WILL KEEP SECRETS
TO PROTECT OTHERS?

Experimental work has the potential to supplement the observational research on the effects of fear on disclosure. Laboratory research has both advantages and disadvantages. In the lab, researchers know whether a transgression occurred, and have control over the variables that may or may not influence children's reporting. On the other hand, researchers do not abuse children or threaten them with serious consequences should they tell. One can therefore question the applicability of experimental research to the disclosure of sexual abuse. More serious transgressions than those studied in the lab might provide stronger motives for disclosure, whereas stronger warnings would increase the need for secrecy. Nevertheless, when considered in tandem with observational work, the experimental data provides useful information confirming the effects of fear on children's disclosure of misdeeds.

There is a quite impressive body of laboratory research suggesting that inducements to secrecy reduce disclosure. Wilson and Pipe (1989), in a study involving 5-year-old children, had a magician perform magic tricks for the child, and then accidentally spill ink on "magic gloves" that the child was wearing. The magician hid the gloves, "saying if they were discovered she (the magician) would be reprimanded and that therefore they should not tell anyone about the ink spill" (pp. 66-67). The child was questioned after 10 days and then 2 months later. The interviewer first asked the child to relate everything that the magician did, and ultimately asked the child whether he or she knew anything about a pair of stained gloves the interviewer had found. None of the children spontaneously mentioned the gloves after 10 days, and 75% failed to do so after 2 months. Twenty-five percent denied knowing anything about the gloves at both interviews when directly asked, and another 33% denied knowing anything at one of the two interviews.

Pipe and Wilson (1994) found similar rates of nondisclosure among 6-year-olds, and less reluctance to disclose among 10-year-olds. Most 6-year-olds failed to mention the gloves in their free recall (75% at two weeks, 81% at two months), and more than 30% failed to reveal what happened after the specific question was asked (40% at two weeks, 32% at two months). The 10-year-olds were less inclined to keep the incident a secret, but nevertheless, more than 30% failed to mention the gloves in free recall (34% at two weeks, 44% at two months), and 16% did not reveal when specifically asked (at both interviews).

Bussey and colleagues (Bussey, Lee, & Richard, 1990) tested 3- and 5-year-olds' willingness to remain silent about a male experimenter who had accidentally broken a prized glass and hidden the pieces. "The experimenter expressed a great deal of concern about the event and asked the child not to disclose." A female experimenter later asked the child questions about the glass, including "Did [the male experimenter] touch the glass?" (if the child had not already revealed this information). Among the 3-year-olds, 14% kept the secret and the rate was 43% of 5-year-olds. If the experimenter sternly told the child not to tell, 43% of the 3-year-olds and 71% of the 5-year-olds either denied that the mishap occurred or refused to discuss it. In a separate paper, Bussey (1993) reported lower rates of nondisclosure among 9-year-olds (approximately 15% after being asked not to tell).

Peters (1990, 1991) examined 5- to 9-year-olds' reluctance to disclose that a thief had stolen a book in their presence, after the thief asked the child to keep the theft a secret. As reported by McGough,

> When the children were asked about the loss of the book in the presence of both their parents and the thief (who lied about the theft), only 5 percent of the children told what they knew. Later, when the thief was not present, nearly one-third (32.5 percent) of the children still feigned ignorance. The children gave two reasons for their denials: they thought they had made a commitment not to tell and they feared him. As one child said, "I think there is going to be some trouble. I'm afraid something bad might happen. That guy might get angry." (1994, p. 91)

The experimental research I have discussed thus far examined children's reluctance to implicate a stranger. What would happen if the transgressor were someone close to the child? "[A] child is three times more likely to be molested by a recognized, trusted adult than by a stranger" (Summit, 1983, p. 182). Most sexually abused children are victimized by someone they know, and most forensic and clinical cases involve intrafamilial abuse (Finkelhor, 1979; Gray, 1993; Smith & Elstein, 1993; Whitcomb et al., 1994). A child will have greater sympathy for a loved one, and is probably less inclined to get that person in trouble. If the loved one is in the child's home, or close to others the child loves, threats and inducements to secrecy may be more effective because the offender has continuing contact with the child and others in the family, and because the child cannot count on being supported by other loved ones should the child reveal.

Bottoms and colleagues (1990) divided their 3- to 4-year-old and 5- to 6-year-old participants into two groups. Both groups of children saw their mother accidentally break the head off a Barbie doll. In the secrecy group, the mother and child had been told not to play with the toys, and the mothers "asked their children to keep the fact they had played with the toys a secret, suggesting the mother would get into trouble if the child told, and offering the child a toy as a present if the child kept the secret" (Bottoms, Goodman, Schwartz-Kenney, Sachsenmaier, & Thomas, 1990; in Pipe & Goodman, 1991, p. 37). In the control group, the mother and child were free to play with the toys, and the mothers did not give their children any instructions about secrecy. Only 1 of the 49 children in both age groups told an interviewer about the doll when asked what happened, and 5-year-olds refused to disclose what their mother had done, even when asked leading questions.

In a study by Devitt and colleagues (1994, described in Honts, 1994; see also Tye, Amato, Honts, Devitt, & Peters, 1999), involving 4- to 11-year-olds, a confederate stole a book in the presence of the child, and told the child "that the theft was a secret and that the child should not tell anyone that the researcher had taken the book." The owner of the book discovered it was missing, and explained that it was needed for an exam the next day. The child was then questioned by the owner and an experimenter, the child and his or her parent were asked to wait for the police to arrive, and the child was then interviewed by a person identified as an officer; 19% of the children failed to name the thief. In a condition in which the child watched as his or her parent stole the book, and the parent told the child to name one of the experimenters as the thief, 81% of the children failed to name the thief (56% falsely accused the experimenter named by the parent, and 25% failed to name anyone).

Ceci and Leichtman (1992) have experimentally demonstrated that the loved one need not be a parent. In a study involving 3- and 4-year-olds, an experimenter spent 20 hours with each child, in order to become a "loved one." The experimenter and the child were told by a nursery school teacher not to play with a toy. While the teacher was gone, the "loved one" touched and broke the toy, and exclaimed, "Gee, I didn't mean to break it. I hope I don't get into trouble." Note that the loved one did not elicit a promise from the child or threaten the child not to tell. The teacher returned and asked the child who broke the toy. "[M]ost children, when confronted with the choice of disclosing that their loved one broke it, either refused to say anything or provided misleading information (e.g., 'A gremlin came in through the window and broke it')" (Ceci & Leichtman, 1992, p. 6).

Experimental work clearly supports the contention that children may be reluctant to reveal the wrongdoing of an adult, particularly when that adult is someone close to the child. Mild inducements not to reveal minor transgressions have profound effects in the laboratory, supporting observational research suggesting that stronger inducements not to reveal sexual abuse have equally profound effects in the real world.

ARE CHILDREN'S COMPLAINTS ALWAYS REPORTED TO THE AUTHORITIES?

"Of the minority of incest secrets that are disclosed to the mother or discovered by the mother, very few are disclosed to outside agencies" (Summit, 1983, p. 187). Even if a victim overcomes reluctance and reports abuse to an adult, this does not guarantee that the abuse allegation is brought to the attention of the authorities. Bagley and Ramsay (1986) found that 75% of children's reports of abuse to an adult were not reported to social services (see also Arata, 1998, noting that of undergraduates who had disclosed their sexual abuse, 10% had subsequent contact with the police; Hanson, Resnick, Saunders, Kilpatrick, & Best, 1999, discussing that of women in a national sample who reported having been molested as children, 13% of cases were reported to the police or other authorities; Palmer, Brown, Rae-Grant, & Loughlin, 1999, in which 6% of cases resulted in police charges; and Russell, 1986, who noted that 47% reported to an adult and 2% to 6% were reported to the police).

Little research has directly addressed why adults fail to report a child's complaint of abuse. The most relevant research has examined the nonoffending mother's reaction to her child's disclosure of abuse. "The mother typically reacts to allegations of sexual abuse with disbelief and protective denial" (Summit, 1983, p. 187). Although the once-popular portrayal of the mother as implicitly condoning incest (Nakashima & Zakus, 1977) has been rejected, research consistently finds that mothers are often ambivalent or unsupportive of the child's claims (Adams-Tucker, 1982; DeJong, 1988; Elliot & Briere, 1994; Everson, Hunter, Runyon, Edelsohn, & Coulter, 1989; Faller, 1988; Heriot, 1996; Leifer, Shapiro, & Kassem, 1993; Myer, 1984/1985; Sas & Cunningham, 1995; Sirles & Franke, 1989; Tufts New England Medical Center, 1984). The research will overstate maternal supportiveness to the extent that it examines the mother's attitude after the disclosure has been validated by authorities. The Tufts study (1984; see also Myer, 1984/1985) found that "[w]hen a mother discovers that her child has been sexually abused, her initial reaction is often shock and denial" (p. 212). If the unsupportive attitude continues, the case is less likely to find its way into the research samples. Indeed, the Tufts (1984) researchers noted that 58% of the families approached for participation in the study refused to do so, largely because they denied abuse or denied that services were needed.

That parental support is related to the child's willingness to reveal abuse when questioned by others is supported by Lawson and Chaffin (1992), who found that in their sample of children with sexually transmitted disease, 63% of children with supportive caretakers disclosed abuse compared with only 17% of children with unsupportive caretakers. Elliot and Briere (1994) found that 78% of children who disclosed abuse had supportive mothers compared to 40% of children who failed to disclose (but who nevertheless could be diagnosed as abused). In both studies, to be "supportive" a parent had to accept the possibility that the child was abused.

The reasons why mothers are often unsupportive of their children's allegations are similar to the reasons why children fail to report. DeJong (1988) notes that

> [s]ome of the internal factors include denial, guilt, frustration, anger, fear of repercussions, feelings of inadequacy, ignorance, previous behavior or emotional problems of the child, or general distrust of or reluctance to involve the police, child protective services, or other agencies in personal matters. External factors would include pressures by family members or friends to protect the abuser [and] specific economic pressures that might arise from loss of support by the abuser. (p. 18)

Similar considerations have been mentioned by other research (Faller, 1988; Herman, 1981; Myer, 1984/1985). DeJong (1988) adds that even after a report is made, a mother may fail to support her child because of the lack of support from the police and social services agencies involved.

In sum, both observational and experimental research supports the existence of accommodation among a large percentage of abused children. Children who are abused often fail to reveal, or reveal only after a delay. Children who reveal are often not believed. Children who are believed are often not reported to social services or the police. Child sexual abuse accommodation is not merely a term of art, but a scientifically supported phenomenon.

Methodological Difficulties
Due to Accommodation and
Its Implications for Recantation

"Treated, reported or investigated cases are the exception, not the norm" (Summit, 1983, p. 186). The sexually abused child has to overcome a number of hurdles in order for his or her case to be brought to official attention. As a result of the child's reluctance to discuss the abuse, and the caretaker's reluctance to believe that abuse occurred, cases that have been substantiated by official action are unrepresentative of sexual abuse because they contain a disproportionate percentage of children who are relatively forthcoming about their abuse. Therefore, observational research supports the existence of accommodation, but is likely to underestimate the frequency with which accommodation occurs.

More than half of all sexual abuse reports are not substantiated by social service investigation (Eckenrode, Munsch, Powers, & Doris, 1988). Substantiation is less likely if the child is not forthcoming with the investigator about abuse. Everson and Boat (1989) interviewed child protective workers regarding 29 cases in which the worker had concluded that abuse had not occurred, and found that "the most frequently cited reason for disbelieving the child's report of abuse was a later retraction by the child. In the words of one worker, 'She admitted it herself, that she had been lying all along.'" (p. 232). In interviews with 20 child protective workers regarding the process by which they evaluate sexual abuse cases, Haskett, Wayland, Hutcheson, & Tavana (1995) found that "[b]y far, the most important factor in this process was the child's verbal disclosure or denial of abuse" (p. 40). That substantiation rates increase with the age of child is likely to be at least partially attributable to older children's greater ability to provide convincing verbal reports of abuse (Eckenrode et al., 1988; Haskett et al., 1995; Winefield & Bradley, 1992).

It is possible that a report could be filed without any previous statement from the child, if the reporter had other reasons for believing that abuse had occurred. In the majority of substantiated cases, however, there was a statement by the child prior to investigation (Bradley & Wood, 1996, of 234 substantiated cases, 6% of reports were filed by the victim and 72% of victims had disclosed to someone else before the report was filed; Farrell, 1988, of 108 substantiated sexual abuse cases, 80% were "self-disclosure"; Whitcomb et al., 1994, of 431 substantiated cases referred to prosecutors, 86% of victims had disclosed the abuse prior to the report).

Whereas cases substantiated by social services may contain a disproportionate number of forthright victims, cases seen by clinicians in self-help groups and in treatment may contain a much higher percentage of abuse victims who failed to report the abuse or who were ambivalent about reporting. As Ceci and Bruck (1995) have argued, "Children in forensic samples may be those who readily disclose, whereas children in clinical samples who delay making disclosures may not go through the criminal system as readily; these may be the children for whom it is difficult to extract a report, and thus they are brought by adults for treatment" (p. 35).

There is some support for the view that forensic and clinical samples look different. Compare two studies: Bradley and Wood (1996) and Sorensen and Snow (1991). In their review of 234 cases of sexual abuse substantiated by social services, Bradley and Wood found that 4% of the children failed to disclose abuse when questioned by social services or the police. Moreover, initial denial of abuse was reported among 6% of the cases, and reluctance to discuss abuse only among 10%. In a review of 116 cases of sexual abuse "in which the authors had been involved as therapists and/or evaluators," and which had been referred to the authors by "child protective service, law enforcement, other mental health personnel and agencies, and private referral" (pp. 4-5), Sorensen and Snow (1991) found that 72% of the children initially denied abuse when questioned by an authority figure or in the formalized investigative process, and 78% exhibited "tentative disclosure" as a middle step, in which they often minimized or claimed to forget aspects of the abuse.

Bradley and Wood (1996) acknowledge that their sample was limited to substantiated cases, but argue that this does not explain why the rate of reluctance to disclose was so low. They emphasize that "caseworkers sometimes responded to an initial denial by scheduling additional interviews or arranging for the child to see a counselor" (p. 889). However, as long as caseworkers *often* close cases based on denials or unconvincing disclosures by ambivalent children, reviews of cases substantiated by social services will exaggerate the extent to which abused children in general are forthcoming about abuse. Because Bradley and Wood did not examine unsubstantiated cases, they were unable to determine how often initial denial was followed up by the investigator. As noted above, research suggests that denial and recantation do indeed reduce the likelihood of substantiation (Everson & Boat, 1989; Haskett et al., 1995; see also Gordon & Jaudes, 1996).

Bradley and Wood (1996) point out that Sorensen and Snow (1991) also examined only substantiated cases of abuse. However, the process by which cases were substantiated in Sorensen and Snow was likely to be quite different. As Ceci and Bruck (1995) suggest, it may be that children referred to Sorensen and Snow for treatment were particularly likely to be ambivalent about disclosing abuse and, therefore, more inconsistent in doing so. Bradley and Wood recognize that children in treatment might look different than children seen by social services, although they speculate that children in treatment *become* reluctant over multiple therapy sessions, rather than *begin* therapy reluctant to disclose.

Besides the issue of substantiation, there are other possible explanations for the differences between Bradley and Wood (1996) and Sorensen and Snow (1991), which will be discussed below. Nevertheless, it is reasonable to assume that research on substantiated cases of abuse will understate the reluctance of abused children to reveal, as well as other symptoms of child sexual abuse accommodation. On the other hand, clinical research that relies on samples of children referred for treatment is likely to contain a disproportionate number of children who are reluctant to disclose. Both samples miss the children for whom accommodation was most effective: those children who never gave any indication of having been abused. Claims regarding the exact percentage of abused children who exhibit accommodation symptoms must be tempered by the characteristics of the populations from which the samples were drawn.

DO ABUSED CHILDREN RECANT?

Whether abused children often recant their allegations of abuse is probably the most controversial element of CSAA. Summit (1983) asserted that "[w]hatever a child says about sexual abuse, she is likely to reverse it" (p. 188). The two studies just described (Bradley & Wood, 1996; Sorensen & Snow, 1991) illustrate the competing claims. Bradley and Wood found that only 4% of children whose abuse was substantiated by child protective services and who originally claimed that abuse occurred subsequently recanted their allegations. In contrast, Sorensen and Snow found that 22% of abused children recanted when questioned by therapists.

Percentages also vary among other research. Jones and McGraw (1987) found a recantation rate of 9% among 309 substantiated cases of sexual abuse investigated by Denver Social Services. Bybee and Mowbray

(1993), examining investigatory records from a single day care abuse case in which 62 children made allegations of abuse, found that 11% of the children recanted abuse at some point during the investigatory process. Keary and Fitzpatrick (1994) found that 14% of the 123 children who had disclosed abuse prior to being seen by a sexual abuse assessment unit failed to repeat their allegation at the investigative interview. Gordon and Jaudes (1996) found that 17% of 103 children reporting abuse during an emergency room interview recanted abuse at the subsequent investigative interview. Gonzalez, Waterman, Kelly, McCord, and Oliveri (1993) found that 27% of 63 children in treatment for ritualistic abuse (in the McMartin case) recanted at some point during therapy.[1] Devoe and Faller (1999) found that 30% of 56 children who had disclosed abuse before being evaluated for sexual abuse failed to disclose abuse at their first interview.

There are several plausible explanations for these differences. One possibility is that many of the children in the studies finding the highest rates of recantation were not, in fact, abused. Ceci and Bruck (1995) raise this point with respect to Sorensen and Snow's (1991) study, both criticizing Snow's interviewing technique and questioning the validity of the criteria whereby the cases were classified as true allegations of abuse. (Specifically, they note that a criminal conviction could be the result of a plea by an innocent defendant afraid of a long sentence should he be convicted after a trial.) The allegations of ritual abuse in the Gonzalez et al. (1993) study could be similarly questioned, given criticism of the investigative methods in the McMartin case and the ultimately inconclusive trial outcome.

To address this problem, one solution is to identify only those cases in which there is clear corroborative evidence that abuse occurred, such as a confession or highly suggestive medical findings. Such a breakdown is possible for the Gordon and Jaudes (1996) study and for Elliot and Briere (1994). In Gordon and Jaudes, 14 children had a sexually transmitted disease; 6 of these children disclosed abuse to the emergency room physician, and 3 subsequently recanted abuse at the investigative interview, for a recantation rate of 50%. In Elliot and Briere, 118 children had evidence of abuse independently of the child's statements.[2] Nineteen of these children never revealed abuse, leaving as many as 99 who may have revealed abuse before the evaluation (the authors do not report the exact number). Because 20 of these children recanted at the evaluation, the recantation rate is at least 20%. Based on this limited data, recantation does not seem to be an artifact of the misclassification of false allegations as true abuse. Rather, recantation rates are quite high among cases one can confidently say are true.

Indeed, the rates of recantation among cases with corroborative evidence are among the highest across the studies. Although this might seem counterintuitive, it reflects the fact that corroborative evidence increases the likelihood that a child will be diagnosed as abused. If a child recants, and there is no other evidence of abuse, it is likely that investigators will fail to conclude that he or she has been abused. On the other hand, if a child recants but there is clear external evidence that abuse occurred, investigators are more likely to diagnose abuse. The result is that a focus on cases with clear evidence of abuse will reveal higher percentages of children who only inconsistently acknowledge that the abuse occurred.

Another explanation for the differences in recantation rates among studies is that they are attributable to the differences, already discussed, between children drawn from substantiated cases of abuse investigated by social services and children drawn from sexual abuse treatment. If recantation decreases the likelihood that abuse is substantiated, then substantiated cases will have a disproportionately small number of children who recant. On the other hand, if recantation increases the likelihood that a child is referred to a therapist, then treatment samples will have a disproportionately large number of recanters.

One can directly test the effects of substantiation on the percentage of abused children who recant by looking more closely at the Gordon and Jaudes (1996) study. The percentages in that study are based on all children reported as abused to social services. Because the authors provide percentages of the cases that were subsequently substantiated by social services investigation, one can determine whether substantiation affects the apparent frequency of recantation. The authors note that "[t]he ability of the state to conclude officially that sexual abuse had occurred was much higher when the child identified the alleged perpetrator in at least the investigative interview than when the child recanted at the second interview" (Gordon & Jaudes, 1996, p. 319). Indeed, the substantiation rate when the child disclosed at both the emergency room interview and the investigative interview was 91%, compared to 29% when the child recanted at the investigative interview. Because recantation decreased the likelihood that cases would be substantiated, one ought to see fewer recantations among substantiated cases than among the cases overall. And this is indeed the pattern. The entire sample contained 141 children. Of the 103 children who reported abuse in the emergency room, 17 (17%) recanted at the investigative interview. The entire group of substantiated cases numbered 108. Of the 83 children who reported abuse in the emergency room, 5% or 6% recanted at the investigative interview.

In addition to the substantiation problem, another factor that increases the difficulty of identifying recantation among abused children is that few of the studies follow the cases beyond the initial investigation. Jones and McGraw (1987) suggest that this leads to an underestimation of recantation in their sample, and Bradley and Wood (1996) speculate that "an abused child who is willing to discuss abuse during an initial [social work] interview may become reluctant to continue the discussion during multiple therapy sessions" (p. 889). Although Bradley and Wood discuss what happened postinvestigation in many of their cases, their information—based on child protective service records—was often spotty (1996, p. 887). In contrast, the two studies on treatment (Gonzalez et al., 1993; Sorensen & Snow, 1991) were able to track children over relatively long periods.

It is reasonable to assume that many children who recant do so only after the negative effects of their disclosure become clear—continued lack of support by a nonoffending parent, inability to return home, the initiation of criminal proceedings against a loved one, to name a few. In my experience as an attorney in child abuse court, I have found that recantation tended to occur after the child had been in foster care for some time, and certainly after the initial phase of child protective services investigation. Unfortunately, I know of no research examining the extent to which recantation occurs over the entire course of legal intervention. A suggestive finding, however, is that by Gray (1993), who analyzed a group of 114 sexual abuse cases that were referred to the prosecutor's office but for whom charges were not filed. In 22% of the rejected cases, the reason for a failure to file charges in the case file was that the "victim changed her story," which "could include simply inconsistent accounts of the abuse, or outright refutation of the original claim" (p. 94). In the county from which the cases were drawn, prosecutors rejected almost 40% of the cases presented to them for prosecution, which would mean that about 8% of all cases presented for prosecution were rejected due to inconsistency, recantation, or both. The findings hint at the problem of recantation after police and social services investigation is complete, because the prosecutor's decision whether to file charges is only one of several hurdles before a case is brought to trial.

A final reason for the differences in recantation rates among studies may be biases in reporting. Bradley and Wood (1996) and Bybee and Mowbray (1993) note that for legal reasons, investigators may not make note of recantation or reluctance in their reports. On the other hand, therapists who believe that accommodation occurs may unconsciously exaggerate the extent to which abused children are inconsistent—a form of confirmatory bias. Exaggeration is especially likely to occur if recantation rates are based on retrospective report, as was used by Sorensen and Snow (1991) and Gonzalez et al. (1993).

For methodological reasons, it is difficult to draw clear conclusions from the research on recantation. There is no evidence that recantation occurs in most cases, and there is equivocal evidence that recantation is rare. I believe an expert is justified in stating that recantation often occurs among children known to have been abused, particularly if the expert's primary goal is to explain how recantation occurs rather than how often. Such a conclusion may seem weak, but only if we are attempting to precisely quantify the frequency with which recantation occurs among abused children. If we are simply trying to teach jurors that recantation does not necessarily mean that the original allegation was false—the usual judicial justification for testimony regarding CSAA—then such a conclusion is helpful without being misleading.

Conclusion

A review of the research on CSAA clearly supports the conclusion that a substantial proportion of abused children exhibit accommodation. The significance of this conclusion must be interpreted in light of the limited purpose for which accommodation is offered in court. If accommodation is intended to prove that abuse occurred, then it must occur more frequently among abused children than among nonabused children. None of the research examined here allows for such a comparison. Indeed, it is somewhat nonsensical to speak of accommodation among nonabused children—for example, how does one define delay in reporting when the child was never abused? On the other hand, if accommodation is intended merely to rebut the assumption that certain witness characteristics prove that abuse did not occur, then it must occur among *some* abused children. The research is relevant for assessing accommodation's utility as rebuttal evidence, and supports its use as such.

Let me end with a caveat. The purpose of this chapter is to refute the criticism that CSAA is unsupported by scientific evidence. Establishing a scientific basis for CSAA testimony goes a long way toward supporting its admissibility in court. It is not a sufficient basis for admissibility, however, because there are other prerequisites to the admissibility of expert testimony. Under the Federal Rules of Evidence, which govern the federal courts and is a model for most states' rules of evidence, an expert's testimony must "assist the trier of fact" (2000, Rule 702). In part this means that the expert must tell the jury something they don't already know.

Do lay people understand the dynamics of sexual abuse? Summit (1983) contended that they do not. At least one critic of CSAA testimony has argued that "it does not take an expert witness to explain that children may delay or recant the telling of an experience as sensitive as sexual abuse" (Mason, 1995, p. 408), and at least one state supreme court has rejected CSAA testimony in part because of this argument (*Commonwealth v. Dunkle*, 1992). Research examining lay people's understanding of sexual abuse is limited (Gray, 1993; Kovera & Borgida, 1997; Morison & Greene, 1992), and provides only moderate support for the assertion that lay people are skeptical of children with CSAA symptoms. For example, Morison and Greene (1992) found that individuals summoned for jury duty "slightly disagreed" with the assertion that "[i]ndividuals should be suspicious about allegations made by a child following a lengthy delay in reporting," whereas sexual abuse experts "disagreed"

(p. 603). Kovera and Borgida (1997) reported that 97% of students and 84% of community members (compared to 97% of experts) agreed with the statement that "delays in reporting child sexual abuse to the police or other authorities are quite common" (see also Gray, 1993). Although Morison and Greene (1992) identified discrepancies between lay and expert opinion, whether those differences are large enough to justify expert testimony is subject to dispute. Moreover, if experts merely testify that *many* rather than *most* children exhibit CSAA, the need for expert testimony is even more questionable.

Ironically, the greatest challenge to CSAA testimony may be that it is a scientific truism rather than a clinical myth. Summit (1992) noted that his article was originally rejected by a psychiatric journal "because the reviewers felt it was so basic it contributed nothing new to the literature" (p. 155; compare Ceci, Bruck, & Rosenthal, 1995, stating that it is "a point of no dispute among researchers" that "truly abused children are often unlikely to disclose sexual abuse out of a sense of embarrassment or fear," p. 506). Whether lay people intuit what researchers think obvious is an open question and awaits further research and argument. At any rate, whatever can be said about CSAA, it certainly cannot be said that it is unscientific. Roland Summit the clinician divined facts even the scientist could accept.

Notes

1. Commentators often cite Sahd (1982) or Goodwin, Sahd, and Rada (1982) for the proposition that 30% of abused children recant. Sahd fails to cite authority for the claim that "[t]he literature indicates that nearly 1/3 of children who report incest consider retracting the allegations at some time" (p. 82). Goodwin and colleagues state that "[r]efusal to talk or testify about the incest is more common than false denial and may occur on the part of as many as 30% of victims" (p. 21). They cite Nakashima and Zakus (1977), but I was unable to find the 30% figure in that article.

2. External evidence included diagnostic medical findings in 64 cases (e.g., hymenal transections to the base, STDs that can be contracted only through sexual contact, semen found in the vaginal canal), confession in 27 cases, a witness to the abuse in 35 cases, and other evidence in 25 cases (pornographic pictures of the child, the child described graphic details of the alleged perpetrator's bedroom when the alleged perpetrator denied the child ever being in his home).

References

Adams-Tucker, C. (1982). Proximate effects of sexual abuse in childhood: A report on 28 children. *American Journal of Psychiatry, 139,* 1252-1256.

Arata, C. M. (1998). To tell or not to tell: Current functioning of child sexual abuse survivors who disclosed their victimization. *Child Maltreatment, 3*, 63-71.

Bagley, C., & Ramsay, R. (1986). Sexual abuse in childhood: Psychosocial outcomes and implications for social work practice. *Journal of Social Work & Human Sexuality, 4*, 33-47.

Berliner, L., & Conte, J. R. (1993). Sexual abuse evaluations: Conceptual and empirical obstacles. *Child Abuse & Neglect, 17*, 111-125.

Bottoms, B. L., Goodman, G. S., Schwartz-Kenney, B., Sachsenmaier, T., & Thomas, S. (1990, March). *Keeping secrets: Implications for children's testimony.* Paper presented at the American Psychology and Law Society Meeting, Williamsburg, VA.

Bradley, A. R., & Wood, J. M. (1996). How do children tell? The disclosure process in child sexual abuse. *Child Abuse & Neglect, 9*, 881-891.

Bussey, K. (1993, March). *Factors influencing children's disclosure of witnessed events.* Paper presented at the Biennial Meeting of the Society for Research in Child Development, New Orleans, LA.

Bussey, K., Lee, K., & Richard, K. (1990). Children's reports of an adult's transgression. Unpublished manuscript.

Bybee, D., & Mowbray, C. T. (1993). An analysis of allegations of sexual abuse in a multi-victim day-care center case. *Child Abuse & Neglect, 17*, 767-783.

Ceci, S. J., & Bruck, M. (1995). *Jeopardy in the courtroom: A scientific analysis of children's testimony.* Washington, DC: American Psychological Association.

Ceci, S. J., Bruck, M., & Rosenthal, R. (1995). Children's allegations of sexual abuse: Forensic and scientific issues: A reply to commentators. *Psychology, Public Policy, & Law, 1*, 494-520.

Ceci, S. J., & Leichtman, M. (1992). "I know that you know that I know that you broke the toy": A brief report of recursive awareness among 3-year-olds. In S. J. Ceci, M. Leichtman, & M. Putnick (Eds.), *Cognitive and social factors in early deception* (pp. 1-9). Hillsdale, NJ: Lawrence Erlbaum.

Commonwealth v. Dunkle, 529 Pa. 168, 602 A.2d 830 (1992).

Daubert v. Merrell-Dow Pharmaceuticals, Inc., 509 U.S. 579 (1993).

Dawes, R. M. (1994). *House of cards: Psychology and psychotherapy built on myth.* New York: Free Press.

DeJong, A. R. (1988). Maternal responses to the sexual abuse of their children. *Pediatrics, 81*, 14-21.

Devitt, M. K., Honts, C. R., Gillund, B. E., Amato, S. L., Peters, D. P., & Norton, M. (1994, March). *A study of the willingness of children to make false accusations about a serious matter.* Paper presented at the American Psychology and Law Society Meeting, Santa Fe, NM.

Devoe, E. R., & Faller, K. C. (1999). The characteristics of disclosure among children who may have been sexually abused. *Child Maltreatment, 4*, 217-227.

Dubowitz, H., Black, M., & Harrington, D. (1992). The diagnosis of child sexual abuse. *American Journal of Diseases of Children, 146*, 688-693.

Eckenrode, J., Munsch, J., Powers, J., & Doris, J. (1988). The nature and substantiation of official sexual abuse reports. *Child Abuse & Neglect, 12*, 311-319.

Elliot, D. M., & Briere, J. (1994). Forensic sexual abuse evaluations of older children disclosures and symptomatology. *Behavioral Sciences & the Law, 12*, 261-277.

Everson, M. D., & Boat, B. W. (1989). False allegations of sexual abuse by children and adolescents. *Journal of the American Academy of Child and Adolescent Psychiatry, 28*, 230-235.

Everson, M. D., Hunter, W. M., Runyon, D. K., Edelsohn, G. A., & Coulter, M. L. (1989). Maternal support following disclosure of incest. *American Journal of Orthopsychiatry, 59*, 197-207.

Faller, K. C. (1988). *Child sexual abuse: An interdisciplinary manual for diagnosis, case management, and treatment.* New York: Columbia.

Farrell, L. T. (1988). Factors that affect a victim's self-disclosure in father-daughter incest. *Child Welfare, 67*, 462-468.

Federal Rules of Evidence. (2000).

Ferguson, D. M., Lynskey, M. T., & Horwood, L. J. (1996). Childhood sexual abuse and psychiatric disorder in young adulthood: I. Prevalence of sexual abuse and factors associated with sexual abuse. *Journal of the American Academy of Child & Adolescent Psychiatry, 35*, 1355-1364.

Finkelhor, D. (1979). *Sexually victimized children.* New York: Free Press.

Finkelhor, D. (1980). Risk factors in the sexual victimization of children. *Child Abuse & Neglect, 4*, 265-273.

Finkelhor, D., Hotaling, G., Lewis, I.A., & Smith, C. (1990). Sexual abuse in a national survey of adult men and women: Prevalence, characteristics, and risk factors. *Child Abuse & Neglect, 14*, 19-28.

Frye v. United States, 54 App. D.C. 46, 293 F. 1013 (1923).

Gonzalez, L. S., Waterman, J., Kelly, R. J., McCord, J., & Oliveri, M. K. (1993). Children's patterns of disclosures and recantations of sexual and ritualistic abuse allegations in psychotherapy. *Child Abuse & Neglect, 17*, 281-289.

Goodman, G. S., Taub, E. P., Jones, D. P. H., England, P., Port, L. K., Rudy, L., & Prado, L. (1992). Testifying in criminal court. *Monographs of the Society for Research in Child Development, 57*(No. 229).

Goodwin, J., Sahd, D., & Rada, R. T. (1982). False accusations and false denials of incest: Clinical myths and clinical realities. In J. Goodwin (Ed.), *Sexual abuse: Incest victims and their families.* Boston: John Wright.

Gordon, S., & Jaudes, P. K. (1996). Sexual abuse evaluations in the emergency department: Is the history reliable? *Child Abuse & Neglect, 20*, 315-322.

Gray, E. (1993). *Unequal justice: The prosecution of child sexual abuse.* New York: Free Press.

Hadden v. State, 690 So.2d 573 (Fl. 1997).

Hanson, R. F., Resnick, H. S., Saunders, B. E., Kilpatrick, D. G., & Best, C. (1999). Factors related to the reporting of childhood rape. *Child Abuse & Neglect, 23*, 559-569.

Haskett, M. E., Wayland, K., Hutcheson, J. S., & Tavana, T. (1995). Substantiation of sexual abuse allegations: Factors involved in the decision-making process. *Journal of Child Sexual Abuse, 4*(2), 19-47.

Hazzard, A., Celano, M., Gould, J., Lawry, S., & Webb, C. (1995). Predicting symptomatology and self-blame among sex abuse victims. *Child Abuse & Neglect, 19*, 707-714.

Herman, J. L. (1981). *Father-daughter incest.* Cambridge, MA: Harvard University Press.

Heriot, J. (1996). Maternal protectiveness following the disclosure of intrafamilial child sexual abuse. *Journal of Interpersonal Violence, 11*, 181-194.

Honts, C. R. (1994). Assessing children's credibility: Scientific and legal issues in 1994. *North Dakota Law Review, 70*, 879-903.

Johnson, R. L., & Shrier, D. K. (1985). Sexual victimization of boys: Experience at an adolescent medicine clinic. *Journal of Adolescent Health Care, 6*, 372-376.

Jones, D. P. H., & McGraw, J. M. (1987). Reliable and fictitious accounts of sexual abuse to children. *Journal of Interpersonal Violence, 2*, 27-45.

Kalman, J. Z. (1998). A modest proposal for a new way to use child sexual abuse accommodation syndrome evidence. *Sexual Assault Report, 1*, 33-34, 42-43.

Keary, K., & Fitzpatrick, C. (1994). Children's disclosure of sexual abuse during formal investigation. *Child Abuse & Neglect, 18*, 543-548.

Kendall-Tackett, K., Williams, L., & Finkelhor, D. (1993). Impact of sexual abuse on children: A review and synthesis of recent empirical studies. *Psychological Bulletin, 13*, 164-180.

Kovera, M. B., & Borgida, E. (1997). Expert testimony in child sexual abuse trials: The admissibility of psychological science [Special Issue]. *Applied Cognitive Psychology, 11*, S105-S129.

Kumho Tire Co., Ltd. v. Carmichael, 526 U.S. 137 (1999).

Lawson, L., & Chaffin, M. (1992). False negatives in sexual abuse disclosure interviews: Incidence and influence of caretakers' belief in abuse in cases of accidental abuse discovery by diagnosis of STD. *Journal of Interpersonal Violence, 7*, 532-542.

Leifer, M., Shapiro, J. P., & Kassem, L. (1993). The impact of maternal history and behavior upon foster placement and adjustment in sexually abused girls. *Child Abuse & Neglect, 17*, 755-766.

Lyon, T. D., & Koehler, J. J. (1996). The relevance ratio: Evaluating the probative value of expert testimony in child sexual abuse cases. *Cornell Law Review, 82*, 43-78.

Mason, M. A. (1995). The child sex abuse syndrome: The other major issue in *State of New Jersey v. Margaret Kelly Michaels. Psychology, Public Policy, & Law, 1*, 399-410.

McGough, L. S. (1994). *Child witnesses: Fragile voices in the American legal system.* New Haven, CT: Yale University Press.

Moore, C., McPhee, J., & Trought, P. (1986). Child abuse: A study of the child's perspective. *Child Abuse & Neglect, 10*, 511-518.

Morison, S., & Greene, E. (1992). Juror and expert knowledge of child sexual abuse. *Child Abuse & Neglect, 16*, 595-613.

Mosteller, R. P. (1996). Syndromes and politics in criminal trials and evidence law. *Duke Law Journal, 46*, 461-516.

Mueller, C. B., & Kirkpatrick, L. C. (1999). *Evidence* (2nd ed.). Gaithersburg, NY: Aspen.

Mueller, C. B., & Kirkpatrick, L. C. (2000). *Evidence under the rules: Text, cases, and problems.* Gaithersburg, NY: Aspen.

Muram, D., Speck, P. M., & Gold, S. S. (1991). Genital abnormalities in female siblings and friends of child victims of sexual abuse. *Child Abuse & Neglect, 15*, 105-110.

Myer, M. H. (1984/1985). A new look at mothers of incest victims. *Journal of Social Work & Human Sexuality, 3*(2-3), 47-58.

Myers, J. E. B. (1992). *Evidence in child abuse and neglect* (2nd ed.). New York: John Wiley.

Nakashima, I. I., & Zakus, G. E. (1977). Incest: Review and clinical experience. *Pediatrics, 60*, 696-701.

Oates, R. K., & Donnelly, A. C. (1997). Influential papers in child abuse. *Child Abuse & Neglect, 21*, 319-326.

Palmer, S. E., Brown, R. A., Rae-Grant, N. I., & Loughlin, M. J. (1999). Responding to children's disclosure of familial abuse: What survivors tell us. *Child Welfare, 78*, 259-282.

People v. Bowker, 203 Cal. App. 3d 385, 249 Cal. Rptr. 886 (1988).

Peters, D. P. (1990, March). *Confrontational stress and children's testimony: Some experimental findings*. Paper presented at the Biennial Meeting of the American Psychology-Law Society, Williamsburg, VA.

Peters, D. P. (1991, April). *Confrontational stress and children's testimony: Some experimental findings*. Paper presented at the Biennial Meeting of the Society for Research in Child Development, Seattle, WA.

Pipe, M., & Goodman, G. S. (1991). Elements of secrecy: Implications for children's testimony. *Behavioral Sciences & the Law, 9*, 33-41.

Pipe, M., & Wilson, J. C. (1994). Cues and secrets: Influences on children's event reports. *Developmental Psychology, 30*, 515-525.

Russell, D. E. H. (1986). *The secret trauma: Incest in the lives of girls and women*. New York: Basic Books.

Sahd, D. (1982). Psychological assessment of sexually abusing families and treatment implications. In W. M. Holder (Ed.), *Sexual abuse of children: Implications for treatment* (pp. 71-86). Englewood, CO: American Humane Association.

Sas, L. D., & Cunningham, A. H. (1995). *Tipping the balance to tell the secret: The public discovery of child sexual abuse*. London, Ontario: London Family Court Clinic.

Sauzier, M. (1989). Disclosure of child sexual abuse: For better or for worse. *Psychiatric Clinics of North America, 12*, 455-469.

Sirles, E. A., & Franke, P. J. (1989). Factors influencing mothers' reactions to intrafamily sexual abuse. *Child Abuse & Neglect, 13*, 131-139.

Smith, B. E., & Elstein, S. G. (1993). *The prosecution of child sexual and physical abuse cases: Final report*. Washington, DC: National Center on Child Abuse & Neglect.

Sorensen, T., & Snow, B. (1991). How children tell: The process of disclosure in child sexual abuse. *Child Welfare, 70*, 3-13.

State v. Foret, 628 So.2d 1116 (La. 1993).

Summit, R. C. (1983). The child sexual abuse accommodation syndrome. *Child Abuse & Neglect, 7*, 177-193.

Summit, R. C. (1992). Abuse of the child sexual abuse accommodation syndrome. *Journal of Child Sexual Abuse, 1*, 153-163.

Tufts New England Medical Center. (1984). *Sexually abused children: Service and research project*. Boston, MA: Author.

Tye, M. C., Amato, S. L., Honts, C. R., Devitt, M. K., & Peters, D. (1999). The willingness of children to lie and the assessment of credibility in an ecologically relevant laboratory setting. *Applied Developmental Science, 3*, 92-109.

Wade, A., & Westcott, H. (1997). No easy answers: Children's perspectives on investigative interviews. In H. Westcott & J. Jones (Eds.), *Perspectives on the memorandum: Policy, practice, and research in investigative interviewing* (pp. 51-65). Hants, UK: Arena.

Whitcomb, D., De Vos, E., Cross, T. P., Peeler, N. A., Runyan, D. K., Hunter, W. M., Everson, M. D., Porter, C. Q., Toth, P. A., & Cropper, C. (1994). *The child victim as a witness: Research report*. Washington, DC: Office of Juvenile Justice and Delinquency Prevention.

Wilson, J. C., & Pipe, M. (1989). The effects of cues on young children's recall of real events. *New Zealand Journal of Psychology, 18*, 65-70.

Winefield, H. R., & Bradley, P. W. (1992). Substantiation of reported child abuse or neglect: Predictors and implications. *Child Abuse & Neglect, 16*, 661-671.

5

Memory and Dimensions of Trauma

Terror May Be "All-Too-Well Remembered" and Betrayal Buried

JENNIFER J. FREYD

> David A. Hoffman, a former child psychologist . . . pleaded guilty in April
> [1994] to gross sexual imposition. . . . Hoffman was charged with the crime
> after a woman remembered being sexually abused during a two-year pe-
> riod, beginning when she was 8 and living in Columbus with her mother.
> . . . The woman is now 26 and lives in Michigan. She had no recollection of
> the abuse until July 1992, said detective John Harris. . . . "She worked in a
> probation office in Grand Rapids, Mich., typing reports," Harris said.
> "Her first memory of the abuse came when she was typing a report re-
> garding a sexual abuse case. Then, whenever she had to type reports in-
> volving sexual abuse, she would become very distraught."

AUTHOR'S NOTE: Some of the material in this chapter is based on an address given by the
author at the 12th Annual Meeting of the International Society for Traumatic Stress Studies,
San Francisco, November 9-13, 1996, and the author's book *Betrayal Trauma: The Logic of
Forgetting Childhood Abuse* (1996). I am indebted to J. Q. Johnson and Jon Conte for helpful
comments on an earlier version of this chapter.

The woman sought therapy. She called Harris after her psychologist urged her to file a police report.

In 1993 . . . [Hoffman] "admitted committing the molesting offenses," Harris said. "That made this case different than most sexual abuse cases. He admitted it." (Medick, 1994)

How can someone forget an event as traumatic as sexual abuse in childhood? In *Betrayal Trauma* (Freyd, 1996), I discuss the logic of forgetting childhood abuse. Betrayal trauma theory proposes that it is adaptive to forget certain kinds of betrayal—as in childhood sexual abuse by a trusted caregiver—and that this forgetting is understandable in terms of what is known about cognitive psychology.

Amnesia for childhood abuse (or so-called memory repression) exists, not for the reduction of suffering, but because not remembering abuse by a caregiver is often necessary for survival. From a logical analysis of developmental pressures and cognitive architecture, we can expect there to be cognitive information blockage under certain conditions—such as sexual abuse by a parent. This information blockage will create various types of "betrayal blindness" and traumatic amnesia.

I began to develop betrayal trauma theory (Freyd, 1991) before I had been directly exposed to Roland Summit's theory of the child sexual abuse accommodation syndrome (CSAAS) (Summit, 1983). My background and expertise through 1991 was in cognitive psychology, at that point an area of study with essentially no overlap with child abuse or traumatic stress studies. Most likely aspects of Summit's contribution did seep through to me even then, by virtue of his having levels of consciousness about child sexual abuse and reactions to that abuse—but I did not directly know of it in 1991. However, by the time I wrote my book I had become well acquainted with the CSAAS and the astounding contribution that Summit has made through his writings, presentations, and personal influence. What has become increasingly apparent is the conceptual congruence between the CSAAS and betrayal trauma theory. I assume, too, that this is not merely coincidental but, in fact, that I had absorbed through cultural transmissions some of Summit's insights explicated in the CSAAS.

The CSAAS and betrayal trauma theory share a core emphasis on the distortion of information for the purpose of preserving a relationship. Whereas the CSAAS includes both conscious and unconscious information distortion (the child may consciously deny abuse when he or she is aware it happened), betrayal trauma focuses on the internalized information distortion in particular (whereby knowledge of abuse is isolated from the victim's conscious memory and awareness).

This chapter summarizes some of the key components of betrayal trauma theory (Freyd, 1996), including discussion of some of my more recent thinking about the possibility that trauma has two separate dimensions and that those two separate dimensions have distinct implications for memory. But first, the controversy.

Controversy and Response

It would hardly seem proper to write about memory for abuse without acknowledging the raging controversy currently preoccupying society, and yet it is tempting to avoid this issue, because that controversy is draining and frustratingly repetitive (Herman, 1992; Olafson, Corwin, & Summit, 1993; Summit, 1988). Questions of disbelief and belief, passionate testimonials, and assertions of scientific authority saturate the conceptual landscape. Not only is this controversy intense, it is quite confusing. Societal, scientific, professional, personal, and moral issues are tangled in what seems, at times, to be a hopeless snarl. In attempting to untangle these issues and find meaning, and to find the opportunity for growth in this controversy, it is essential that we integrate a rational and scientific approach, drawing on many disciplines with a moral and compassionate stance. In this regard, those of us struggling with the recovered memory field can do no better than to look to Roland Summit's response to the controversy that has adhered to him and his CSAAS. Summit steers a clear course by correcting the errors of attribution without succumbing to ad hominem attack or exaggeration (e.g., 1992; see also Freyd, 1996, pp. 50-51, for a description of Summit's response to a 1994 *New Yorker* editorial). In such responsible actions and communications, Roland Summit offers a model of responsiveness, rationality, compassion, and dignity.

Either perspective alone—that is, a purely scientific/rational analysis or a purely humane/compassionate response—will not work as an effective or ethical way to respond to the issues of recovered memory. Indeed, either perspective in isolation may lead to great damage. Further-more, because the controversy involves disagreement about a complex reality, it is essential to attempt to articulate the separate questions, un-knowns, and issues. If we take care to pose separate questions we can discover which ones, in fact, we know the answers to, which ones we don't know the answers to, and which ones research might eventually let us answer.

There are some questions we can answer. Although the debate some-times appears to be about whether people can and do sometimes forget and later remember abuse, this is really a nonissue because we know they can and do forget and later remember abuse. Indeed, there is good reason to believe that both essentially false memories and essentially true memories of abuse are possible given what is known about cogni-tive mechanisms (see Freyd, 1996; Morton, in press; Schachter, 1996; Schooler, Bendiksen, & Ambadar, 1997). Furthermore, not only are these theoretical possibilities, but there is a large and growing body of evi-dence documenting the occurrence of both recovered memories and false memories (e.g., see Butler, 1996; Corwin & Olafson, 1997; Freyd, 1996; Lindsay & Briere, in press; Scheflin & Brown, 1996; Schooler et al., 1997). This means that we can answer in the affirmative the questions "Are essentially true recovered memories possible?" and "Are alleged recovered memories of abuse sometimes essentially true?" and "Are al-leged recovered memories of abuse sometimes essentially false?"

Similarly, the scientific debate is not (or should not be) fundamentally about whether memory is sometimes essentially false. All viewpoints must invoke the concept of memory distortion. Whether you have a false memory of a happy childhood, or a false memory of having been sexu-ally abused, you have a memory distortion. These memory distortions are arguably different; in one case you're emphasizing an error of omis-sion and another an error of commission. Regardless, memory is dis-torted from objective reality. Most people will also have to invoke some notion of human suggestibility. We are influenced either by suggestive family members, a suggestive culture, or overzealous therapists, books, or self-help movements. In either case, false memories of abuse or false memories of a happy childhood, there are powerful suggestive influ-ences, and humans are receptive to such influences.

Research on the disparity between memory and external events is of potential relevance to those interested in recovered memories. Thus, the large body of research showing that memory is a reconstructive process and is never or rarely perfectly accurate is clearly relevant to understanding the limits of veracity in any reported memory of trauma. Similarly, research on suggestibility is pertinent. The now-famous studies—in which whole narratives of being lost in a shopping mall are "implanted" into the minds of relatives of research assistants after an inducing sequence involving the research assistant claiming to have witnessed the "false" event (e.g., Loftus & Ketcham, 1994)—are relevant for understanding the ability of family members to distort memory, just as they are relevant for understanding the ability of therapists to distort memory.

Because both true and false memories are possible, it is very important we not reflexively assume, without additional and compelling information, that a recovered memory of sexual abuse is neither necessarily true nor necessarily false. Furthermore, it is quite likely that most memories contain both accurate and inaccurate components, that most memories, whether recovered or continuously accessible, are a perplexing mixture of true and false. Interestingly, there is evidence that recovered memories of sexual abuse are no more or less likely to be inaccurate than continuously accessible memories of sexual abuse (Pope & Brown, 1996; Scheflin & Brown, 1996). Dalenberg (1996), for instance, noted that "Memories of abuse were found to be equally accurate whether recovered or continuously remembered" (p. 229). Using a prospective method, Williams (1995) investigated the memories of women who as children, 17 years earlier, had been admitted into a hospital emergency room for sexual assault. Williams observed that "in general, the women with recovered memories had no more inconsistencies in their accounts than did the women who had always remembered" (p. 660), further commenting, "In fact, when one considers the basic elements of the abuse, their retrospective reports are remarkably consistent with what had been reported in the 1970s" (p. 662).

Not only are there limits to what we can legitimately determine about a given recovered memory (or a given denial of an accusation) without additional and compelling information, so, too, are there currently limits about what we can determine about the probabilities or frequencies of truth and falsity in these domains. Thus, two important questions arise that we cannot answer immediately: First, given a recovered memory, what is the probability that it is essentially true (or false)? Second (and equally important to keep in mind), given a denial of accusation of sexual abuse, what is the probability that the denial is essentially true (or false)? These important questions about overall frequencies and probabilities will perhaps yield to answers with future research. Even if the probability, based on overall frequencies, that a recovered memory is true is either very high or very low overall, it will be important to remember that individual cases will require and deserve individual scrutiny.

Currently determining the accuracy of memory (both continuously accessible and recovered) for events that are long past, private, and potentially of criminal or ethical significance is a true scientific, societal, and forensic puzzle. Yet perhaps one confusing aspect of the "memory debate" is that in many of the most charged disputes involving recovered memories, the underlying charged issue driving the dispute is often not really about memory per se. When the dispute becomes most heated, the real issue is whether the alleged abuse happened; arguments about memory are surface disputes (and often very confused surface disputes). Because the stakes are so high, there is a tremendous struggle for the authority to define reality, and the struggle in individual cases interacts dramatically with the struggle for authority in the media, scientific world, and popular culture. To argue a position about the scientific status of memory (or to claim a scientist or science supports one's own viewpoint) may give a kind of authority and legitimacy that is then used to attempt to win the underlying dispute about the abuse allegation. Although there are genuine scientific issues implicated in memory for abuse, we must be careful not to allow the science and scientific debate to be misused and corrupted.

Given the high personal and legal stakes, it is important for memory scientists to attempt to sort out the true applicability of memory research to these very heated disputes. Sometimes the pressure to make laboratory studies of memory research bear on a particular side of the contested memories leads to exaggerated claims of applicability (Freyd, 1996; Freyd & Gleaves, 1996; Gleaves, 1996; Gleaves & Freyd, 1997).

Memory researchers *can* contribute by finding the scientifically tractable questions about memory for abuse, the questions we have a hope of answering, answer these first, and then return to the retrospective problem.

Two important prospective and scientific questions can be posed immediately. First, given someone who did not experience parental sexual abuse, what is the probability (within various manipulations and contexts) that this person can be induced to falsely remember sexual abuse? This question is very difficult to answer because we have no way to know for certain if someone did not experience sexual abuse and because it is not ethical to induce a false memory of sexual abuse. Some research suggests that there is no evidence for a majority of false memories of abuse (e.g., Andrews et al., 1999) or evidence supporting the construct of a false memory *syndrome* (Hovdestad & Kristiansen, 1996), although there is general consensus that some cases of false memories of abuse have been documented and that the general research on misinformation and human suggestibility is relevant to this question (Schooler et al., 1997). The second question is one that we do know something about. Given someone who did experience parental sexual abuse, what is the probability that the memory becomes unavailable and then later available? Here we have data (see next section) and although we don't know exactly, we can estimate that it is at least .15 and probably much higher. Given this data, the next questions, and the ones that are my focus, are why and how this failure to remember abuse occurs.

The Phenomenon of Forgetting Abuse

Systematic studies indicate that a substantial minority of people who are now adults living in the United States were sexually abused in their childhood. (See Figure 5.1 for findings from four separate large community samples [Finkelhor, 1979; Kinsey, Pomeroy, Martin, & Gebhard, 1953; Russell, 1986; Timnick, 1985].)

In addition, empirical evidence—both systematic studies involving statistical tests and more detailed case reports like the opening case described by Medick (1994)—indicates that of those who were abused, forgetting the abuse is a real and relatively frequent phenomenon. But the

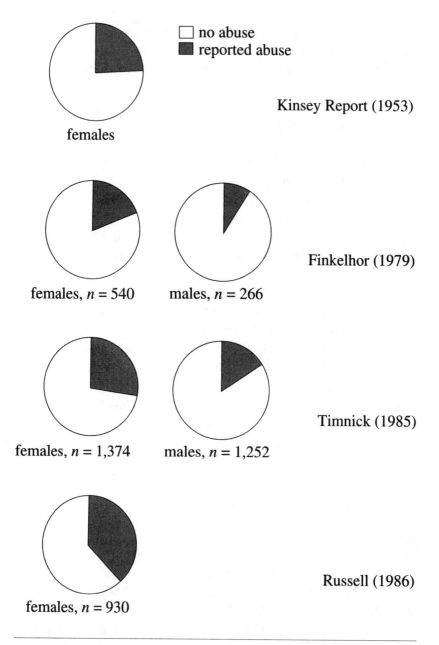

Figure 5.1. Prevalence Rates of Childhood Sexual Abuse from Four Samples

reality of this phenomenon is apparently difficult to accept. As Ross Cheit (quoted in Freyd, 1996) said, "Long-lost memories of sexual abuse can resurface. I know, because it happened to me. But I also know that I might not have believed that this was possible if [it] hadn't occurred to me."

(See Figure 5.2 for amnesia rates estimated from four studies of adult abuse survivors [Feldman-Summers & Pope, 1994, professional psychologists who reported childhood abuse; Herman & Schatzow, 1987, women in an incest survivors group; Loftus, Polonsky, & Fullilove, 1994, low-income women in a substance abuse program who reported childhood abuse; Williams, 1994a, 1994b, 1995, women who had been admitted into an emergency room as children for treatment of sexual abuse]. These studies were chosen in part due to the diversity of populations studied.) The results from these four studies are consistent with a rapidly growing body of literature showing similar results for a wide variety of populations and methodologies (e.g., Briere & Conte, 1993; Burgess, Hartman, & Baker, 1995; Elliott & Briere, 1995; van der Kolk & Fisler, 1995). Indeed, in an important recent review by Scheflin and Brown (1996), of 25 studies assessing amnesia rates for abuse, the authors note that every study was found to reveal that some abused people had periods of forgetting the abuse. Scheflin and Brown state "A reasonable conclusion is that amnesia for childhood sexual abuse is a robust finding across studies using very different samples and methods of assessment" (1996, p. 143).

Three of the studies depicted in Figure 5.2 (and the majority of studies reviewed by Sheflin & Brown, 1996) employed a retrospective methodology; that is, adults were asked about their abuse experiences, and they were also asked about the persistence of their memory for that abuse experience. They were asked if there was ever a time when they were not conscious of the abuse they could now remember. In the fourth case portrayed in Figure 5.2, the study was conducted using a prospective methodology (for additional prospective studies on amnesia for abuse, see Burgess et al., 1995; Widom & Morris, 1997). Linda Meyer Williams began with hospital records of people who were admitted into an emergency room (ER), and found these people 17 years later and attempted to assess whether they could remember the abusive event that brought

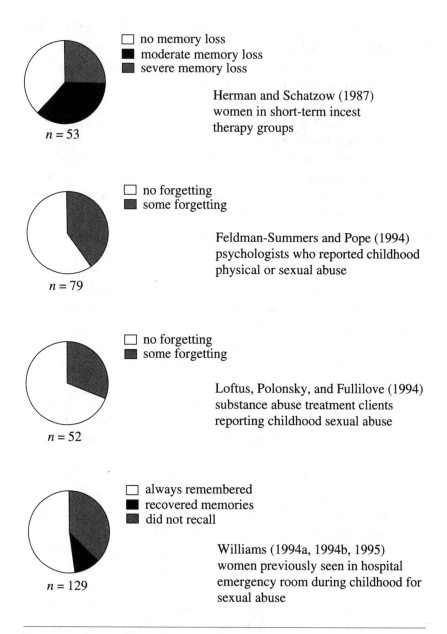

Herman and Schatzow (1987)
women in short-term incest
therapy groups

Feldman-Summers and Pope (1994)
psychologists who reported childhood
physical or sexual abuse

Loftus, Polonsky, and Fullilove (1994)
substance abuse treatment clients
reporting childhood sexual abuse

Williams (1994a, 1994b, 1995)
women previously seen in hospital
emergency room during childhood for
sexual abuse

Figure 5.2. Rates of Forgetting Sexual Abuse from Three Retrospective
Studies and One Prospective Study

SOURCE: From *Betrayal Trauma: The Logic of Forgetting Childhood Abuse,* by J. J. Freyd, 1996, Cambridge,
MA: Harvard University Press. Copyright © 1996 by Harvard University Press. Reprinted with permission.

them into the ER. Interviewers attempted to determine if the now-adult sexual assault victims could remember either the event for which they were brought to the ER or any other abuse by that same perpetrator. Williams went to great pains to determine if they could remember but simply did not report the event. It's a difficult problem and one that cannot be entirely answered, but Williams (1994a, 1994b) noted that a large percentage—38%—did not report the abuse that had led to their hospital admission as children, nor did they report any other abuse by the same offender. Of the women who did recall the abuse that was documented in their 1970s records, approximately one in six reported some previous period when they had forgotten it. That is, approximately 10% of her total sample reported recovered memories. This suggests that close to half (48%) of the women in Williams's study—women with documented sexual abuse histories—could not remember the abuse at the time of the interview or some time before that (see Figure 5.2).

More recent and very useful articles (Bowman & Mertz, 1996; Brewin, 1996; Butler, 1996; Scheflin & Brown, 1996) summarize the strong evidence for recovered memories. Taken together, a growing number of different studies on a variety of different populations using different methodologies all propose the finding that a sizable minority of those who experienced abuse also had a period when they could not remember the abuse. Furthermore, I am not aware of any recent study of abuse and memory using sound methodology that fails to find evidence of amnesia for the abuse. Perhaps it is the power of the systematic data that is causing some of the cultural preoccupation with the issue of memory for abuse; the implications of these systematic studies are quite disturbing. If we take the two sets of prevalence depicted in Figures 5.1 and 5.2 together and extrapolate from percentage to frequency in the populations— that is, the number of people who have been abused at all, and the number of people who have forgotten—we're left with a substantial number of people who have forgotten abuse.

Two-Dimensional Model

In answering questions about what happens when somebody has been abused, and what happens to their awareness, one of the first things to consider is why they would possibly be motivated to forget. The commonsense reason is that they forget because it's painful to remember. This answer—we forget because the memory is emotionally painful—is insufficient to account for the data and is theoretically circular.

As a first step, it is important to realize that one must distinguish between the observable phenomena of forgetting abuse (*what* we can observe), the motivations that might be going on for that forgetting (*why* it happens), and the mechanisms that might be underlying the forgetting (*how* it happens). These three types of issues—what, why, and how—are often tangled. For example, Elizabeth Loftus and Katherine Ketcham, in their 1994 book *The Myth of Repressed Memory*, wrote,

> When we begin to look for memories we have lost, we enter a strange psychic realm called repression. The concept of repression presumes a certain power of the mind. Those who believe in repression have faith in the mind's ability to defend itself from emotionally overwhelming events by removing certain experiences and emotions from conscious awareness. (p. 7)

This typifies an intermixing of phenomena ("what") with presumed motivations ("why") and presumed mechanisms ("how"). In untangling these phenomena, the first thing to acknowledge is a profusion of terminology that is very confusing because the terminology doesn't map consistently onto these different issues. I prefer "knowledge isolation" (Freyd, 1996). We also have observable phenomena, that is, experiencing a significant event, the forgetting of it, and the later remembering of it. And we have proposed motivations and possible mechanisms. From this point I will treat these as separate issues. They may, in fact, interact in interesting ways, but first we need to consider them as conceptually separate (see Table 5.1).

We now focus on the motivation question: Why do children and adults sometimes fail to remember significant traumatic events? Is the motivation for forgetting simply the avoidance of pain, as common sense would seem to suggest? The most common reason given for why people forget is indeed that the forgetting is to ease pain. Daniel Goleman (1985) put it this way:

Table 5.1 Disentangling Concepts of "Memory Repression"

Terminology	Repression, dissociation, dissociative amnesia, traumatic amnesia, knowledge isolation
Observable Phenomena	Experiencing significant event, but not consciously recollecting significant aspects of it. Later recollecting the event
Proposed Motivations	Avoidance of: • Pain • Being overwhelmed • Threats to self-perception • Threats to assumptions of meaningful world • Information threatening a necessary attachment
Possible Mechanisms	• Selective attention • Inhibition of consolidation after initial encoding • State-dependent learning • Inhibition of accessing information already well-stored

> Repression is the quintessential lacuna; it lessens mental pain by attenuating awareness, as does its close cousin, denial.
>
> The defense mechanisms . . . are recipes for the ways we keep secrets from ourselves. The defenses are diversionary, activated in tandem with painful information; their function is to buffer that pain by skewing attention. (pp. 112-113)

In addition to demonstrating the confusion of phenomena motivation and mechanism, I think this also typifies the assumption that pain and avoidance of pain is the primary motivation for repression. I believe that this is not correct; the primary motivation for forgetting information in these cases is to preserve a necessary relationship (more on this follows), and that we're just not lucky enough to be designed to be able to stop feeling pain because we don't like pain (unless we take drugs).

The important thing to consider is the role of betrayal in the traumas that induce amnesia (and how the response to betrayal relates to relationship preservation). Ross Cheit, who recovered memories of sexual abuse by a camp counselor, wrote

The concept of trauma never seemed right to me, it didn't fit my story. There were no threats, I never sensed danger, I didn't fear him, he was nice to me. But the letters [sent home from camp, that Cheit read as an adult] were just devastating, because the letters were the first time that I thought about these actions in terms of what this man meant to me in my life, in terms of a relationship rather than in terms of just actions. And I read these letters, and I realized how important he was to me. I thought he was a great guy. I really admired him. I read the letters and the whole thing shifted from just "those acts" to complete betrayal. (Freyd, 1996, pp. 9, 11)

Figure 5.3 displays a two-dimensional model of trauma. Without question, some traumas that involve betrayal are terrorizing. Some terrorizing events, however, don't involve betrayal (or, at least, great amounts of betrayal), and some betrayals are not particularly terrorizing, at least at the time that it's occurring. The things that we call traumatic can be thought of as falling into four quadrants of space, created by two dimensions, as shown in Figure 5.3. (There are really more than just two dimensions here, but for now these are the two I'd like to separate from one another.) One is a dimension labeled as "terror, or fear inducing." This dimension corresponds to threats to life—things that actually can cause you bodily harm, and often do. These are terrorizing events. Another dimension is the dimension of betrayal and threats to social relationships. As depicted, some traumas are high on both these dimensions. For instance, sadistic abuse by a caregiver, the Holocaust, some combat experiences, and much childhood sexual abuse, are both terrorizing and involve a betrayal of a relationship. But some traumas that lead to forms of traumatic stress are high on one dimension but not so high on the other. From this viewpoint, some of the things we see in response to trauma—such as hyperarousal—and some of the biology of fear (including various sensory and emotional memory effects; see van der Kolk, 1994) are well captured by the events that are high in terror, but that amnesia is especially likely to occur for the events that are high in betrayal.

It is important to realize that although sexual abuse is arguably the kind of trauma most highly likely to be replete with betrayal (both betrayal by the perpetrator and betrayal by the bystanders), other sorts of trauma can and do involve betrayal and thus can and do create amnesia. Betrayal trauma theory leads to specific predictions about the factors related to betrayal and social interactions (i.e., the vertical dimension of

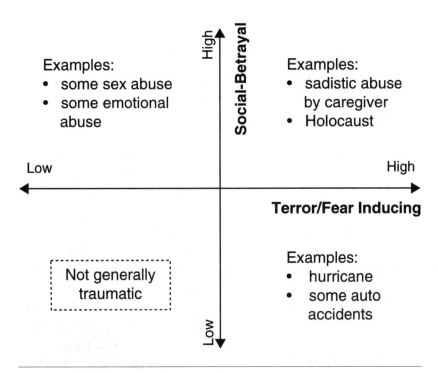

Figure 5.3. The Two-Dimensional Model of Trauma
SOURCE: Copyright © 1996, Jennifer J. Freyd.

trauma depicted in Figure 5.3) that will make amnesia most probable. Table 5.2 presents seven of these factors that emerge from betrayal trauma theory.

The first factor is the most directly relevant to the nature of the relationship and betrayal. The remaining six factors have to do with the impact of social environment and communication on the cognitive feasibility of amnesia (some of this will be taken up in the section below on the cognitive model, but for more detail see Freyd, 1996). It is important to stress two caveats. First, these factors are predicted to be statistically and significantly related to the probability of amnesia with all other factors held constant, but they are not presented as an exhaustive set of necessary and sufficient conditions for amnesia. Other factors, in fact, determine the probability of amnesia, including genetically determined potentialities that vary from person to person and including coping habits developed due to past experience with trauma. Additional factors are

Table 5.2 Factors Predicted to Be Related to Amnesia Rates

Betrayal Trauma Theory Predicts Amnesia Greatest When

---

1. Abuse by parent or important caregiver (betrayal)
2. Explicit threats demanding silence
3. Abuse context different from non-abuse context
4. Isolation during abuse
5. Young at age of abuse
6. Alternative reality defining statements by offender
7. Lack of discussion of abuse

SOURCE: From *Betrayal Trauma: The Logic of Forgetting Childhood Abuse,* by J. J. Freyd, 1996, Cambridge, MA: Harvard University Press. Copyright © 1996 by Harvard University Press. Reprinted with permission.

also relevant for predicting amnesia that stems from other dimensions of external trauma, such as possible effects of fear on memory consolidation due to changes in brain chemistry or structure (e.g., see Bremner et al., 1995; van der Kolk, 1994). Presumably, multiple motivations and mechanisms for forgetting traumatic events exist. The list of factors in Table 5.2 is thus considered neither exhaustive nor completely determinant, but instead is presented as those factors predicted to relate to amnesia that emerge from betrayal trauma theory for testing. Ultimately, it would be beneficial to compare each of these factors with other factors on the list and off the list for their potency in predicting amnesia.

It is not difficult to see from Table 5.2 that childhood sexual abuse perpetrated in secret by a parent is apt to be highly loaded on all seven factors and, therefore, an example of a kind of trauma that would have a relatively high probability of being forgotten. However, other traumas are also potentially highly loaded on at least some of these seven factors, and it follows that amnesia would be predicted to occur with some frequency for these other traumas. Patience H. C. Mason, editor of the newsletter *The Post-Traumatic Gazette,* sent me a description of a war trauma resulting in amnesia that fits this perspective (Mason, personal communication, February 6, 1997).

Many veterans have repressed memories, have forgotten whole periods of their tours, usually the most traumatic. My husband, who was a helicopter pilot and wrote a book about his experiences (*Chickenhawk*) [Mason, 1983], has seen a photograph of himself in front of an area strewn with body parts of enemy soldiers who had tried to overrun Plei Me and still cannot remember being there or seeing them. One of the official symptoms of PTSD is forgetting all or part of a trauma. Some of us also believe betrayal is a major component in PTSD in veterans. Jonathan Shay, MD, discusses its importance in *Achilles in Vietnam* [Shay, 1994]. At a conference on My Lai's 25th Anniversary at Tulane University . . . Hugh Thompson (the helicopter pilot who landed at My Lai and tried to stop the killing) revealed that he forgot about My Lai for two years. He would probably still not remember it if The New York Times and other papers hadn't broken the story. I may have been the only person in the audience who realized the incredible significance of that moment. . . . I later interviewed Mr. Thompson for my newsletter, The Post-Traumatic Gazette. This is the part of my article on his experiences:

History doesn't lie. Perhaps the most impressive example of a repressed memory is that of Hugh Thompson. Mr. Thompson was a helicopter pilot in Vietnam. On March 16th, 1968, he was flying his scout helicopter around a town called Pinkville. He kept seeing dead civilians. Whenever he called in that a wounded civilian needed help, he would see them dead when next he flew over. He didn't understand what was going on. He became angry and desperate. Finally he landed and called in help for one group, having his crew chief and gunner aim their weapons at the Americans to stop them. Later his crew chief waded into a ditch full of bodies and pulled a small wounded child out. They flew the child to a local hospital. The kid was the age of Hugh Thompson's own son at home. The whole experience was extremely traumatic for him. Two years later, when the Army investigators came to interview him about what he was doing on March 16, 1968, they got really angry at him and thought he was "giving them the run-around," as he put it in a recent phone interview with me. At that time he remembered nothing. He knew he had been in Vietnam on that date, that was all. "They said they had my flight records. Finally they asked me if I remembered hitting a tree with my helicopter. 'Oh, yeah. I remember that.' I said. Then things started coming back." He had a vague memory of pulling a gun on an American officer and thought he was in trouble for that. He had forgotten the whole My Lai Massacre. All of his heroic actions are documented in the US Army's report on My Lai. Over the course of several days of questioning by Army investigators it all came back to him, the horror, the dead women, children and old people, the fact that none of the authorities would listen or investigate. He had repressed the memory. He still does not remember all the details. The helplessness and horror he felt at what he saw were clear in his voice as he spoke about it last year at Tulane University at a conference on My Lai. When Hugh tried to get someone to listen to him about the massacre, no one would. Even the US Army and the Nixon Administration never used the "no such thing as repressed memories" defense when they were trying to cover up My Lai.

Unfortunately not all repressed memories have such a body of hard historical evidence to back them up.

Hugh Thompson's case fits all of the criteria for betrayal trauma set
forth in Jennifer Freyd's book: 1. The betrayal was by his caregivers, the
high ranking officers who were responsible for his life in Vietnam. 2. He
was threatened. He was told to forget it by people who could control
whether he lived or died just by the missions they sent him on. 3. It happened in a different context: My Lai was away from the base where he
lived. 4. Isolation: He was the only one who tried to stop the massacre or
even reported My Lai. 5. Youth: He was a relatively inexperienced WO-1,
the lowest ranking pilot. 6. Alternative reality defining statements by the
higher ups: They kept saying it hadn't happened. 7. Lack of discussion: No
one talked about what had happened. There was no one he could talk to
about it. (Mason, 1997)

The more the victim is dependent on the perpetrator, the more power
the perpetrator has over the victim in a trusted and intimate relationship, the more the crime is one of betrayal. Betrayal trauma theory proposes that betrayal by a trusted caregiver is the core factor in determining amnesia for a trauma. In addition, the social nature of this dimension
also affects how people respond to a trauma: If you're not allowed to talk
about the trauma and you're treated in a certain way, a terrorizing
trauma can become high in the social betrayal dimension, depending on
how people respond to you after you've had that trauma (thus affecting
many of the factors listed in Table 5.2).

Why are betrayals at the core in producing amnesia? Consider three
conceptual issues and then put them together. The first is the role of
"psychic" pain. Although it seems commonsensical that we can elimi-
nate pain because we don't like pain, if you stop and consider what pain
must be doing for us in a design sense, this doesn't make sense. Why do
we experience pain (whether so-called physical or psychic pain) at all?
Let's consider physical pain first. Presumably, we're designed to experience pain because it motivates changes in behavior: If we're very hungry
we're motivated to go eat; if we're very tired, to go sleep; if we're in pain
because of an inflamed injury, we're motivated to stop using that part of
the body and to rest. Similarly, if we feel psychological pain in response
to relationship events, we're motivated to leave the relationship or insist
on change. Sometimes, however, we don't experience pain we would
normally experience. Why would that happen? This happens when the

normal response to pain would actually be a threat or risk to survival. We're motivated to block pain when that normal response is going to get us into trouble; when does that happen? In the animal world, that can happen when a creature, under attack by a predator but injured, must fight or escape, but can't stop and heal its wounds. In fact, humans and other animals have a natural analgesic system, called the stress response, that will block pain under certain circumstances (Kelly, 1985). This is also the case with psychological or "psychic" pain—that humans can block it under the right circumstances—but perhaps it's just a little harder to figure out when that's going to happen.

The key to blocking psychic pain, according to betrayal trauma theory, is when the experience of pain may pose a survival hazard. Furthermore, often not only is the psychic pain itself blocked, but the information that leads to the pain reaction is isolated from other mental operations such as consciousness. The survival hazard has to do with the simultaneous need to remain attached to a caregiver (or, psychologically, this may be better understood to be the need to remain connected to an important attachment figure), and the conflicting "normal" response to betrayal. That normal response includes (potentially extreme) psychological pain and resulting behavioral changes affecting the relationship. Thus, three critical constructs develop: (a) the relationship between pain and changes in behavior (and related to that the relationship between blocking pain in order to thwart the normal changes in behavior), (b) the overwhelming importance of attachment (and very real dependence) to humans, and (c) the "normal" or, at least potential, exquisite sensitivity we have to betrayal and the resulting behavioral outcomes of that sensitivity.

Strong evidence suggests that humans—creatures born physically immature and vulnerable and forever social—arrive in this world both physically and psychologically dependent on others, and, in fact, psychologically (and sometimes physically) remain dependent on others throughout the life span (although the degree of dependence ideally decreases with maturity). The early extreme physical dependence of human infants and children on their caregivers is presumably part of what has driven the evolution of innate attachment mechanisms that operate in humans of all ages, especially newborns. These attachment mechanisms result in powerful affective responses (love) and a whole cascade of behaviors that ensure relationship stability. That we remain a social species throughout the life span, and that our dependence on others never dissipates completely, may combine with or even interact powerfully with our physical vulnerability.

To some extent, we share aspects of this vulnerability, social propensity, and attachment system with some of our primate relatives. In 1959, Harlow published his classic study "Love in Infant Monkeys." Harlow separated newborn monkeys from their mothers and put them into cages containing artificial mothers. In one experiment, the infant had a choice of mothers: one mother was made of wire with a rubber nipple that provided milk for the infant, the other mother had no nipple but was made of soft cloth. The infants chose to spend their time with the cloth mother, indicating that attachments are not primarily based on food and that the infant had a drive to meet its attachment needs. When the infants were frightened, they chose the cloth monkey and clung to it. Harlow also studied the effects of this social deprivation on the infants' development. He found that the infants who were deprived of social contact during their first year of life did not develop into psychologically healthy monkeys; they were generally stressed and depressed and exposure to another monkey caused them to withdraw into a corner and rock and show other signs of distress. The good news is that researchers have found that these deprived monkeys may recover with time if they are allowed to live with normally raised monkeys (sometimes referred to as "monkey therapists"). When those previously deprived monkeys who apparently had recovered were later stressed, however, they easily regressed, showing signs of the harm that was done to them as infants. They also were not able to become suitable parents: They tended to neglect their infants if they were forced into pregnancy, and even abuse and kill their infants.

This similarity between human response and monkey response to early social deprivation indicates that much of the attachment system is probably innately programmed. It's now widely recognized that the physical and mental survival of human infants and children depends on a successful attachment between the child and caregiver (Bowlby, 1969, 1988). Under healthy conditions during the first year of a human's life, the caregiver and the infant are responding to one another, developing a deep, affectionate, intimate, and enduring relationship. Because attachment is of so much significance to the human, there is a complex system of emotional, cognitive, and behavioral processes that ensure that under normal conditions attachment develops. It is important to keep in mind that this is a reciprocal relationship. The infant is not a passive recipient; rather, the infant is actually doing things to be lovable, and in being lovable the infant is ensuring the attachment and dedication of the caregiver. An infant who is unable to respond in a lovable way risks not being cared for, and although very mature parents will presumably, ideally, still care for their infant, many parents will likely pull away and not be as good parents, simply because the infant is not responding in the normal, lovable, adorable way. The fundamental importance of attachment to human psychological well being has been demonstrated for infants, children, and adults (e.g., Ainsworth, 1982; Kobak & Sceery, 1988; Main, Kaplan, & Cassidy, 1985).

What happens when a human child—charged by life with the duty to become attached to and elicit attachment from his or her caregiver—is betrayed by that very caregiver? Why are amnesia and unawareness adaptive in these cases? This takes us to the last piece of the puzzle that must be added to the understanding of pain and attachment. We are exquisite detectors of betrayal under many situations. Cosmides (1989), an evolutionary psychologist, has postulated that humans have a naturally evolved mental mechanism devoted specifically to detecting cheaters. Her argument is that our evolution took place in a social context and that we had to become very good at determining whether or not people were sticking to their social contract. So, we are adept and quick at detecting cheating. Evidence marshaled for this viewpoint comes from laboratory studies conducted using reasoning tasks. Cosmides has found that people can do well on laboratory reasoning tasks if the situation involves detecting a violation of a social contract (cheating) but significantly less well for logically identical problems not involving the detection of cheating.

Whether one agrees with the evolutionary perspective or not, a fair amount of evidence indicates that we are very motivated to detect cheating and betrayal under some conditions. If the choice exists, it would be completely logical for you to stop interacting with somebody who is cheating you. And, as adults, often we do have that choice. When we're very aware that we have been cheated—for instance, when we've been billed incorrectly—it can make us very angry to feel that we've been deceived.

We are frequently sensitive to cheating when we have the choice, and we know we have the choice to avoid the cheater. But what if we don't have the choice? The sensitivity to betrayal brings pain, and the pain of betrayal can be extraordinarily great. When the betrayer is someone we're dependent on, the very mechanisms that normally protect us—sensitivity to cheating and the pain that motivates us to change things so that we will no longer be in danger—become problematic. An infant or child who is responding to cheating in the "normal" way would pull back from that relationship, become less lovable and less likely to inspire the very nurturing he or she is dependent on. Child abuse is especially likely to produce a social conflict of betrayal for the victim. If a child processes the betrayal in the usual way, he or she will be motivated to stop interacting with the betrayer. Essentially, the child needs to ignore the betrayal to preserve the attachment. Thus, for a child dependent on a caregiver, the trauma of abuse, by the very nature of it, demands that information about the abuse be blocked from mental mechanisms that control attachment and attachment behavior. How is a child to manage this on a long-term, and sometimes nearly daily, basis? How is the child to succeed at maintaining this necessary relationship when a natural response is to withdraw from the source of the pain? It is just this dilemma that is captured by betrayal trauma and, therefore, the child blocks the pain of the abuse and betrayal by isolating knowledge of the abuse/betrayal from awareness and memory. Various avenues for achieving this isolation develop, one being conscious memories without affect, and another the isolation of knowledge of the event itself from awareness.

The How Question:
Many Kinds of Memory

Thus far a theory has been suggested about *why* abuse is forgotten; now we move to the *how* question. How could a child experience repeated instances of abuse, fail to remember the events, and yet eventually be able to recover the memories? For this to happen, there must be a disruption of the sort of processing that leads to consciously accessible memory, and still maintain the continuation of other sorts of processing that lead to some kinds of memory for the events. We can understand the phenomenon of forgetting and remembering abuse using concepts from cognitive science. There's nothing necessarily mysterious about forgetting abusive events, considering what we already know about cognitive architecture.

Here, I consider a number of concepts from cognitive science—parallel processing, selective attention and memory, different kinds of memory, different mental codes, shareability (which is a theory about how knowledge sharing changes the nature of the knowledge), the fact that processing complex events takes time, and laboratory studies on memory inhibition.

Memory psychologists tend to divide memory into the three very general processes depicted in Figure 5.4: (a) the processes of encoding information or putting material into memory, (b) the processes of storing information, and (c) the processes of retrieval or recovering information from memory. We know that there can be breakdowns in any one of these three overall components of the memory process. We also know that there is often a relationship between the nature of encoding and the nature of retrieval. Thus, depending on how something has been encoded, it may be easier or harder to retrieve it.

The model presented in Figure 5.4 implies serial processing: Things go in, they're stored, and they come out. In real life, when we're interacting with the complex world, we are, in fact, encountering multiple events that are happening at once and we're processing them in parallel. That is, not only are there multiple events, but we're processing each event in a number of different ways simultaneously and in parallel.

Another aspect of memory that we know well from cognitive science is the extent to which all aspects of information processing—from perception, attention, problem solving, and memory—are very active and very selective. As actors in a complex world, we are confronted with far too much information to absorb, process, and comprehend all of it, and we therefore need to select the information we're going to perceive, pro-

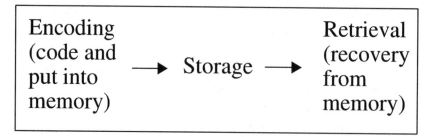

Figure 5.4. Traditional Model of Memory
SOURCE: From *Betrayal Trauma: The Logic of Forgetting Childhood Abuse,* by J. J. Freyd, 1996, Cambridge, MA: Harvard University Press. Copyright © 1996 by Harvard University Press. Reprinted with permission.

cess, and remember. William James (1890) pointed out, "If we remembered everything we should on most occasions be as ill off as if we remembered nothing" (p. 68). Certainly this is true for perception as well.

Two profoundly relevant aspects of selective attention exist to understand memory for trauma. One is that you can select information to attend to, and the other is that the selection process is not perfect; it is not all or none. As an example, if you are watching a television show with a noisy family around you, you may be able to partially ignore the noisy family, selecting the television as your primary focus (even if it is not as loud as the events around you). However, if that noisy family includes your teenage son announcing his plans to erase the hard drive on your computer, you are likely to suddenly disengage from the television set and select your son's speech stream as your primary focus. Taken further, from the perspective of the child who is motivated to isolate from consciousness information about an abusive event by a caregiver (a betrayal trauma), these facts about selective attention mean that the child can instead select other information simultaneously available for focus concentration, and at the same time the child cannot completely avoid some processing of the abusive event. In other words, the simultaneous reality of the sound of a radio in the room next door, the visual details of the wallpaper in the current room, the feel of an insect crawling on a part of the body not involved in the abusive event—all of these may be events that can be focused on instead of the abusive event. This selective attention toward alternative events and away from the abusive event will certainly make it more likely the abusive event is unavailable to conscious memory, and yet, the selection of information is unlikely to be only partially effective, in that some of the physical reality of the event that is affecting the nervous system will be registered.

Distinctions in memory are very important for understanding memory for trauma, and psychologists make many distinctions based on behavioral and on neurophysiological data, especially based on people with brain lesions who have various amnesias. Three important distinctions are depicted in Figure 5.5: (a) a distinction in how material is learned (intentional versus incidental), (b) a distinction about the kind of material it is (declarative knowledge you can state versus knowledge you cannot state such as skills learned), and (c) a distinction in how material is retrieved from memory (explicitly versus implicitly). Most learning that occurs is incidental, not intentional. Humans learn, not just because we plan to learn, but because we're learning machines—we cannot stop learning. The distinction in knowledge is extremely important. Declarative knowledge is the knowledge you have that you know you know. It tends to be the material you can verbalize. Within declarative knowledge there are various distinctions, including semantic knowledge, such as the meanings of words and all the things you generally know you know, versus episodic knowledge, such as your memory for events. Semantic and episodic knowledge are things you can declare in some way, but most of our knowledge is nondeclarative.

Nondeclarative knowledge represents all the skills you have, all the conditioning you've been subjected to, which means a great deal of the socializing you've absorbed, perceptual learning, and many other kinds of behavioral knowledge. Indeed, arguably most knowledge is nondeclarative. You know it (how to ride a bicycle, how to sing "Happy Birthday"), but you can't declare the specifics of that knowledge. This distinction (see Squire, 1992) is related to, but not exactly the same as, a distinction in how you retrieve information from memory (see Roediger, 1990). Here the issue is whether you explicitly are trying to recall something, or you implicitly are demonstrating your memory. Most of the time, we are using implicit memory; we're not trying to remember but our memory is guiding our behavior. Most nondeclarative knowledge can be accessed only implicitly, but, in fact, you can have explicit retrieval of both nondeclarative and declarative knowledge and implicit retrieval of both.

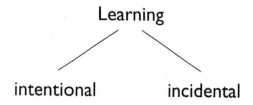

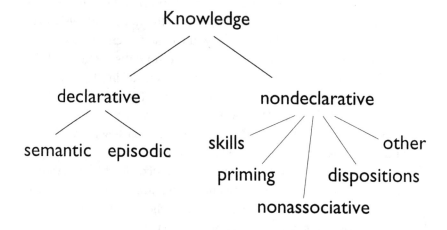

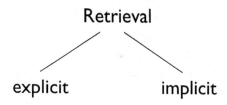

Figure 5.5. Three Distinctions in Memory
SOURCE: Copyright © 1996, Jennifer J. Freyd.

Figure 5.6 illustrates what I call the iceberg model of kinds of memory. It represents graphically that we have many kinds of memory. It also demonstrates that declarative, explicit memories are just the tip of the iceberg. They are the ones we're really conscious of, the ones we might think of when we first hear the word *memory,* the category in which autobiographical memories fall. These are the things we can say we know. But most of memory is not above the conscious line and instead, it involves all the shifts in judgment that have occurred, all the effects of socialization, all the learning that has occurred at the level of skills and motor behaviors. Most of memory is below this line.

Going back to the notion of parallel processing, if you consider the possibility that you've got a blockage in processing, you can imagine that you've got a blockage that's going to lead to explicit and declarative memories, but you also have fully functioning processing that's going to lead to procedural and implicit memories. For the abused child, this means that an event can be experienced and processed in ways that allow some information to enter those processing mechanisms that learn behaviors and habits and perceptual associations while simultaneously being blocked from those mechanisms that support consciously accessible episodic event memories. This means an abused child may have sensory memories of abuse that are dissociated from a conscious understanding of their source, and that an abused child may also learn a range of behaviors from the abuse (including behaviors eventually expressed during parenting), yet all the while not having access to a clear narrative account of the abusive events.

Shareability theory is a hypothesis developed (Freyd, 1983, 1990) not for traumatic memories, but because information that is shared tends to become more discrete and categorical. The theory says that through knowledge sharing, internal material becomes more categorical and is the spontaneous property of two people, or a group of people, communicating. Categorical information can have stability across space and time, and shareability theory presumes that the sharing of information spontaneously causes this emergent property of categorization. However, if a traumatic experience was never coded into shareable format, it's likely to be stored in mental codes that are continuous, sensory, and dynamic. Memory for perceptual experiences that have not been encoded in a declarative way is stored using mental coding that's quite different from the kind of declarative coding that we use. And sharing the information allows an integration of information between these different mental codes that might not otherwise be occurring. This means private knowledge may be structurally different from shared or public

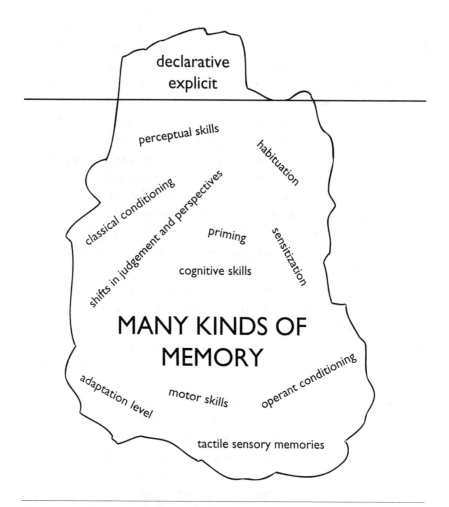

Figure 5.6. The Iceberg Model of Different Kinds of Memory
SOURCE: Copyright © 1996, Jennifer J. Freyd.

knowledge. Consider that child abuse experiences are likely to have never been discussed for years, maybe never. If a child never speaks of the trauma, we would expect from shareability theory that the memory for that trauma would be qualitatively different from memories that have been socially shared.

Processing complex events takes time, and because it takes time means that one way we can disrupt the storage of memories into normal full memory is by blocking the repeated processing of information via feedback loops that support mental rehearsal and consolidation of information (Browne, 1990). When I say it takes time, I mean lots of time— Consider a time when you first learned of distressing news, news that would largely impact your life. You can probably also recall that you were very actively processing this significant information for hours, days, maybe even weeks. In this processing time, consolidation is occurring. If you stop this processing time, you leave traces for the event that have a very fragmented, unfinished feel to them because you haven't continued the normal consolidation. For example, if you learn that someone you care about is moving far away, you may process that information over the next few days. Consider what occurs when you inhibit that normal processing.

Finally, we know from laboratory studies on memory inhibition that it's possible for people to go through the processing of a memory and lay down a very good memory and still not be able to remember it. This occurs when a block is created to the retrieval cues. Under the right laboratory conditions, this can be induced; typically, these experiments are done for very neutral stimuli, like words on a list. But that block can also be released under the right conditions. We know that it's cognitively possible to have not only the blockage of information in the encoding stage, but even the blockage of information after encoding that's affecting retrieval (Anderson & Bjork, 1994; Anderson & Spellman, 1995). If these laboratory results can be generalized to event memory (and that is yet to be tested empirically), then we would expect that the abused child could, in fact, later inhibit an already formed memory of the abuse. Until further experimentation on the generalizability of these laboratory findings on memory inhibition is performed, we can say that there are known cognitive mechanisms discovered in laboratory experiments for inhibiting and later recovering memories.

Putting this all together, we can answer the question of how it is cognitively plausible to forget and remember abusive events. Rather than saying there's one way to forget and one way to remember abuse, we can recognize that there are many ways information can be forgotten and later remembered. We have multiple mental mechanisms processing information in parallel. Attention is selective, and different kinds of memory are tied to different mental processes using different mental codes. In normal memories, these codes are associated with one another, but in traumatic memories, because of those blockages, they may not be. But the sharing of information, either at the time of the event or much later, as in a therapeutic relationship, may facilitate integration between different codes. That processing complex events takes time implies that knowledge can be isolated by interrupting the extended processing of complex events. The finding that even well-formed memories can be inhibited and later recovered suggests, but does not prove, that this may be true for abuse memories, too.

In sum, there are multiple ways for the abused child to disrupt knowledge integration and awareness of the abuse and yet still facilitate the important and crucial relationship. This cognitive perspective also suggests that there are multiple ways for the adult survivor of childhood abuse to recover these memories, and that these different ways will depend, in part, on how the memories were isolated in the first place. At the same time, this cognitive plausibility does not negate the potential for false memories to occur. Indeed, the cognitive mechanisms that support knowledge isolation and recovery may be in part the same mechanisms that may support memory errors (see also Freyd, 1996; Morton, in press; Schachter, 1996; Schooler et al., 1997).

Implications, Predictions, and Summary

Betrayal trauma theory has implications for the sequelae of child sexual abuse, for societal and personal healing, and also for an awareness of everyday betrayal (things that are less traumatic than childhood sexual abuse) (Freyd, 1996). Adulthood and everyday betrayals—a boss who speaks in a patronizing voice, a spouse who flirts with a friend —also often leave little marks on conscious awareness. The human response of not knowing—of not remembering—betrayals may be ubiquitous.

Betrayal trauma theory makes testable predictions about when forgetting abuse is most likely (see Table 5.2). For instance, it predicts that amnesia will be more likely the more dependent the victim is on the perpetrator. Reanalyses of extant data (Cameron, 1993; Feldman-Summers & Pope, 1994; Williams, 1994a, 1995), in which information was gathered about both the relationship of perpetrator to victim and the persistence of memory, are consistent with this prediction (Freyd, 1996). Only one study claims to find that persistence of memory is unrelated to whether the abuse was incestuous (Loftus, Polonsky, & Fullilove, 1994). However, reanalysis of the data collected for that study indicated that the "highest amnesia rates are among those woman abused by a parent and that family relatedness per se does not predict amnesia" so that the data are "equivocal on the relationship between betrayal and amnesia" (Freyd, 1996, p. 156). In addition, two oft-cited studies (Briere & Conte, 1993; Herman & Schatzow, 1987) reporting very high rates of amnesia for abuse (62% and 59.3%, respectively) both also have very high rates of incestuous abuse in their samples (100% and 89.8%, respectively).

In summary, betrayal trauma theory provides a logic to amnesia for childhood abuse. Betrayal is a violation of trust; if you can choose whom to interact with, it's best to be very aware of betrayal. Where escape is not a viable option, however, the ability humans have to detect betrayal may need to be stifled. When a child distrusts a parent, the child risks alienating that parent further and that, in turn, results in more abuse and less love and care. Amnesia for the abuse can be adaptive, allowing a dependent child to remain attached to the abusive caregiver, thus eliciting some degree of life-sustaining nurturing and protection. And various degrees of amnesia—from partial to robust, with various onsets from the time of the event to afterward—and various consequences can be understood in terms of what cognitive science currently informs us about memory and attention.

The psychological effects of trauma can be understood to depend on at least two separate dimensions of trauma: immediate bodily threat that may be only too well remembered, and betrayal that may be forgotten in order to preserve a relationship (Freyd, 1996), as much as a child may deny, delay, or even retract an allegation of abuse to preserve his or her world (Summit, 1983).

References

Ainsworth, M. D. (1982). Attachment: Retrospect and prospect. In C. M. Parkes & J. Stevenson-Hinde (Eds.), *The place of attachment in human behavior* (pp. 3-30). New York: Basic Books.

Anderson, M. C., & Bjork, R. A. (1994). Mechanisms of inhibition in long-term memory: A new taxonomy. In D. Dagenbach & T. Carr (Eds.), *Inhibitory processes in attention, memory and language* (pp. 265-325). San Diego: Academic Press.

Anderson, M. C., & Spellman, B. A. (1995). On the status of inhibitory mechanisms in cognition: Memory retrieval as a model case. *Psychological Review, 102,* 68-100.

Andrews, B., Brewin, C. R., Ochera, J., Morton, J., Bekerian, D., Davies, G. M., & Mollon, P. (1999). Characteristics, context and consequences of memory recovery among adults in therapy. *British Journal of Psychiatry, 175,* 141-146.

Bowlby, J. (1969). *Attachment and loss.* New York: Basic Books.

Bowlby, J. (1988). *A secure base: Parent-child attachment and healthy human development.* New York: Basic Books.

Bowman, C. G., & Mertz, E. (1996). What should the courts do about memories of sexual abuse? Towards a balanced approach. *Judge's Journal, 35*(4), 7-17.

Bremner, J. D., Randall, P., Scott, T. M., Bronen, R. A., Seibyl, J. P., Southwick, S. M., Delaney, R. C., McCarthy, G., Charney, D. S., & Innis, R. B. (1995). MRI-based measurement of hippocampal volume in patients with combat-related posttraumatic stress disorder. *American Journal of Psychiatry, 152,* 973-981.

Brewin, C. R. (1996). Clinical and experimental approaches to understanding repression. In J. D. Read & D. S. Lindsay (Eds.), *Recollections of trauma: Scientific research and clinical practice.* New York: Plenum.

Briere, J., & Conte, J. (1993). Self-reported amnesia for abuse in adults molested as children. *Journal of Traumatic Stress, 6*(1), 21-29.

Brown, D., Scheflin, A. W., & Hammond, D. C. (1997). *Memory, trauma treatment, and the law.* New York: Norton.

Browne, I. (1990). Psychological trauma, or unexperienced experience. *ReVision, 12*(4), 21-34.

Burgess, A. W., Hartman, C. R., & Baker, T. (1995). Memory presentations of childhood sexual abuse. *Journal of Psychosocial Nursing, 33*(9), 9-16.

Butler, K. (1996). The latest on recovered memory. *Family Therapy Networker, 20*(6), 36-37.

Cameron, C. (1993, April). Recovering memories of childhood sexual abuse: A longitudinal report. Paper presented at the Western Psychological Association Convention, Phoenix, AZ.

Corwin, D. L., & Olafson, E. (1997). Videotaped discovery of a reportedly unrecallable memory of child sexual abuse: Comparison with a childhood interview videotaped 11 years before. *Child Maltreatment, 2*(2), 91-112.

Cosmides, L. (1989). The logic of social exchange: Has natural selection shaped how humans reason? Studies with the Wason Selection Task. *Cognition, 31,* 187-276.

Dalenberg, C. J. (1996). Accuracy, timing and circumstances of disclosure in therapy of recovered and continuous memories of abuse. *Journal of Psychiatry and Law, 24*(2), 229-275.

Elliott, E., & Briere, J. (1995). Posttraumatic stress associated with delayed recall of sexual abuse: A general population study. *Journal of Traumatic Stress, 8*(4), 629-647.

Feldman-Summers, S., & Pope, K. S. (1994). The experience of "forgetting" childhood abuse: A national survey of psychologists. *Journal of Consulting and Clinical Psychology, 62,* 636-639.

Finkelhor, D. (1979). *Sexually victimized children.* New York: Free Press.

Freyd, J. J. (1983). Shareability: The social psychology of epistemology. *Cognitive Science, 7,* 191-210.

Freyd, J. J. (1990). Natural selection or shareability? *Behavioral and Brain Sciences, 13,* 732-734.

Freyd, J. J. (1991, August). Memory repression, dissociative states, and other cognitive control processes involved in adult sequelae of childhood trauma. Paper presented at the Second Annual Conference on Psychodynamics—Cognitive Science Interface, Langley Porter Psychiatric Institute, University of California, San Francisco.

Freyd, J. J. (1996). *Betrayal trauma: The logic of forgetting childhood abuse.* Cambridge, MA: Harvard University Press.

Freyd, J. J., & Gleaves, D. H. (1996). "Remembering" words not presented in lists: Relevance to the current recovered/false memory controversy. *Journal of Experimental Psychology: Learning, Memory and Cognition, 22*(3), 811-813.

Freyd, J. J., DePrince, A. P., & Zurbriggen, E. L. (in press). Self-reported memory for abuse depends upon victim-perpetrator relationship. *Journal of Trauma & Dissociation, 2,*(3).

Freyd, J. J., & Quina, K. (2000). Feminist ethics in the practice of science: The contested memory controversy as an example. In M. Brabeck (Ed.), *Practicing feminist ethics in psychology* (pp. 101-124). Washington, DC: American Psychological Association.

Gleaves, D. H. (1996). The evidence for "repression": An examination of Holmes (1990) and the implications for the recovered memory controversy. *Journal of Child Sexual Abuse, 5*(1), 1-19.

Gleaves, D. H., & Freyd, J. J. (1997). Questioning additional claims about the "false memory syndrome" epidemic. *American Psychologist, 52,* 993-994.

Goleman, D. (1985). *Vital lies, simple truths: The psychology of self-deception.* New York: Simon & Schuster.

Harlow, H. F. (1959). "Love in infant monkeys." *Scientific American, 200,* 68-74.

Herman, J. L. (1992). *Trauma and recovery.* New York: Basic Books.

Herman, J. L., & Schatzow, E. (1987). Recovery and verification of memories of childhood sexual trauma. *Psychoanalytic Psychology, 4*(1), 1-14.

Hovdestad, W. E., & Kristiansen, C. M. (1996). A field study of "false memory syndrome": Construct validity and incidence. *Journal of Psychiatry and Law, 24*(2), 299-338.

James, W. (1890). *Principles of psychology.* New York: Holt.

Kelly, D. D. (1985). Central representations of pain and analgesia. In E. R. Kandel & J. H. Schwartz (Eds.), *Principles of Neural Science* (pp. 331-343). New York: Elsevier.

Kinsey, A. C., Pomeroy, W. B., Martin, C. E., & Gebhard, P. H. (1953). *Sexual behavior in the human female.* Philadelphia: W. B. Saunders.

Kobak, R. R., & Sceery, A. (1988). Attachment in late adolescence: Working models, affect regulation, and perception of self and others. *Child Development, 59,* 135-146.

Lindsay, D. S., & Briere, J. (in press). The controversy regarding recovered memories of childhood sexual abuse: Pitfalls, bridges and future directions. *Journal of Interpersonal Violence.*

Loftus, E. F., & Ketcham, K. (1994). *The myth of repressed memory: False memories and allegations of sexual abuse.* New York: St. Martin's.

Loftus, E. F., Polonsky, S., & Fullilove, M. T. (1994). Memories of childhood sexual abuse: Remembering and repressing. *Psychology of Women Quarterly, 18,* 67-84.

Main, M., Kaplan, N., & Cassidy, J. (1985). Security in infancy, childhood, and adulthood: A move to the level of representation. *Monographs of the Society for Research in Child Development, 50,*(1-2), 66-104.

Mason, P. H. C. (1997). False memory syndrome vs. lying perpetrator syndrome. *Post-Traumatic Gazette, 1*(4), p. 4.

Mason, R. (1983). *Chickenhawk.* New York: Viking.

Medick, E. (1994, June 16). Women's repressed memory of abuse leads to conviction. *Columbus Dispatch,* p. 1A.

Morton, J. (in press). Cognitive perspectives on recovered memories. In J. Sandler (Ed.), *Recovered memories of abuse: True or false.* London: Karnac Books.

Olafson, E., Corwin, D. L, & Summit, R. C. (1993). Modern history of child sexual abuse awareness: Cycles of discovery and suppression. *Child Abuse & Neglect, 17*, 7-24.

Pope, K. S., & Brown, L. S. (1996). *Recovered memories of abuse: Assessment, therapy, forensics.* Washington, DC: American Psychological Association.

Roediger H. L., III. (1990). Implicit memory: Retention without remembering. *American Psychologist, 45*(9), 1043-1056.

Russell, D. E. H. (1986). *The secret trauma: Incest in the lives of girls and women.* New York: Basic Books.

Schachter, D. L. (1996). *Searching for memory: The brain, the mind, and the past.* New York: Basic Books.

Scheflin, A. W., & Brown, D. (1996). Repressed memory or dissociative amnesia: What the science says. *Journal of Psychiatry & Law, 24*, 143-188.

Schooler, J. W., Bendiksen, M., & Ambadar, Z. (1997). Taking the middle line: Can we accommodate both fabricated and recovered memories of sexual abuse? In M. A. Conway (Ed.), *Recovered memories and false memories.* Oxford: Oxford University Press.

Shay, J. (1994). *Achilles in Vietnam: Combat trauma and the undoing of character.* New York: Atheneum.

Squire, L. R. (1992). Memory and the hippocampus: A synthesis from findings with rats, monkeys, and humans. *Psychological Review, 99*(2), 195-231.

Summit, R. C. (1983). The child sexual abuse accommodation syndrome. *Child Abuse & Neglect, 7*, 177-193.

Summit, R. C. (1988). Hidden victims, hidden pain: Societal avoidance of child sexual abuse. In G. E. Wyatt & G. J. Powell (Eds.), *Lasting effects of child sexual abuse* (pp. 39-60). Newbury Park, CA: Sage.

Summit, R. C. (1992). Abuse of the child sexual abuse accommodation syndrome (Case conference: Mental health/social service issues and case studies). *Journal of Child Sexual Abuse, 1*(4), 153-163.

Timnick, L. (1985, August 25). 22% in survey were child abuse victims. *Los Angeles Times,* pp. 1, 34.

van der Kolk, B. A. (1994). The body keeps the score: Memory and the evolving psychobiology of posttraumatic stress. *Harvard Review of Psychiatry, 1*(5), 253-265.

van der Kolk, B. A., & Fisler, R. (1995). Dissociation and the fragmentary nature of traumatic memories: Overview and exploratory study. *Journal of Traumatic Stress, 8*, 505-525.

Widom, C. S., & Morris, S. (1997). Accuracy of adult recollections of childhood victimization: II. Childhood sexual abuse. *Psychological Assessment, 9*(1), 34-46.

Williams, L. M. (1994a). Recall of childhood trauma: A prospective study of women's memories of child sexual abuse. *Journal of Consulting and Clinical Psychology, 62,*(6), 1167-1176.

Williams, L. M. (1994b). What does it mean to forget child sexual abuse? A reply to Loftus, Garry, and Feldman (1994). *Journal of Consulting and Clinical Psychology,62*(6), 1182-1186.

Williams, L. M. (1995). Recovered memories of abuse in women with documented child sexual victimization histories. *Journal of Traumatic Stress, 8*, 649-674.

AUTHOR'S POSTSCRIPT: This chapter was completed in 1997. In the interim, the in-press version of the paper inspired a number of new empirical studies and theoretical developments, including the following:

DePrince, A. P., & Freyd, J. J. (in press). Memory and dissociative tendencies: The roles of attentional context and word meaning in a directed forgetting task. *Journal of Trauma & Dissociation, 2,*(2).

DePrince, A. P., & Freyd, J. J. (in press). The intersection of gender and betrayal in traumatic exposure and trauma sequelae. In R. Kimerling, P. C. Oumette, & J. Wolfe (Eds.), *Gender and posttraumatic stress disorder: Clinical, research, and program-level applications.* New York: Guilford.

DePrince, A. P., & Freyd, J. J. (in press). The harm of trauma: Pathological fear, shattered assumptions, or betrayal? In J. Kauffman (Ed.), *Loss of the assumptive world. Philadelphia: Taylor & Francis.*

DePrince, A. P. (2001). Trauma and posttraumatic responses: an examination of fear and betrayal. Doctoral dissertation, University of Oregon, 2001.

DePrince, A. P., & Freyd, J. J. (1999). Dissociative tendencies, attention, and memory. *Psychological Science, 10,* 449-452.

Freyd, J. J. (1998). Science in the memory debate. *Ethics & Behavior, 8,* 101-113.

Freyd, J. J. (1999). Blind to betrayal: New perspectives on memory for trauma. *The Harvard Mental Health Letter, 15*(12), 4-6.

Freyd, J. J., & DePrince, A. P. (2001). Perspectives on memory for trauma and cognitive processes associated with dissociative tendencies. *Journal of Aggression, Maltreatment, & Trauma, 4,* 137-163.

Freyd, J. J., DePrince, A. P., & Zurbriggen, E. L. (in press). Self-reported memory for abuse depends upon victim-perpetrator relationship. *Journal of Trauma & Dissociation, 2,*(3).

Freyd, J. J., & Quina, K. (2000). Feminist ethics in the practice of science: The contested memory controversy as an example. In M. Brabeck (Ed.), *Practicing feminist ethics in psychology (pp. 101-124). Washington, DC: American Psychological Association.*

Stoler, L., Quina, K., DePrince, A. P., &. Freyd, J. J. (in press). Repressed memories. In J. Worrell (Ed.), *Encyclopedia of Gender.* San Diego: Academic.

Veldhuis, C. B., & Freyd, J. J. (1999). Groomed for silence, groomed for betrayal. In M. Rivera (Ed.), *Fragment by fragment: Feminist perspectives on memory and child sexual abuse* (pp. 253-282). Charlottetown, PEI Canada: Gynergy Books.

6

Not Necessarily Politically Correct Reflections and Thoughts on Approaches to the Treatment of Traumatic Material in Dissociative Identity Disorder Patients

RICHARD P. KLUFT

The literature of the mental health professions literally has exploded with advice on how to avoid the contamination of patients' recollections and how to avoid creating false memories of childhood abuse. Warnings against practices alleged to have such nefarious effects abound. Perusing this literature, a visitor from another galaxy might conclude that from the mid-1990s through the first years of the new millennium, the most compelling imperative in the psychotherapy of those who allege that they have been traumatized is the prevention of the recovery of materials that might cast aspersions on third parties to the treatment. Further, such a visitor might surmise that honing the expertise of the therapist and more effectively pursuing the recovery of the patient have become minor considerations at this moment in history.

Unfortunately, were such an interpretation offered by an extra-galactic scholar, it would contain an element of truth. Despite the questionable scientific and clinical status of the concerns that have been raised about so-called false memory (Pope, 1996), despite the fact that the prevalence of so-called false memories is unknown (Brown, 1995; Brown, Scheflin, & Hammond, 1997), and despite the possibility that the sources of so-called false memories that are volunteered or thought to have been produced in therapy may not have their origins within the treatment (Brown et al., 1997; Kluft, 1995a, 1995b, 1996a, 1998), the vigorous and often vicious polarized debate that surrounds these issues has become a central focus of contemporary psychotherapeutic thought.

The so-called false memory debate has captured center stage with the attention-grabbing peremptory force of a group of terrorists seizing and holding hostage the passengers of an aircraft or ship. Admittedly, the comparison is provocative, but it captures an essential aspect of the impact of this contention on the helping professions. Without the central scientific issues having been established or demonstrated to the point of a preponderance of the evidence, let alone to the level of proof beyond a reasonable doubt, psychotherapists and psychotherapy itself have been subjected to withering attacks on the basis of allegations emerging from this debate. Careers have been ruined, jobs have been lost, therapists' offices have been picketed, lawsuits have been encouraged and filed, and the bloodlust of the media has been incited (to which the media have responded with an enthusiastic voracity that would elicit heartfelt professional admiration from a great white shark or a school of piranha). The processes involved with such events have neither patience nor circumspection. They are forced to their crises with much remaining unknown and partially, if not largely, incompletely apprehended or understood. The media and the legal system often appear to be driving clinical practice. It is clear that the only safe course of conduct that will result in a therapist's "release" from this siege is capitulation to the political (represented as scientific) agendas of those analogized to the terrorists. Of course, they must be granted amnesty for their actions, because, after all, their cause was just (or so they say).

When one explores many of the recommendations that are put forth, one rapidly appreciates that most of them are too sweeping and draconian to apply under realistic clinical circumstances. Furthermore, most of them assume that the therapist's interventions, even if they are few and subtle, have an amazing potency to wreak destructive havoc on the patient's autobiographical memory. The assumption is made that the patient is highly suggestible and extremely malleable to the therapist's slightest efforts and most covert influences. Such assumptions often make the clinician's head whirl with incredulity and confusion. All too often, the therapist, using the most forceful and pervasive suggestive efforts over an extended period, has failed to make a meaningful impact on the patient's psychopathology and understanding of his or her circumstances. Yet the clinician is asked, nonetheless, to believe that a casual remark or an unfortunate inquiry made of the allegedly highly suggestible patient has instigated a horrifically complex series of consequences, all of which may have lasting, if not permanent, impacts.

The situation becomes somewhat more comprehensible when one appreciates that many of the advices that have been put forward have sprung from the word processors of authorities who have had little, if any, connection with the trauma field. Many are not even involved in the treatment of patients. Their expertise is soi-disant, self-ascribed, auctorial, or inferred/deduced/extended from their contributions of unquestioned importance in peripherally related fields of scholarship. Whitfield (1995), a thoughtful student of this intriguing phenomenon, has described it as the "false expert syndrome."

In this chapter, I will begin with a review of some of the problems associated with the study of dissociative identity disorder (DID) patients' accounts of trauma. Then, I will share results of an empirical investigation of the possibility of encountering the recovery of both accurate memories once covered over by amnesia and inaccurate yet believed-in memories of trauma in the therapy setting. I will explore the implications of these findings. Next, I will offer some observations about how I attempt to practice in the face of these realizations, with specific attention to a number of crucial topics, such as the therapeutic alliance with the traumatized patient, and the use of techniques that facilitate therapy. Finally, I shall offer some discussion and concluding remarks. In this process, I will not attempt to tell clinicians what they should or should not do. That has been done already by many others, most of whom have far less experience in treating traumatized individuals than I. It is easier for such people to offer such advice because they are less aware of how difficult it is to conduct the evaluation and psychotherapy of suffering patients. They often deduce advice from laboratory studies, in which the experimenter controls the situation and many of the variables under study with a degree of power and discretion about the selection of alternatives that have little resemblance to the options that might be realistically available in a complex and crisis-ridden clinical situation. I will illustrate aspects of my own efforts to struggle with the issues and questions that are encountered. My remarks will not be comprehensive; they will focus only on certain selected concerns.

Dissociative Identity Disorder and Trauma

A curious paradox pervades the discussion of DID and trauma. On the one hand, few conditions are more strongly associated with exogenous traumatization. The vast majority of contemporary DID patients allege severe childhood mistreatment (e.g., Coons, Bowman, & Milstein, 1989; Putnam, Guroff, Silberman, Barban, & Post, 1986; Ross et al., 1991; Schultz, Braun, & Kluft, 1989). On the other hand, few groups of patients have been so consistently challenged with respect to their credibility (e.g., Frankel, 1992; Piper, 1994; Simpson, 1995). Both as individuals and as a class of patients, their efforts to have others appreciate their plights are often greeted with skepticism, if not overt disbelief.

Anecdotal reports link DID to traumatic antecedents. Schreiber's (1973) classic *Sybil* is a paradigm of such accounts. Individual reports in the lay literature were followed by occasional case studies and small series with documentation of trauma (e.g., Bliss, 1984; Bowman, Blix, & Coons, 1985; Fagan & McMahon, 1984; Kluft, 1984b).

Survey studies report this connection. Putnam et al. (1986) found that 97% of their subjects alleged childhood traumatization (see also Coons, Bowman, & Milstein, 1989; Ross, Heber, Norton, & Anderson, 1989; Ross et al., 1991; Ross et al., 1990; Ross, Norton, & Wozney, 1989; Schultz et al., 1989).

Despite these accounts, doubts of the accuracy of allegations made by DID patients were widespread, especially regarding allegations of satanic ritual abuse (which had not been inquired after in the above accounts). Controversy surrounding such reports created profound rifts within the dissociative disorders field, with many prominent figures taking strong stances against their veracity (e.g., Ganaway, 1989; Putnam, 1991), others attempting to study the clinical syndrome of patients making such reports (Young, Braun, & Sachs, 1991), and still others remaining convinced of their veracity (Freisen, 1991). A number of books have attempted to grapple responsibly with how to treat patients with such given histories (Fraser, 1997; Ross, 1995; Sackheim & Devine, 1992). At this time, it is my impression that most sophisticated practitioners in the dissociative disorders field believe that most, if not all, reports of satanic ritual abuse in transgenerational cults are not historically accurate; however, many consider it within the realm of possibility that some such circumstances may exist. Elsewhere I have discussed some of the dynamics that might make it comprehensible for a patient's defensive processes to result in his or her making such reports (Kluft, 1997b).

Furthermore, doubts were raised about the association of genuine trauma with DID by Frankel (1992), among others. Global dismissal of the allegations of trauma made by DID patients has become a staple item in the public addresses of many professionals and academics who argue against the possibility of the recovery of accurate repressed memories (e.g., McHugh, 1995). It has become commonplace to find the accounts of DID patients dismissed out of hand in academic settings.

Despite such attacks, a reasonable body of corroborative evidence indicates that accounts of trauma by DID patients should be taken seriously. In 1984, Bliss documented some allegations made by eight of nine (89%) DID patients. In 1986, Coons and Milstein were able to corroborate some abuse accounts in 85% of 20 DID patients. Hornstein and Putnam, in 1992, reported that 95% of 66 children and adolescents with dissociative disorders had documented abuse, and in 1994, Coons described corroborating the presence of abuse in 95% of a similar population of 22 young people.

Although it had become clear from these studies that DID populations as a rule have suffered genuine childhood traumatization, corroboration or disconfirmation of accounts of specific abuses given in therapy was not specifically addressed. That is, one could be reasonably assured that a DID patient actually had been abused (or suffered some other overwhelming childhood experiences [Kluft, 1984a, 1984b]), but there was not much data that spoke to whether a DID patient's own specific accounts of trauma had been confirmed. Thus, whereas traumatization could be regarded as likely, if not established, the patient's baseline auto-biographical memories of traumatization, and the patient's recovered memories of traumatization, remained to be studied. The DID patient could be assumed to have encountered misfortune, but it could not be assumed that the actual allegations made by the DID patient were accu-rate. This had profound implications for the clinical setting, in which the identity of the abuser may be crucial in the process of the therapy, and of major importance to the patient's management of his or her life, let alone regarding forensic considerations.

Recently, Kluft (1995b, 1997a, 1998, 1999c) studied the charts of 34 DID patients in treatment with him for an average of five and a half years for evidence of the confirmation or disconfirmation of abuse allegations. Only eyewitness corroborations (uncontradicted by other eyewitnesses), confessions of abusers, and legal documents such as police and court re-ports were accepted. For example, if one sibling insisted an event had oc-curred but another sibling also alleged to have been present insisted that it had not occurred, the event was not tabulated as confirmed. Under these circumstances, 19 DID patients, or 56%, had a total of 34 corrobo-rated specific instances of abuse (see Table 6.1).

Of the 19, 10 patients, or 53%, had always retained conscious aware-ness of the abuses that were later confirmed; these abuses had been re-ported, usually having been mentioned (without specific details) during the first few interviews. However, 13 of the 19, or 68%, obtained corrobo-ration of abusive events that had not been recalled prior to their treat-ments. Four patients, 21%, received confirmation of both always recalled and belatedly recovered memories. Furthermore, for three, or 9%, there were definitive disconfirmations of abuse scenarios reported sincerely as historical events. Two of the patients (67%) who had allegations dis-credited also had confirmed instances of mistreatment. Therefore, nei-ther does an instance of confirmation allow one to infer the accuracy of other allegations, nor does a disconfirmation allow one to conclude that other allegations may be discounted. The complexity that one can en-counter in a clinical setting is demonstrated in Table 6.2, which illus-trates the findings in one individual subject, a female licensed health care professional.

Table 6.1 Sources of Confirmation of Abuse Allegations for 19 DID Patients

(C = Always Recalled; R = Recovered in Therapy)	Total	C	R
Confirmation by a Sibling Who Witnessed Abuse*	12	4	8
Confirmation by One Parent of Abuse by the Other Parent	5	3	2
Confession by Abusive Parent (Deathbed or Serious Illness)	4	1	3
Confession by Abusive Parent (Other Circumstances)	3	1	2
Confirmation by Police/Court Records	3	2	1
Confirmation to Author by Abusive Therapist	2	1	1
Confirmation by a Childhood Neighbor of Witnessed Abuse	1		1
Confession by Abusive Sibling (During Terminal Illness)	1		1
Confession of Abusive Sibling (Other Circumstances)	1		1
Confirmation by Relative (Neither Parent Nor Sib)	1		1
Confirmation by Friend Who Witnessed and Interrupted Abuse Attempt	1		1
Totals	34	12	22

SOURCE: From "The confirmation and disconfirmation of memories of abuse in dissociative identity disorder patients: A naturalistic clinical study, by R. P. Kluft, 1995, *Dissociation, 8*, 253-258. Reprinted (with corrections) with permission.
NOTE: For three patients sibs confirmed both C and R material; one report unclassified because the dissociative handling of the incident involved depersonalization and derealization, but not frank amnesia.

What are the implications of this study? A total of 34 abuse scenarios were confirmed and three were disconfirmed. Therefore, the most striking finding is that most allegations of abuse were neither confirmed nor disconfirmed. These 37 abuse scenarios constitute only a small fraction of the mistreatments that these patients had alleged. Furthermore, most of the confirmations occurred rather late in these patients' therapies. Therefore, the majority of the psychotherapy of this group of traumatized patients took place under the aegis of genuine uncertainty about their pasts. In addition, this study demonstrates that materials that are not initially within a patient's awareness, but recovered in treatment, may prove to be accurate. The dissociation or repression of traumatic memories and their recovery is a genuine clinical phenomenon, discounters to the contrary.

The confirmation that pseudomemories or confabulations are a clinical phenomenon is consistent with the stances of many who disparage

Table 6.2   Confirmations and Disconfirmations in an Illustrative Case of
                  DID: A Professional Woman in her 40s

Alleged Abuse	Source of Confirmation or Disconfirmation
Father-Daughter Incest (general)	Three Sisters, One Brother, and Mother Were Aware of Incest; Father Confessed and Apologized While Terminally Ill
Father-Daughter Incest (Specific incidents)	Three Sisters, One Brother, and Mother Recall Walking in on Specific Episodes; Patient Recovered the Memories in Hypnosis and Asked Them for Confirmation
Incest-Rape by Brother	Confession by Brother Dying of Cancer Confirmed Hypnotically Recovered Memory
Abuse by Physician Mentor	No Data
Satanic Ritual Abuse	School Records Demonstrate Patient Was Not at Location of Alleged Abuses

SOURCE: From "True lies, false truths, and naturalistic clinical data: Applying clinical research findings to the false memory debate," by R. P. Kluft, 1996, paper presented at Trauma and Memory: An International Research Conference at the University of New Hampshire, Durham. Reprinted with permission.

clinicians for creating false memories. However, only in one instance was there evidence to suggest that treatment played a role in the generation of an inaccurate memory—one patient's account appears to have occurred due to contamination in a group therapy session. The other two inaccurate accounts stemmed from patients' confusion of fantasy with reality. The role of fantasy-proneness (Wilson & Barber, 1983), that is, the capacity for experiencing one's mental productions with a vividness and verisimilitude commensurate with the experience of historical events, in generating a confusion of fantasy for reality, must be considered a potent factor in the production of pseudomemories (see Belli & Loftus, 1994, and Kluft, in press, for further discussion of the distortion of reality monitoring in this context). In dealing with DID patients, the interactions of the alters in their inner worlds, their so-called third reality, may also be mistaken for events that have occurred in external reality and may be regarded by the patient and reported in therapy as historical occurrences. Therefore, in the treatment of DID patients, the clinician may encounter reports of traumatization that include accurate and inaccurate accounts and admixtures of both as well as those of uncertain veracity (Kluft, 1984b, 1995a, 1995b, 1996a, 1997a). It is likely that all forms of permutations and combinations of accuracy may occur (Kluft, 1984b). The extreme stances (a) that all memories that emerge in the course of therapy must be accorded credibility or (b) that all memories that emerge in the course of therapy must be denied credibility a priori are without scientific standing. Neither the concerns of those who feel that the clinician is obtaining a more complete portrait of the patient's trying past as more reports of trauma are recovered nor the worries of those who feel that confabulation explains the recovery of additional reports can be discounted.

The circumspect clinician must treat with the humbling awareness that he or she will probably never know the accuracy of the vast majority of the reports that are offered by the patient. We are more adept at healing our patients than we are skilled at establishing historical truth. This is especially true in the early stages of treatment, when the patient is often acutely in need of support. Most of the confirmations in this study were in the cases of patients who had been in psychotherapy for a protracted time.

Although recently figures associated with lay groups advocating for a skeptical stance toward recovered memories have suggested that therapists should investigate allegations prior to the commencement of psychotherapy, four facts make this an unrealistic consideration. First, psychotherapists do not have investigative skills, nor do they have resources with which to undertake genuine investigations. Interviewing an alleged abuser who denies abusing the patient provides no more credible data than does the patient's initial allegations of abuse. Choosing to accord credibility to one person's word against another's when neither individual's allegations are corroborated is not scientific evidence. Second, confirmations are usually made late in treatment, usually after a family constellation has changed, a consideration that will be discussed below. Therefore, one will rarely get the information one wants antecedent to the need to address the patient's therapeutic needs. If the patients in the Kluft (1995b, 1997a 1998, 1999c) studies had been treated as if they were untraumatized because there was no corroboration available at the beginning of treatment, this assumption would have been inaccurate, and resulted in a misdirected and reality-distorting treatment. Third, in almost all instances, confidentiality belongs to the patient, and neither the frame of therapy nor confidentiality can be violated without the patient's permission, which should, if given, be based on informed consent. It is most important to establish the foundation of the treatment, and to create for the patient a sense of safety within the treatment setting and process. Fourth, it is poor therapy. Few who allege abuse could accept or tolerate their therapist's immediately violating the frame of treatment or deferring their treatment needs as they try to verify their allegations with the purported abusers. Patients need support and empathy when they share their understandings of their lives, not contradiction, confrontation, and challenge. Most patients wish to avoid stressful confrontations, and have no intention of sharing their thoughts with their families. A good percentage are unsure about their allegations, and would not want to impose the unnecessary pain of raising such issues when they cannot be sure of their accuracy. The prime rule of the healing arts, from Hippocrates to the present, has been, "First, do no harm." Pressuring a patient to break the treatment frame, forfeit the confidentiality of therapy, and make public his or her most shameful and upsetting material as a precondition of dealing with a deeply personal pain is as sadistic as it is unethical. It runs the risk of destroying the therapy rather than establishing it, and can cause grievous hardship to significant others in the patient's life.

Approaching Traumatic Material in the Treatment of DID

OVERVIEW

The treatment of the traumatized is a triphasic process. Herman (1992) has described a stage of safety, followed by a stage of remembrance and mourning, and culminating in a stage of reintegration. Of course, these stages are hypothetical entities. They reflect emphases rather than absolutes, and indicate a progressive shift of focus toward new goals for the treatment as earlier goals are achieved. Safety is a preoccupation throughout the treatment, traumata and their consequences are often preoccupations from the first session to the last, and every intervention that enhances the cohesion of the patient's mentation and sense of self, and the facility of his or her affect regulation, enhances integration.

The phases of DID treatment are completely consistent with Herman's overall scheme (Kluft, 1991, 1993a). For example, using the nine-stage model of Kluft (1991), which is consistent with the frames of Braun (1986) and Putnam (1989), the phase of safety consists of (1) the establishment of the psychotherapy, (2) initial interventions, and (3) history gathering and mapping. Remembrance and mourning is the equivalent of (4) metabolism of the trauma. Reconnection consists of (5) moving toward integration/resolution, (6) integration/resolution, (7) learning new coping skills, (8) solidification of gains and working through, and (9) follow-up.

INITIAL HISTORY TAKING

Taking the history of a DID patient is a very complex process; it can appear to be "a never-ending tale." However, in general, there are three stages of history taking. First, an initial clinical history is taken, as one would for any patient. Second, in the phase of history gathering and mapping, a general history is taken from each major alter or group of alters, so that the clinician has a rough idea of what to expect in the work on traumatic material. Third, as each alter tells its own story, offers its perspectives on the given history of other alters, and abreacts or otherwise works through its traumata, still more history is given. Clearly the earliest given history is least likely to have been shaped by the therapy, but is also the least likely to be complete.

In the first stages of the DID treatment model noted above, there is a deemphasis on making inquiry about trauma except insofar as it emerges in (a) the freely offered history of the patient given through the host and the alters that spontaneously emerge in order to offer a baseline account of life during the evaluation process, and (b) the patient's responses to mild inquiries about unpleasant life experiences. I will address the subject of initial mild inquiries because many individuals recently have maintained that no such inquiry should be made, that any inquiry holds within it the potential for encouraging a confabulation.

In clinical work, one is usually, if not always, on the horns of a dilemma. Alternative approaches, each with their unique assets and liabil-
ities, compete within one's mind to inform the course of treatment. Judgments are made, each of which has its consequences. When taking a
history, one is not only trying to discover how the patient came to be who
he or she has become, but also, in the process, indicating that certain
topics are of potential importance to the therapy. One is also giving implicit permission, if not encouragement, to the patient to provide further
information, should it come to his or her attention. Frequently, I find that
my patients refer to my early inquiries at a later date, and provide additional data about either their history or symptomatology.

All too often, the price of an inadequate history is a misdirected therapy. Special considerations obtain in the treatment of the traumatized individual; it requires certain cautions and restraints. If one does not take
the trouble to inquire whether trauma may play a role in the patient's
psychopathology, false steps are not unlikely. For example, a therapist
who had made no inquiries about trauma was working with a patient
who was too ashamed about her traumatic past to volunteer it spontaneously. When the therapist commented on the early signs of her erotic
transference to him, she felt the therapist was making a statement that
she had brought the abuse she had suffered on herself because she was
so provocative and sexually preoccupied. She made a serious suicide
attempt. Another therapist who had not attempted to elicit a history of
trauma did not appreciate that her patient, a student mental health professional, was making an inappropriate choice by selecting a placement
with a program that treated a sexually traumatized population. The patient was triggered into flashbacks at every case presentation and conference. After months of agony, she revealed her plight to a supervisor and
sought to transfer to another placement, only to learn it was too late for
reassignment. She strongly considered dropping out of school. Trans-
ferring to a therapist familiar with the treatment of trauma, she was able
to obtain appropriate treatment and completed her academic year at a
painful but manageable level of discomfort.

This would argue for routine inquiry about trauma as part of every
work-up. However, the problem is not that straightforward. The therapist's inquiries are an implicit set of instructions about what is important

to discuss in therapy, about how to be a good patient. Is it possible for initial inquiries to encourage a patient to de-center his or her therapy, or even to create de novo confabulations that mirror the therapist's inquiries? It appears that the answer is a qualified but not unequivocal yes (Brown, 1995; Brown, Scheflin, & Hammond, 1997). However, even among those most skeptical about the possibility of the recovery of unavailable memories and firmly convinced of the risks of instigating confabulations, most doubt that the latter process is instigated by a mere handful of questions (e.g., Lindsay & Read, 1994). Although one cannot rule out the possibility that a rare individual will launch a confabulation at the implicit behest of a single circumspect inquiry, the circumstances that are likely to promote confabulation are much more elaborate (Brown, 1995). Should the initial screening inquiries about trauma lead to answers that beget further pointed inquiries and expressions of interest from the interviewer, or should initial negative responses be greeted by confrontation of the interviewee's assumed denial, processes are set in motion that shift the tone of routine history taking to the ambience of interrogatory suggestibility (Gudjohnsson, 1992), a set of circumstances in which differential responses are differentially reinforced, and the subject is likely to endorse as true accounts that are more shaped by the qualities of the interviewer's interventions than by the baseline configuration of the patient's autobiographical memory.

It is clear that when taking a history of abuse is done circumspectly, only a very small percentage of interviewees are at risk for responding with a confabulated answer. However, should the inquiry be sustained, pressured, and leading, the risk that false information may be generated by a larger percentage of interviewees begins to climb.

THE STANCE OF THE THERAPIST TOWARD
INITIAL ALLEGATIONS OF MISTREATMENT

One of the most difficult and often frankly impossible challenges in the management of abuse allegations surfaces early in the evaluation and treatment of the DID patient. One must offer the patient empathy, which is essential for the treatment to continue, without immediately tendering real or apparent validation of the alleged abuses, which is a course that may be fraught with peril. If the clinician appears excessively skeptical, detached, scrupulous, equivocating, and technical about responses to the patient's accounts of mistreatment, it will be virtually impossible to establish a holding environment or for the patient to feel accepted and understood. Conversely, should the therapist rapidly endorse the patient's account, and leap to make exculpatory statements on behalf of the patient and indict the alleged abusers, the therapist will have created short-term security at the cost of long-term uncertainty. There are several reasons for this. First, working out how to understand the impact of abuse is a major task of the therapy that will involve substantial effort on the part of patient and therapist alike. An early unequivocal stance by the therapist may (a) intellectualize what must be a profoundly affective experience for the patient; (b) instruct the patient how the therapist wants the patient to feel, depriving the patient of the experience of searching for and ascertaining his or her own truth; (c) imply the patient should take a hostile and rejecting stance toward an individual with whom many attachment concerns must be addressed; (d) prematurely and inappropriately disambiguate what is probably a highly complex relationship that will require years of study to understand and disentangle; (e) place the patient, who may wish to retain a relationship with the abuser, in a loyalty conflict between the therapist and the complexly perceived abuser; (f) endorse the account of one alter or group of alters despite the fact that another group may volunteer an alternate perception and understanding; (g) lend the authority of the therapist to an inaccurate allegation; and (h) make it difficult for the patient to know how to proceed should he or she begin to entertain doubts about what he or she has said.

Therefore, it is useful, without either challenging or endorsing the patient's account, to both express empathy and make some baseline inquiries that, without becoming adversarial, elicit some forms of information that may prove useful at a later time. I will empathize, "That sounds like a very upsetting experience," and inquire further "How did you understand that?" "What was that like for you?" "How did you try to cope with that?" I will ask my patient whether the information has always been retained in memory, whether it has been unavailable at times, or whether it has come to awareness more recently. If the latter, I will try to understand the context in which it came to awareness, and appreciate (without making an issue of it) any potential triggers, contaminants, or social pressures that may have played a role in the patient's new awareness. If it was established in a prior therapy, I will learn as much about this as I can, with regard to both the process and any techniques that may have played a role. I do not assume that there is any correlation between the application of a particular technique and the accuracy of the material that is retrieved, because it is my experience that reasonably accurate material may be retrieved with all sorts of techniques (Kluft, 1995b), and that social influence factors surrounding the expectations and the use of the technique are more potent concerns than the technique itself (Kluft, 1997a). I also will inquire about the form of the apparent memory, whether it was reassembled from a series of fragmentary images and sensory impressions, or returned in a more comprehensive form.

Almost invariably one encounters problems in the attempt to be cautious about validations. An occasional patient will insist on being believed from the first as a precondition of treatment. I do not hesitate to tell a patient that I cannot serve him or her well if I am told what to think. I will tell the patient that I do not insist on being trusted from the first, because only in the process of our working together can he or she get a sense of how trustworthy I am. I tell the patient that I encourage my patients to approach such matters thoughtfully, and do not insist on a leap of faith. I insist on the same prerogative for myself. I then say that I am being placed in an impossible position by such a request. I have only heard a fraction of what I will ultimately hear from many parts of the mind, and I owe it to all parts to keep an open mind until the therapy has offered all parts of the mind a chance to express their perceptions adequately. I may add words to the effect, "I'm surprised to hear you make such a request. How could you expect to be helped by a therapist who could be bullied into what he should think before he has had a chance to get to know you and your situation in a reasonable amount of depth?" I have even told an occasional patient that if he or she thinks someone can make such important decisions on the basis of someone's insistence, he or she is desperately in need of treatment, because he or she will be prone to misunderstanding and revictimization all of his or her life. In more than 20 years of taking such stances, I have had only three patients decline to work with me because of my expressed position.

Often, a patient will indicate it is difficult to express deeply personal material without advance reassurance that he or she will be believed. To this I respond with empathic agreement, and the patient almost invariably proceeds. Some patients will make sarcastic remarks to the effect, "But of course, you don't really believe me," or fret, "If you believe me . . . " Again, my first approach is empathic, that is, "It must be very uncomfortable to be taking the risk of sharing these experiences, all the while wondering what I am thinking." When a patient shoots back, "Well, wouldn't you be?" I am inclined to say "Yes, I would," if the patient's shame, pain, and embarrassment seem to prevail, and to comment on the affect if anger seems predominant. To one patient, whose attempts to persuade me to believe her reached epic proportions, I remarked that the only other people who had tried so hard to persuade me of a point of view were used car salesmen, insurance agents, and managed care reviewers. She chuckled, and got the message.

The profound effort of the patient to convince the therapist to make a determination of what is the case is a frequent problem in the treatment of the traumatized, and often is best understood as a variant of projective identification (Chu, 1994, 1998) or object-coercive persuasion (Kramer, 1983). Although I am sympathetic with the "political" stance of empowering and validating the victim and facilitating the transition from victim to survivor, I am convinced that this is a level of discourse that disempowers good therapy. It is my experience that premature validation carries some of the same risks that Freud discussed in his comments on secrets in psychotherapy (Freud, 1915-1917/1961-1963). Freud argued that a secret left unexplored sooner or later becomes that repository of most of the central dynamics of the treatment, which is defeated by the implicit agreement to leave that secret unexplored. In the matter under discussion, the unexplored assertion that is validated from the first and allowed to stand outside of the therapeutic process sooner or later becomes the focus of major difficulties in the treatment.

For example, recently a patient of mine attacked me because we had considerable treatment time spent on material she now disbelieves. I empathized with her distress. We reviewed how we had decided to explore the material despite its uncertain veracity, and discussed the pluses and minuses of what she had experienced in its exploration. We came to the conclusion that one of the main benefits had been that once the affect associated with the apparent memories had been reduced, she had become able to reassess her life history and determine, as best she could, that this material was inaccurate. She appreciated that this material had served the function of prolonging her pathological attachment to certain family members, which the therapy had succeeded in reducing considerably.

ESTABLISHING THE THERAPEUTIC ALLIANCE

The establishment of the therapeutic alliance with DID patients is a complex matter, reviewed elsewhere in detail (Kluft, 1993b). Here I want to emphasize only a small number of concerns that deal directly with the management of traumatic material. I appreciate that much of what I say may be contrary to the opinions and practices of others.

I try to teach my patients that work with traumatic material is useful as a means to an end, in the service of a therapy that has their recovery as its goal. Uncovering the past is not an objective in and of itself, and cannot be allowed to take on a life of its own that overwhelms the major objectives of the therapy. I take strong issue with patients who insist that they must know the truth in order to recover, and am willing to argue this point before going further. I point out that many major schools of therapy (e.g., cognitive-behavioral, Ericksonian hypnosis) and the healing practices of many cultures (e.g., Navaho, Korean animism) do not emphasize individual autobiographical memory and its reconstruction, and that many successful healing traditions and schools of therapy have been based on ideas that have since been disproven (Ellenberger, 1970), but have certain common factors that contribute to the restoration of morale (Frank, 1972, 1975).

I try to socialize my patients to a particular attitude toward new insights and recovered material that is consistent with psychoanalytic practice—that they should be taken to the couch, not to the bank (and most certainly not to third parties or to the courts). I encourage processing in depth and at length, and discourage taking action until the material and its implications have been studied, understood, its implications appreciated, its likely veracity assessed, and the implications of taking any actions are truly comprehended. I discourage impulsivity. I try to teach my patients that good therapy is a reasonable approximation to strict frame therapy as described in a rather rigid form by Langs (1981). I encourage containing treatment within the therapeutic dyad—we agree to "slug it out ourselves" without the intrusion of others and their agendas. Currently, I will not continue to treat a DID patient who insists on participating in incest-related or dissociative disorder support groups that are not run by trained professionals, which one patient of mine described as "self-helpless groups." It is terribly difficult to treat DID, and to do so under the scrutiny of the patient's group members and others with whom they share the details of their sessions is not tenable. I have seen too many instances of vicarious traumatization, reenactment, intrusion, and contamination in such settings. Likewise, patients who tend to process their sessions with their friends, who may also have abuse, dissociative backgrounds, or both, are in danger of complicating their recovery process. I tend to interpret such behaviors in terms of the pathological dynamics that I observe in each individual case.

I tell my patients that whenever possible, we will adhere to a "top-down" approach to traumatic material. That is, we will first deal with what is known and recalled, and allow the successful processing of the known to serve as our major avenue into what is currently unknown. The exceptions concern intrusive disruptive symptoms, which often can be explored with great benefit to the patient's comfort, and which may accelerate the therapy, but cannot be approached rapidly without the possibility of suggestion being introduced (Kluft, 1997c). In such instances, a clinical decision must be made in the context of informed consent.

There are many advantages to the top-down approach, discussed elsewhere (Kluft, 1997b), but the main concern here is facilitated management of allegations that often stir incredulity. For example, suppose a patient has always retained vague conscious memories of sexual molestation by an uncle, and abruptly presents a series of dreams in which she sees black-hooded figures around a fire, and hears the screaming of someone in terrible pain. She wonders if they indicate satanic ritual abuse. Of course, I would wonder why these dreams are emerging, and search for both dynamic information and contributions to day residue. However, I might tell the patient that I am not sure what the dreams may be telling us, but that I am confident that therapy should focus on what we know to be the case, and later, if there are further indications, we may address materials that seem so much more difficult to understand and deal with. As I have observed elsewhere (Kluft, 1997b), such material can become a coercive misdirection or diversion to the therapy. In fact, I maintain that this is one of the many unconscious or even planned motivations for its emergence in many cases.

If one suggests to the patient who raises the issue of, for example, satanic ritual abuse, that such material should be pursued at a later date, one of three courses usually follows. In the first, the more mundane material is worked through, and the patient gets well even though the more remarkable material never returns. One might conclude that the satanic material never returned because it was an artifact or happenstance that was not reinforced, and it does not represent historical reality. Conversely, however, it might be that whatever issues were raised by historical ritual abuse may have been worked through in therapy directed at derivatives of these experiences and issues. In a second scenario, after more routine material has been processed, satanic material emerges and is processed, and the patient recovers. One might infer that after dealing with less traumatic material, more genuine traumatic material came through and was processed. Conversely, one might argue that the patient's various conflicts and issues were insufficiently resolved by work with the genuine traumatic material, and that the satanic material has served as the vehicle by which they might be addressed, even though it is not historically accurate. In a third series of events, a patient might not be able to put aside concerns about additional remarkable abuse scenarios, despite the therapist's efforts and directions. One might argue that the genuine pain of these experiences was so compelling that it had to be addressed, or, on the other hand, that these productions are the product of a mind too overwhelmed to accept stabilization.

I try to make it clear to my patients that early in therapy we will contain traumatic material as best we can, and shut it down as soon as we have dealt with enough to allow the patient to decompress (Kluft, 1989, 1997c). We will also take an interpretive focus when such material emerges, trying to understand why it is coming up when it does, and what its emergence means in the overall treatment.

Regarding the techniques that will be used to explore and process traumatic memories, I try to teach my patients about memory, and about the effects on memory that certain techniques are thought capable of exerting. I offer observations on issues raised both in the scientific literature and the media. Hypnosis, drug-facilitated interviewing, eye movement desensitization and reprocessing, and the exploration of dreams receive attention. I explore their pluses and minuses, and indicate that whenever one or another appears to be appropriate to advance the therapy, we can discuss the pros and cons of proceeding. This usually occurs in the context of an overall informed consent process.

I regard the process of obtaining informed consent as an important aspect of establishing the therapeutic alliance. Here I will note only that I spend some time offering my patients a succinct and nonobsessional plain English overview of the concerns that have been raised over the impact of various techniques on memory. This usually occurs in the context of an overall informed consent process.

THE ISSUE OF INFORMED CONSENT

It is essential to appreciate that (a) it is possible for inaccurate allegations and recollections to emerge in the context of therapy, and (b) in a litigious era, often avoiding even the appearance of potential impropriety may become very important. If a patient comes to therapy with an inaccurate notion of his or her past stimulated by a provocative talk show, years later his or her attorney will leave no stone unturned to buttress the argument that the recollection in question was iatrogenic in origin, even if it was "Oprahgenic" (i.e., triggered by a talk show). Even with impeccable technique, there is no sure way to guard against the operation of the patient's expectations, the agendas of those who influence the patient, and other problematic extratherapeutic influences. The patient comes with given traits, which may include hypnotizability, dissociativity, and fantasy-proneness. Sometimes approaches that currently are derided are in fact excellent therapeutic techniques in selected circumstances. There is no ultimate treatment condom with which to practice safe psychotherapy.

The current false memory debate does not require our jettisoning the current therapeutic armamentarium or the invention of novel psycho-therapeutic processes and techniques. It does require a compassionate approach to patient care that acknowledges what Appelbaum and Gutheil (1991) have described as "the principle of informed uncertainty" and a set of interventions that they have discussed under the heading of "informed consent as a process." I do not advocate imposing a scholarly review of the current literature on the patient. That would have the potential of being pedantic, defensive, and confusing in the clinical context. It would smack of a preemptive defense against an anticipated lawsuit rather than an empathic effort to address the needs of a suffering patient. Furthermore, most of the scientific literature on memory is without demonstrated ecological validity—it may not be truly representative of what occurs in the clinical context. A more informal explanation, flexible, empathic, and tailored to the unique complaints and concerns of the individual patient, seems a more appropriate type of intervention.

All patients should be treated under the aegis of informed consent, despite the conceptual difficulties of applying this construct to psychotherapy (Appelbaum & Gutheil, 1991). Informed consent is often considered a veritable procedure, to be done at a particular time, and memorialized in some written form. Although there has been discussion of using a particular consent form for procedures that involve work with memory (Brown et al., 1995; Hammond et al., 1995), additional considerations are relevant. Drawing on Appelbaum and Gutheil (1991), first, when one is using a written form, it may be understood that it covers only what it specifically enumerates. Psychotherapy is such a diverse process that no form could address all conceivable possibilities. Second, it is very important to appreciate that patients rarely comprehend and retain all of the instructions they are given. Can we truly say that the therapist's efforts to educate the patient for today's informed consent will be powerful determinants of decisions made by the patient three or four months or years hence? Third, the perceived meanings and consequences to the patient of procedures discussed for the purpose of obtaining informed consent may be different at different points in time. For example, if informed consent for the use of hypnosis for some purpose is

obtained before the issue of the possibility of abuse has arisen, the patient's attitudes, expectations, and emotions may be relatively neutral,
or positive toward hypnosis due to the hope of some relief of suffering or
gaining some crucial understanding. It cannot be assumed that the same
will be the case once abuse is under discussion, with potentially profound implications for important relationships, for one's sense of one's
self, one's sense of safety in the world, and the possibility of uncovering
material that may induce a delayed posttraumatic stress disorder
and/or related phenomena. It will be advisable to revisit the issue of informed consent again, with additional considerations.

For these and other reasons, I endorse the concept of informed consent as a process (Appelbaum & Gutheil, 1991). In my own practice I
have begun to use an informal outline of 12 steps, considerations, or both
(Table 6.3) when dealing with traumatic material or explorations that
may discover traumatic materials (Kluft, 1994b).

The most important step is the last, "Repeat p.r.n." I regard the informed consent process as coextensive with the therapy itself. At times
my "refresher course" may be no more extensive than a brief reminder:
"Remember, we can't take what we come up with to the bank. We take it
to the microscope of therapy." At times I feel a need to briefly review
many, if not all, of these steps. I want my patient and me to be partners in
a health-promoting discovery and exploration, not members of a lynch
mob or a dedicated group of defenders or apologists.

The therapist who treats trauma and deals with allegations of trauma
of uncertain veracity must bear in mind that the current furor over the
accuracy of memory has, with few exceptions (e.g., Finkelhor, 1987),
failed to explore the deeper meanings of a patient's making an inaccurate allegation. Ganaway (1989, 1994), whether one agrees with his formulations or finds them less than helpful, is to be congratulated for insisting on exploring the dynamic implications of memories that may not
be accurate. Unfortunately, his a priori assumptions demonstrate ample
confirmatory bias, and his arguments illustrate motivated skepticism.
That is, he finds what he wants to find in patients' productions and is
more critical of material that opposes his point of view than he is of material that appears consistent with his stance. This makes the endorsement
of his specific formulations a leap of faith, unlikely to be taken by those

Table 6.3

1. Elicit and correct erroneous expectations and beliefs

2. Determine whether the planned interventions will impede other agendas of the patient

3. Review current knowledge and media representations with the patient

4. Review the implications of the above for therapy

5. Explain that recovery does not require "the truth"

6. Outline the potential benefits of the proposed intervention or treatment

7. Explain the complexity of potential contaminants

8. Request the patient to verbalize his/her understanding

9. Solicit and answer the patient's questions

10. Document informed consent

11. Record if advisable

12. Repeat p.r.n.

who do not accept those assumptions from the first. Nothwithstanding these shortcomings, I encourage readers to study their efforts to come to grips with this thorny subject. Elsewhere I have discussed the limited subject of what would motivate patients to report satanic ritual abuse experiences (Kluft, 1997b).

It is essential to appreciate that any allegation, whether accurate or erroneous, may serve defensive functions for a particular patient at a particular moment in time. Unless this aspect of an allegation is borne in mind from the first by the therapist, he or she may unwittingly reinforce belief in an allegation until it becomes a fact for the patient, regardless of its veracity.

An aspect of informed consent often overlooked in the current climate relates to item 6 in Table 6.3. In what can become a mad dash to self-exculpation, it is easy to forget what brought the patient to treatment in the first place. I try to explain the potential benefits of every intervention.

My own approach is modeled on verbalizations I have heard Thomas Gutheil, M.D., use in workshop settings, examples of which are presented in Appelbaum and Gutheil (1991). Our "conversation" may consist of a number of observations over a series of sessions. I try to convey the difference between scientific concepts of truth, legal concepts of truth, and clinical concepts of truth. I try to convey to the patient that what emerges in the course of therapy is to be considered food for thought in the therapy, not pure historical reality on which one should feel entitled or compelled to act. Limitations of space preclude my elaboration on these points, but the flavor of what I might say is conveyed in the brief verbalizations below (which also appear in approximately the same form in Kluft, 1997b, and are based on verbalizations taught by Thomas Gutheil in the context of discussing medications and their side effects).

> I wish I could assure you that your flashbacks, dreams, and symptoms add up to certainty about what actually happened to you, but the truth of the matter is that we can't take that leap and count these things as definitive proof. We'll have to explore them in connection with everything else we learn together in order to sort out what they mean.

> I appreciate how strongly you are driven to find and know the truth about what happened to you, and together we'll do our best to figure that out as best we can. But I want you to know from the first that psychotherapy is a lot better at healing you and figuring out how your mind understands the world than it is at recovering your actual history. Whatever comes up we'll explore at length and in depth. We'll have to fight the tendency to jump to premature conclusions about what actually happened to you.

> When we use hypnosis to explore this block in your memory, we will be looking for hypotheses for further exploration. If we find something, whatever we find will be the starting point for more ongoing work—not the end of a quest or search. The nature of your hypnotic experience may give whatever we come up with the personal experience that it is very real. That and the fact you may visualize it can make it seem like what you have actually experienced and seen it, but that can be real deceptive. We tend to think that if we see it has to have occurred. To demonstrate that, I'll give you the experience of seeing under hypnosis something that has not occurred, so you can understand what I mean. Remember, we're looking for hypotheses. Moses didn't come down the mountain with what you may find in hypnosis engraved on a slab of stone, but it sure can feel that way.

> I appreciate that you want to confront your uncle about what you have come to believe occurred to you, and maybe even to sue him, and I understand that you are being encouraged to do so by some well-meaning friends and relatives who have your best interests at heart, and believe that this will empower you and help you recover more rapidly. I know you hope he will confess and apologize. But please consider this. What you have remembered may or may not be accurate. Only external confirmation

can demonstrate its accuracy beyond a doubt, and abusers are not likely to confess. What may help you recover in our work together is not necessarily acceptable as scientific or legal proof. I can't stand up in court and say your recollections are accurate, only that they are possible and that work with them has helped you recover from your problems and symptoms. Confrontations like the one you propose are unlikely to bring about what you want. Even if you feel stronger as a result, all sorts of hell may break loose. Do a real cost-benefit analysis. You must think this through and consider the possible consequences. They include your being rejected and repudiated, not only by those you dislike, but those with whom you want to maintain a relationship. Others may be hurt, whether you intend this or not. Your uncle may or may not be guilty, but living without the confrontation is one hell of a lot easier than making the confrontation and one day realizing it may have been in error. Bear in mind that such confrontations and lawsuits may slow down your recovery for years, and that our court system, which is designed to protect the rights of the accused, is about as friendly to accusations such as yours as a meat grinder. I am not saying that it is fair that your uncle may "get away" with what you think he did to you. But please weigh the whole situation carefully. I advise you to study this matter at length and depth before taking any irretrievable step. The best revenge is living well.

ISSUES RELATING TO TRAUMATIC MEMORY IN THE PROCESS OF THE THERAPY OF DID

As the treatment of DID continues stage by stage, each provides new concerns in the management of traumatic memories. Most of the issues relevant to the management of this material in the first two stages—establishing the therapy and initial interventions—have been discussed above. Here I will note only a few matters from early in the treatment, and then deal with each subsequent stage separately.

EARLY CONCERNS

One of the most thorny difficulties early in the treatment of DID is the tension between allowing the free and open-ended discussion of trauma prior to any interventions, which is optimal for the taking of an untainted history, and the necessity to preclude the patient's becoming overwhelmed by the premature discovery and exploration of traumatic material. In the clinical setting, the principle primum non nocere, or, "first, do no harm," almost invariably must prevail. Fine (1991) states this strongly when she describes the early stages of treatment as a phase of "suppression" or "suppression of affect." Clinical experience indicates that containment must be prioritized over extensive exploration unless forensic considerations preclude the use of techniques, such as hypnosis, that may be optimal to assure the patient's stability (Kluft, 1993a, 1993b).

Furthermore, at this stage, the alters' robust senses of separateness have not yet been eroded. One is confronted with "multiple reality disorder" as the alters understand and explain their experiences from different assumptions, different databases, and with different cognitive operations (Kluft, 1991, 1996a, in press; see also Fine, 1988, 1991, 1993). As a result, if one tries to bring the alters' accounts into accord prematurely, one often initiates a period of internal warfare replete with self-injury, intensification of resistance, and the alters' coercing one another to endorse versions of reality that are congenial to the coercers. In short, the pursuit of "truth" becomes dangerous, and introduces pressures that might distort the alters' baseline accounts.

HISTORY GATHERING AND MAPPING

In this phase, the patient has mastered the capacity to achieve self-stabilization in the face of mild to moderate distress. Now it becomes useful to get "the lay of the land" in order to better conduct the remainder of the treatment. While the clinician most concerned about memory distortion might want to proceed without intrusive inquiry and allow materials to emerge spontaneously, exposed to minimal opportunity for confabulation, the clinician concerned about the patient's safety and comfort might prefer to gain a perspective that would minimize the likelihood that the patient will decompensate and suffer unduly.

If one simply moves toward dealing with what has been presented, the processing of one trauma in one alter may precipitate the reliving of analogous traumatic materials by many alters, leaving the patient in disarray, with potential for decompensation, inability to function, and self-harm or suicide. If one takes the time to identify as many alters as possible and to take some history from each, one may be able to make interventions that isolate most of the alters from the alter with which trauma work is being done (e.g., Fine, 1991, 1993; Kluft, 1988, 1994a, 1996a). This is an approach associated with far fewer crises. A serendipitous informal study of this issue occurred in the early days of EMDR (Eye Movement Desensitization and Reprocessing). Clinicians unaware that they were dealing with DID patients would begin work with traumatic material, only to find the patients spontaneously switching, becoming very agitated, and not infrequently decompensating. Faced with many such experiences, EMDR training now emphasizes the importance of identifying dissociative patients before beginning treatment and making strenuous efforts to support them through the process (Shapiro, 1995; see also Kluft, 1999a).

When taking histories from alters in this stage, one is not pressing for details but for themes, and one is eager to desist the moment it appears that the patient is becoming overwhelmed or that other alters are determined to punish the alter that is making revelations. Therefore, often the history of alter A is taken from an alter that is coconscious with A but does not experience its affect. If alter B threatens alter A for making a revelation, inquiry switches to alter B, who usually will ultimately give the outline of alter A's story as it explains why it should not be told or believed. This usually sidesteps the inner warfare.

One should come out of this stage with a rough idea about the alter system and the concerns, both past and current, of each alter or group of alters. It makes a big difference whether pursuing a particular issue will mobilize one alter or one dozen, and often such knowledge is instrumental in treatment planning.

Only if the patient can apply the lessons of the first two stages of the therapy to this third stage is it safe to continue to trauma work. Otherwise, the treatment should remain primarily supportive (Kluft, 1997c).

METABOLISM OF TRAUMA

In this stage, alters will tell and abreact or otherwise process their traumatic experiences. However this is pursued, the therapy must prioritize the resolution of the impact of the trauma rather than the preservation of memory in its pristine form. As noted earlier, traumatic material is addressed and processed in the service of recovery, and the prospect of recovery cannot be sacrificed to theoretical concerns. The patient enters this stage already well informed about the vicissitudes of memory, but will have to be reminded from time to time, especially when impelled to take precipitous action on what has been revealed.

A major concern is that traumatic memory, whether one wishes to argue for its being primarily recovered in its original form or reconstructive, often, if not usually, appears to have elements of both. Even when the major theme of a traumatic scenario seems well established in fact, its exposition in a particular abreactive account may well contain elements that are confabulated to fill in gaps and details. This is a time for caution, because the intense affect, undoubted (and undoubting) sincerity, and the vivid detail of many accounts are likely to convince the credulous that the events in question must have occurred, and are likely to convince the skeptical that the events must have been confabulated. In fact, the clinical research evidence presented earlier casts severe doubt on both polar stances.

In the course of working through traumatic material and processing it, the material may undergo a series of transitions. More incidents may emerge. Incidents experienced piecemeal by several alters may be reassembled because work with one alter spills into work with another. New understandings may be reached, and subsequent materials may bear their imprints. In short, myriad processes are mobilized that may result in changes as the material is retrieved serially for work in session after session. In many treatments, the impact of such processes is barely perceptible; in others, it is dramatic and impressive.

Another aspect of this stage of therapy is the stance taken toward memory materials by the therapist. Several may be identified, none of which should be understood as rigorously established or mutually exclusive. Many therapists allow the memories to speak for themselves, and comment on them as they would any other important material.

This is typical of dynamically oriented therapists. Others actively try to use the material to help the patient correct misperceptions about the patient's self and significant others. This is characteristic of cognitively oriented therapists. Another group might try to modify the memories to make them easier to live with, or to facilitate an experience of mastery under circumstances under which the patient felt helpless and unable to control what occurred. Such therapists might actively try to change a given memory, to encourage the imagination of scenarios in which more favorable outcomes occurred, or both.

My own practice is to follow the patient's lead and the patient's need. Usually, I start with a dynamic perspective, and move toward cognitive interventions if my patients do not demonstrate spontaneous movement toward a more appropriate perspective on what befell them. I make no active efforts to modify memory, but I will use techniques to enhance mastery, including replaying the scenario with a more favorable ending, or as it might have transpired if the patient encountered such a potential risk with assistance, with full adult capacities, or both. My limiting case in this latter instance is the concept of ecological validity as it is discussed in the EMDR literature (Shapiro, 1995). Initially, I try to add nothing to the patient's processing of the material that is not within the realm of the possible, although after the processing itself, I may use clearly fantasy-based scenarios to restore my patients' injured sense of self and to clear up the sequelae of "body memories" (e.g., Kluft, 1994a).

The management of somatic "body memories" and apparent relivings of physical aspects of trauma is an area in which the most effective clinical techniques perforce involve the risk of suggesting confabulations, and the anticipated reward for the patient's production and processing of a "memory" is a highly desired symptomatic relief. Although body memory in this context is understood to be a metaphor (for another perspective, see van der Kolk, 1994), the essential idea is that physical discomforts may constitute a signifier of a flashback or memory that is not necessarily consciously available in the alter present in session. The signifier is understood to be, in the framework of Braun's (1988) BASK (behavior, affect, sensation, knowledge) model of dissociation, an intrusion of the sensations associated with a trauma.

The exploration of such sensations is based on the assumption that it is possible that a hidden traumatic event is manifesting itself through the sensations, which appear to be unexplained orphan symptoms, perhaps signifying a medical problem. For example, in the 1970s, I saw a patient on a surgical floor in my role as consultation-liaison psychiatrist. She complained of a mass in her anus that moved and caused her great pain. No mass was found. I discovered the patient had DID and took her into treatment. Months later, I explored the symptom with hypnosis, and the patient, in an alter unknown to me, began to abreact an experience of anal rape. The abreaction led to the integration of that alter, and the cessation of the symptom. Although the accuracy of the particular incident that was abreacted is uncertain, this patient's childhood sexual abuse was both documented by social service records and acknowledged by her prostitute mother.

The clinician must make a careful clinically based determination as to whether the benefits of achieving the rapid resolution of a symptom outweigh the drawbacks associated with the possibility that the patient may come up with an inaccurate recollection. Usually by the time such issues arise in treatment, the therapist and patient have reached an understanding about the vicissitudes of memory and an agreement with regard to the prioritization of recovery over retaining a theoretically "pristine" autobiographic recollection.

The sense of a continuity of autobiographic memory is an essential aspect of achieving a coherent sense of self. Therefore, in the psychotherapy of the DID patient, or any patient, it may be necessary to give priority to attaining such an outcome, and accept that historical memory may suffer some inevitable rearrangement in this process.

MOVING TOWARD INTEGRATION/RESOLUTION

As alters share more and more, with mutual identification, empathy, and cooperation, they move toward resolution, a more effective functioning of the alter system, and, in more successfully treated cases, on to integration, the undoing of the dissociative defenses and the blending of the alter personalities. These processes are discussed at length elsewhere (Kluft, 1993a). Relevant to memory is that as alters come together in the integration process, their different memories become condensed and blended into a more or less coherent narrative personal truth (see Spence, 1982). Some degree of editing and secondary revision is virtually inevitable. For example, in the integration of three alters, one of which experienced a trauma, one of which identified with the traumatizer, and one of which had no recollection of the event, three very disparate versions of events must become reconciled and their contradictions addressed.

When resolution is sought, but integration is not, a decision must be made by the alters in their cooperation as to what version of autobiographical memory will become the patient's overall working memory, and will guide decision making. For example, which of the three versions of memory in the above example will guide interactions with the individual in question? As certain versions are de facto endorsed repeatedly, and others disregarded, it is quite possible that memory will be affected.

INTEGRATION/RESOLUTION

In this stage, the tentative conclusions of the prior stage are formalized by the mental restructuring that is understood to occur, especially if the outcome is integration. It is not uncommon for discordant percepts to be redissociated, and result in the later failure of the apparent integration (Kluft, 1986). Many patients integrate their separate selves before they integrate the memories associated with those separate selves. Often when two alters join, the fused alter holds in memory two rather than one version of many historical events. Periods of uncertainty may occur, and impulsive attempts to resolve the confusion of having alternative versions of important events in mind are not infrequent. Some fluctuations of the patient's perceptions of his or her past may occur.

LEARNING NEW COPING SKILLS

Although this phase is mostly concerned with learning to live with "single personality disorder" (Kluft, 1988b), it often has a major impact on the patient's ultimate understanding of his or her autobiographic memory. As patients focus on their residual problems and interpersonal difficulties, they often deduce from them which version of historical events should be accorded credibility. A version that ostensibly explains why they have the difficulties that they do is likely to be endorsed more readily by patient and therapist alike. For example, a patient's alters, now integrated, had differed widely over which understanding of her father's behavior was accurate. He was never accused of abusive behavior. For some, he was perfect; for others, he was tyrannical, demanding, demeaning, and impossible to please. As a unified person, she was torn

between these two versions of her father. However, when she appreciated that she had experienced herself as terrified of male authority figures, and had been certain that they would be critical of her and humili-
ate her, she concluded that her own behavior and feelings were
consistent with the more negative view of her father. Over a period of
weeks, she came to believe that her father was indeed very difficult, and
that she had defended herself against dealing with this by idealizing
him. Gradually, her accounts of her father became consistently apprecia-
tive of his less-than-perfect manner toward her.

SOLIDIFICATION OF GAINS
AND WORKING THROUGH

Not uncommonly, in this phase, the issues dealt with earlier in the
therapy are revisited in the transference. However, the transference by
now has undergone some degree of modification as discordant percepts
have come together in the course of the treatment. What is projected on
the therapist is likely to be a reconstructed percept. The reconstruction of
the past from the transference, however helpful in the healing of the
patient, is undertaken with the interpretation of projections that themselves are, to a certain degree at this point in treatment, an outcome of the
therapeutic process as well as a representation of the patient's intra-
psychic concerns. Consequently, understandings and constructions
reached at this stage of the treatment are often drawn from derivatives
that are some distance from the original material and may have been
subject to distortion. Although it is my clinical experience that what
emerges this late in the treatment has excellent verisimilitude when external corroboration is possible, because most material is neither confirmed nor disconfirmed, all possibilities, including that of pseudomemory, remain open.

FOLLOW-UP

During this final phase of treatment, it is not uncommon for memories
that are subjectively understood to have been dissociated, but not
"filed" in an alter, to emerge gradually and require attention. It is my experience that the memories that come up this late often are more useful

in helping patients grasp the complexity of their object relationships with those who are alleged to have abused them than they are likely to yield major new historical information. The recovered and recovering DID patient will be involved in a lifelong process of coming to grips with what has occurred and its ramifications throughout all aspects of his or her life. Memories will be rethought continuously by some, and intermittently by others. By this time, there are relatively few concerns about the historical accuracy of memory for most patients, and memory is understood mostly in terms of the light it casts on contemporary concerns and issues.

Remarks on Particular Interventions

It has been intriguing to follow current attacks on the credibility of material that is recovered with the use of more active approaches, such as hypnosis or drug-facilitated interviews. Here I will focus on hypnosis as an exemplar. This focus on hypnosis becomes extremely relevant when it is appreciated that DID patients are highly hypnotizable (Frischholz, Lipman, Braun, & Sachs, 1992) and that even if heterohypnosis is omitted, spontaneous trance and autohypnosis are sure to make their appearance in the course of the treatment of DID. Elsewhere I have reviewed this subject in-depth (Kluft, 1997a). Here I will make only some general remarks. I intend for my remarks on hypnosis to be understood as a commentary on interpersonal influence, of which hypnosis is only one variety.

Hypnosis is often discussed as if it were a particular type of intervention or treatment. In fact, hypnosis is very difficult to define, and major debates surround its conceptualization. Lynn and Rhue (1991) have recently reviewed most major theories. Hypnosis is not a uniform phenomenon. Two subjects with the same degree of hypnotizability may have very different hypnotic talents, some of which are far more relevant than others to the vicissitudes of memory. Furthermore, there is consensus that hypnosis is a facilitator of treatment rather than a treatment in and of itself. In the service of suggestive inquiries it facilitates them, but in the service of permissive inquiries it facilitates a rather different sort of intervention.

Consequently, many modern comments and cautions about hypnosis are discussing a caricatured straw man version of hypnosis that bears only a tangential relationship to hypnosis as it is understood at a more sophisticated level. Even the research findings that are cited to illustrate the likelihood of hypnosis creating pseudomemories must be reexamined and reevaluated. Much of what has been attributed to hypnosis is more correlated with the hypnotizability of the subject and the demand characteristics of the situation. McConkey (1992) found that once these other factors were accounted for, the degree of distortion was not affected by the induction of hypnosis.

Therefore, the fact that hypnosis can be associated with memory distortion, even if the relevant factors do not include the hypnosis itself, has been misrepresented to the extent that what is possible (although not due to hypnosis itself) is represented as characteristic of hypnosis itself, and such distortion is often represented as if it were the likely, if not the inevitable, outcome of its use. On this basis, its exclusion from trauma work has been recommended. Inappropriate interpersonal influence is associated with an increased likelihood of pseudomemories, and often attributed to hypnosis.

In this context we will return to the naturalistic study of the confirmation and disconfirmation of the trauma memories of DID patients alluded to earlier (Kluft, 1995b). Of the 13 patients who recovered 22 memories in treatment that later were confirmed by external corroboration, 19 of these memories (86%) were recovered with the facilitating help of hypnosis. The remainder emerged in the course of psychoanalytic psychotherapy or EMDR. None of the three memories that were disconfirmed had been discovered with hypnosis. In fact, all had been represented as consciously available material.

This finding, although far from conclusive, certainly casts doubt on the notion that hypnosis has no place in the treatment of the traumatized due to its tendency to create pseudomemories. When used gently and circumspectly, without the exertion of either undue influences, suggestions, or both, it may have a very legitimate role in work with the traumatized. It is important to appreciate that most stereotypic notions about the potential dangers of hypnosis implicitly assume that highly suggestive inquiries have been made under its aegis. If a person is placed in a trance and subjected to highly leading interrogatories, mishap is not un-likely, but the percentage of false materials one may encounter remains unknown. If a person is placed in a trance and subjected to highly per-missive inquiries, mishap is not likely, but the percentage of true and false materials one may encounter remains unknown.

For example, if a person is placed in a trance and asked to explore a time for which there is amnesia, and is exposed to verbalizations such as, "Who is the man there? Is it your uncle? Is he wearing clothes?" it is not inconceivable that this sequence might cause the visualization of a man, who would then take on the appearance of the uncle, and finally, be seen as naked. This percept, visualized, might hoodwink the mind's reality monitoring capacities, and be registered inaccurately as a historical rec-ollection. A pseudomemory might be the result.

Contrast this to the situation that prevails should a person be placed in a trance and asked to explore a time for which there is amnesia, and be exposed to verbalizations such as, "Please share whatever you observe." "Please tell me if you are able to identify the person you have observed." "Please indicate if there is anything more that you observe." Under these circumstances there are far fewer pressures toward pseudomemory for-mation. This latter type of inquiry is more characteristic of my clinical practice, and was used with those patients whose recovered memories were confirmed. Transcripts indicate that my most frequent verbaliza-tion I made to my patients was, "Whatever's there," that is, declining to lead. Usually, that was the only verbalization I made until the memory had been shared. Hopefully, this illustration may demonstrate why it is not inconceivable that accurate memories can be found with hypnosis. I note that leading questions do not inevitably lead to confabulation, and that nonleading questions do not guarantee uncontaminated recollec-tions. For example, the patient may come to the session with unappreci-ated and unvoiced expectations that dictate what will be found far more than the therapist's interventions.

Concluding Remarks

The treatment of the traumatized is a challenging endeavor, and work with DID patients is one of the most demanding aspects of trauma work.

Although it is always tempting to consider therapeutic approaches that do not address the traumatic pasts of DID patients—that offer the hope of bypassing the pain and tumult of working with difficult material and the distress that often attends this effort—the literature offers little justification for such a strategy. Although DID patients can improve considerably with adaptationalist strategies, and can be helped by treatments that reconfigure the alter system toward smoother function and better adaptation, they do not resolve the DID itself. The only therapies that succeed in achieving this objective are those that engage and resolve the traumatic material, regardless of its historical veracity (Kluft, 1996a). These are the strategic integrationalist and the tactical integrationalist perspectives, or an integration-oriented application of ego-state therapy, which approach the painful material via the undoing of defenses and the application of adroit techniques of intervention, respectively (Kluft, 1993a, 1999b).

Because it is not within our capacity to heal the DID patient to the point of integration without venturing into the uncertain waters of autobiographical memory, it is essential to do so in an informed, circumspect, and compassionate manner. We must not be frightened away from good clinical work by the stormy debates that rage around many of the most central issues of our field. If we wait until they are resolved beyond all dispute, we may wait forever, or at least beyond the likely spans of our own lives, let alone beyond the urgent clinical needs of our patients. In the absence of definitive answers, we must do the best we can, using available knowledge with an awareness of its limitations. We cannot allow the perfect to become the enemy of the good, and timorously abandon the legitimate clinical needs of a generation of trauma patients.

References

Appelbaum, P. S., & Gutheil, T. G. (1991). *Clinical handbook of psychiatry and the law* (2nd ed.). Baltimore: Williams & Wilkins.

Belli, R. F., & Loftus, E. F. (1994). Recovered memories of childhood abuse: A source monitoring perspective. In S. J. Lynn & J. W. Rhue (Eds.), *Dissociation: Clinical and theoretical perspectives* (pp. 415-433). New York: Guilford.

Bliss, E. L. (1984). Spontaneous self-hypnosis in multiple personality disorder. *Psychiatric Clinics of North America, 7,* 135-148.

Bowman, E. L., Blix, S., & Coons, P. M. (1985). Multiple personality in adolescence: Relationship to incestual abuse. *Journal of the American Academy of Child Psychiatry, 24,* 109-114.

Braun, B. G. (Ed.). (1986). *Treatment of multiple personality disorder.* Washington, DC: American Psychiatric Press.

Braun, B. G. (1988). The BASK (behavior, affect, sensation, knowledge) model of dissociation. *Dissociation, 1*(1), 4-23.

Brown, D. (1995). Pseudomemories, the standard of science, and the standard of care in trauma treatment. *American Journal of Clinical Hypnosis, 37,* 1-24.

Brown, D., Scheflin, A., & Hammond, D. C. (1997). *Memory, trauma treatment, and the law.* New York: Norton.

Ceci, S. J., & Bruck, M. (1993). Suggestibility of the child witness: A historical review and synthesis. *Psychological Bulletin, 113,* 403-439.

Chu, J. (1994, June). *Pitfalls in the treatment of trauma victims.* Workshop at the Eastern Regional Conference on Trauma and Dissociation, Alexandria, VA.

Chu, J. (1998). *Rebuilding shattered lives.* New York: Wiley.

Coons, P. M. (1994). Confirmation of childhood abuse in childhood and adolescent cases of multiple personality disorder and dissociative disorder not otherwise specified. *Journal of Nervous and Mental Disease, 182,* 462-464.

Coons, P. M., Bowman, E. S., & Milstein, V. (1989). Multiple personality disorder: A clinical investigation of 50 cases. *Journal of Nervous and Mental Disease, 176,* 519-527.

Coons, P. M., & Milstein, V. (1986). Psychosexual disturbances in multiple personality: Characteristics, etiology, and treatment. *Journal of Clinical Psychiatry, 47,* 106-110.

Ellenberger, H. (1970). *The discovery of the unconscious.* New York: Basic Books.

Fagan, J., & McMahon, P. P. (1984). Incipient multiple personality in children: Four cases. *Journal of Nervous and Mental Disease, 172,* 26-36.

Fine, C. G. (1988). Thoughts on the cognitive perceptual substrates of multiple personality disorder. *Dissociation, 1*(4), 5-10.

Fine, C. G. (1991). Treatment stabilization and crisis prevention: Pacing the therapy of the multiple personality disorder patient. *Psychiatric Clinics of North America, 14,* 661-676.

Fine, C. G. (1993). A tactical integrationist perspective on the treatment of multiple personality disorder. In R. P. Kluft & C. G. Fine (Eds.), *Clinical perspectives on multiple personality disorder* (pp. 135-154). Washington, DC: American Psychiatric Press.

Finkelhor, D. (1987). The sexual abuse of children: Current research reviewed. *Psychiatric Annals, 17,* 233-241.

Frank, J. D. (1972). *Persuasion and healing: A comparative study of psychopathology* (2nd ed.). Baltimore: Johns Hopkins University Press.

Frank, J. D. (1975). General psychotherapy: The restoration of morale. In D. X. Freedman & J. E. Dryud (Eds.), *American handbook of psychiatry* (2nd ed., Vol. 5, pp. 117-132). New York: Basic Books.

Frankel, F. H. (1992). Adult reconstruction of childhood events in the multiple personality disorder literature. *American Journal of Psychiatry, 150,* 954-958.

Fraser, G. A. (Ed.). (1997). *The phenomenon of ritualized abuse.* Washington, DC: American Psychiatric Press.

Freisen, J. G. (1991). *Uncovering the mystery of MPD.* San Bernardino, CA: Here's Life Publishers.

Freud, S. (1961, 1963). Introductory lectures on psycho-analysis (Parts 1-3). In J. Strachey (Ed. and Trans.), *The standard edition of the complete psychological works of Sigmund Freud* (Vols. 15 & 16). London: Hogarth Press. (Original work published 1915-1917)

Frischholz, E. J., Lipman, L. S., Braun, B. G., & Sachs, R. G. (1992). Psychopathology, hypnotizability, and dissociation. *American Journal of Psychiatry, 149*, 1521-1525.

Ganaway, G. K. (1989). Historical truth versus narrative truth: Clarifying the role of exogenous trauma in the etiology of multiple personality and its variants. *Dissociation, 2*, 205-220.

Ganaway, G. K. (1994). Hypnosis, childhood trauma, and dissociative identity disorder: Toward an integrative theory. *International Journal of Clinical and Experimental Hypnosis, 43*, 127-144.

Gudjohnsson, G. H. (1992). *The psychology of interrogations, confessions and testimony.* New York: John Wiley.

Hammond, D. C., Garver, R. B., Mutter, C. B., Crasilneck, H. B., Frischholz, E., Gravitz, M. A., Hibler, N. S., Olson, J., Scheflin, A., Spiegel, H., & Wester, W. (1995). *Clinical hypnosis and memory: Guidelines for clinicians and for forensic hypnosis.* Chicago: American Society of Clinical Hypnosis Press.

Herman, J. L. (1992). *Trauma and recovery.* Cambridge, MA: Harvard University Press.

Hornstein, N. L., & Putnam, F. W. (1992). Clinical phenomenology of child and adolescent multiple personality disorder. *Journal of the American Academy of Child and Adolescent Psychiatry, 31*, 1055-1077.

Kluft, R. P. (1984a). Treatment of multiple personality disorder. *Psychiatric Clinics of North America, 7*, 9-29.

Kluft, R. P. (1984b). Multiple personality in childhood. *Psychiatric Clinics of North America, 7*, 121-134.

Kluft, R. P. (1986). Personality unification in multiple personality disorder: A follow-up study. In B. G. Braun (Ed.), *Treatment of multiple personality disorder* (pp. 29-60). Washington, DC: American Psychiatric Press.

Kluft, R. P. (1988a). On treating the older patient with multiple personality disorder: "Race against time" or "make haste slowly"? *American Journal of Clinical Hypnosis, 30*, 257-266.

Kluft, R. P. (1988b). The postunification treatment of multiple personality disorder: First findings. *American Journal of Psychotherapy, 42*, 212-228.

Kluft, R. P. (1989). Playing for time: Temporizing techniques in the treatment of multiple personality disorder. *American Journal of Clinical Hypnosis, 32*.

Kluft, R. P. (1991). Multiple personality disorder. In A. Tasman & S. M. Goldfinger (Eds.), *American Psychiatric Press review of psychiatry* (Vol. 10, pp. 161-188). Washington, DC: American Psychiatric Press.

Kluft, R. P. (1993a). The treatment of dissociative disorder patients: An overview of discoveries, successes, and failures. *Dissociation, 6*, 87-101.

Kluft, R. P. (1993b). The initial stages of psychotherapy in the treatment of multiple personality disorder patients. *Dissociation, 6*, 145-161.

Kluft, R. P. (1994a). Applications of hypnotic interventions. *Hypnos, 21*, 205-223.

Kluft, R. P. (1994b, March). *Informed consent in the treatment of dissociative identity disorder.* Paper presented at the Scientific Sessions of the American Society of Clinical Hypnosis, Philadelphia, PA.

Kluft, R. P. (1995a). Current controversies surrounding multiple personality disorder. In L. Cohen, L. Uyehara, & M. Elin (Eds.), *Dissociative identity disorder* (pp. 347-377). Northvale, NJ: Jason Aronson.

Kluft, R. P. (1995b). The confirmation and disconfirmation of memories of abuse in dissociative identity disorder patients: A naturalistic clinical study. *Dissociation, 8,* 253-258.

Kluft, R. P. (1996a). Treating the traumatic memories of patients with dissociative identity disorder. *American Journal of Psychiatry, 153,* 103-110 (Festschrift Supplement).

Kluft, R. P. (1996b, July). *True lies, false truths, and naturalistic clinical data: Applying clinical research findings to the false memory debate.* Paper presented at Trauma and Memory: An International Research Conference at the University of New Hampshire, Durham.

Kluft, R. P. (1997a). The argument for the reality of the delayed recall of trauma. In P. S. Appelbaum, L. Uyehara, & M. Elin (Eds.), *Trauma and memory: Clinical and legal controversies* (pp. 25-57). Northvale, NJ: Jason Aronson.

Kluft, R. P. (1997b). An overview of the treatment of patients alleging that they have suffered ritualized or sadistic abuse. In G. A. Fraser (Ed.), *The phenomenon of ritualized abuse* (pp. 31-64). Washington, DC: American Psychiatric Press.

Kluft, R. P. (1997c). Treatment of traumatic memories: Always? never? sometimes? now? later? *Dissociation, 10,* 80-90.

Kluft, R. P. (1998). Reflections on the traumatic memories of dissociative identity disorder patients. In S. J. Lynn & K. McConkey (Eds.), *Truth in memory* (pp. 304-322). New York: Guilford.

Kluft, R. P. (1999a). Current issues in dissociative identity disorder. *Journal of Practical Psychiatry and Behavioral Health, 5,* 3-19.

Kluft, R. P. (1999b). An overview of the psychotherapy of dissociative identity disorder. *American Journal of Psychotherapy, 53,* 289-319.

Kluft, R. P. (1999c). True lies, false truths, and naturalistic raw data. In L. M. Williams & V. L. Banyard (Eds.), *Trauma & memory* (pp. 319-329). Thousand Oaks, CA: Sage.

Kluft, R. P. (in press). Body-ego integration in dissociative identity disorder. In J. M. Goodwin & R. Attias (Eds.), *Splintered reflections: Images of the body in trauma* (pp. 239-255). New York: Basic Books.

Kramer, S. (1983). Object-coercive doubting: A pathological defensive response to maternal incest. *Journal of the American Psychoanalytic Association, 31,* 325-351 (Supplement).

Langs, R. (1981). *Resistances and interventions: The nature of therapeutic work.* Northvale, NJ: Jason Aronson.

Lindsay, D. S., & Read, J. D. (1994). Psychotherapy and memories of childhood sexual abuse: A cognitive perspective. *Applied Cognitive Psychology, 8,* 281-338.

Lynn, S. J., & Rhue, J. W. (Eds.). (1991). *Theories of hypnosis: Current models and perspectives.* New York: Guilford.

McConkey, K. M. (1992). The effect of hypnotic procedures on remembering: The experimental findings and their implications for forensic hypnosis. In E. Fromm & M. R. Nash (Eds.), *Contemporary hypnosis research* (pp. 405-426). New York: Guilford Press.

Piper, A., Jr. (1994). Multiple personality disorder: A critical review. *British Journal of Psychiatry, 164,* 600-612.

Pope, K. S. (1996). Memory, abuse, and science: Questioning claims about the false memory syndrome epidemic. *American Psychologist, 51,* 957-974.

Putnam, F. W. (1989). *The diagnosis and treatment of multiple personality disorder.* New York: Guilford.

Putnam, F. W. (1991). *The satanic ritual abuse controversy. Child Abuse & Neglect,* 15, 175-179.

Putnam, F. W., Guroff, J. J., Silberman, E. K., Barban, L., & Post, R. (1986). The clinical phenomenology of multiple personality disorder: Review of 100 recent cases. *Journal of Clinical Psychiatry, 47,* 285-293.

Ross, C. A. (1995). *Satanic ritual abuse: Principles of treatment.* Toronto: University of Toronto Press.

Ross, C. A., Heber, S., Norton, G. R., & Anderson, G. (1989). Differences between multiple personality disorder and other diagnostic groups on structure interview. *Journal of Nervous and Mental Disease, 179,* 487-491.

Ross, C. A., Miller, S. D., Bjornson, L., Reagor, P., Fraser, G. A., & Anderson, G. (1991). Abuse histories in 102 cases of multiple personality disorder. *Canadian Journal of Psychiatry, 36,* 97-101.

Ross, C. A., Miller, S. D., Reagor, P., Bjornson, L., Fraser, G. A., & Anderson, G. (1990). Structured interview data on 102 cases of multiple personality disorder from four centers. *American Journal of Psychiatry, 147,* 596-601.

Ross, C. A., Norton, G. R., & Wozney, K. (1989). Multiple personality disorder: An analysis of 236 cases. *Canadian Journal of Psychiatry, 34,* 413-418.

Sackheim, D. K., & Devine, S. E. (1992). *Out of darkness: Exploring satanism and ritual abuse.* New York: Lexington Books.

Schreiber, F. R. (1973). *Sybil.* Chicago: Henry Regnery.

Schultz, R., Braun, B. G., & Kluft, R. P. (1989). Multiple personality disorder: Phenomenology of selected variables in comparison to major depression. *Dissociation, 2,* 45-51.

Shapiro, F. (1995). *Eye movement desensitization and reprocessing: Basic principles, protocols, and procedures.* New York: Guilford.

Simpson, M. A. (1995). Gullible's travels, or the importance of being multiple. In L. Cohen, J. Berzoff, & M. Elin (Eds.), *Dissociative identity disorder* (pp. 87-134). Northvale, NJ: Jason Aronson.

Spence, D. P. (1982). *Narrative truth and historical truth: Meaning and interpretation in psychoanalysis.* New York: Norton.

van der Kolk, B. A. (1994). The body keeps the score: Memory and the evolving psychobiology of posttraumatic stress. *Harvard Review of Psychiatry, 1*(5), 253-265.

Whitfield, C. L. (1995). *Memory and abuse: Remembering and healing the effects of trauma.* Deerfield Beach, FL: Health Communications.

Wilson, S., & Barber, T. (1983). The fantasy-prone personality: Implications for understanding imagery, hypnosis, and parapsychological phenomena. In A. Sheikh (Ed.), *Imagery: Current theory, research, and applications* (pp. 340-387). New York: John Wiley.

Young, W. C., Sachs, R. G., & Braun, B. G. (1991). Patients reporting ritual abuse in childhood: A clinical syndrome. *Child Abuse & Neglect, 15,* 181-189.

Index